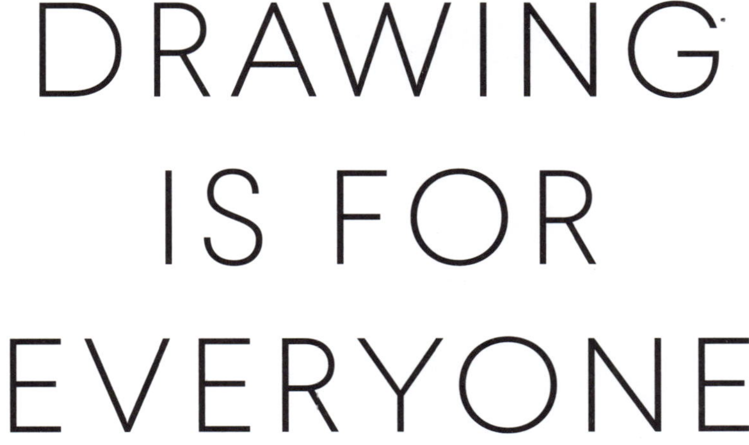

DRAWING IS FOR EVERYONE

Simple Lessons to Make Your Creative Practice a Daily Habit

KATERI EWING

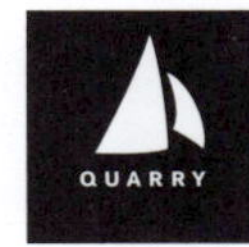

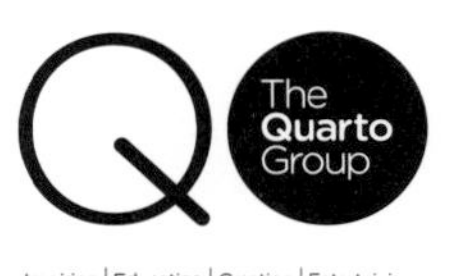

Brimming with creative inspiration, how-to projects, and useful information to enrich your everyday life, quarto.com is a favorite destination for those pursuing their interests and passions.

First Published in 2021 by Quarry Books,
an imprint of The Quarto Group,
100 Cummings Center, Suite 265-D,
Beverly, MA 01915, USA.
T (978) 282-9590 F (978) 283-2742 Quarto.com

Quarry Books titles are also available at discount for retail, wholesale, promotional, and bulk purchase. For details, contact the Special Sales Manager by email at specialsales@quarto.com or by mail at The Quarto Group, Attn: Special Sales Manager, 100 Cummings Center, Suite 265-D, Beverly, MA 01915, USA.

10 9 8 7 6 5 4 3 2

ISBN: 978-0-7603-7066-7

Digital edition published in 2021
eISBN: 978-0-7603-7067-4

Library of Congress Cataloging-in-Publication Data
is available

Design: Debbie Berne
Cover Image: Kateri Ewing
Photography: Kateri Ewing

Printed in China

This book is dedicated to anyone who has ever desired to make drawing a part of their life but was too afraid to fail. All our fears and hesitations are only layers of dust to be swept away from our true and innate creative, sparkling natures. I created this book for you, with love.

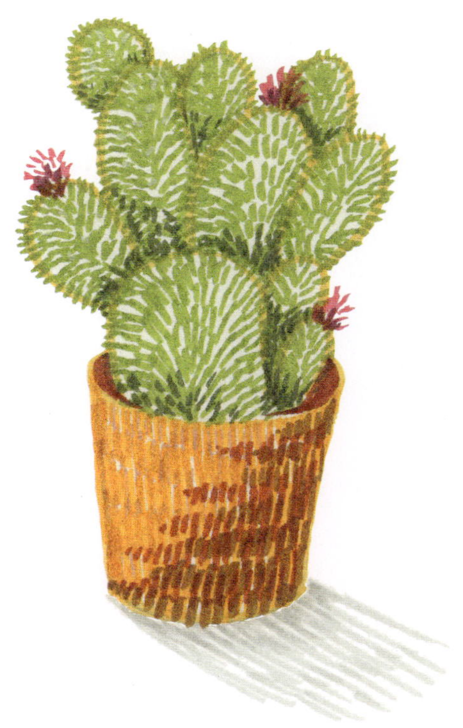

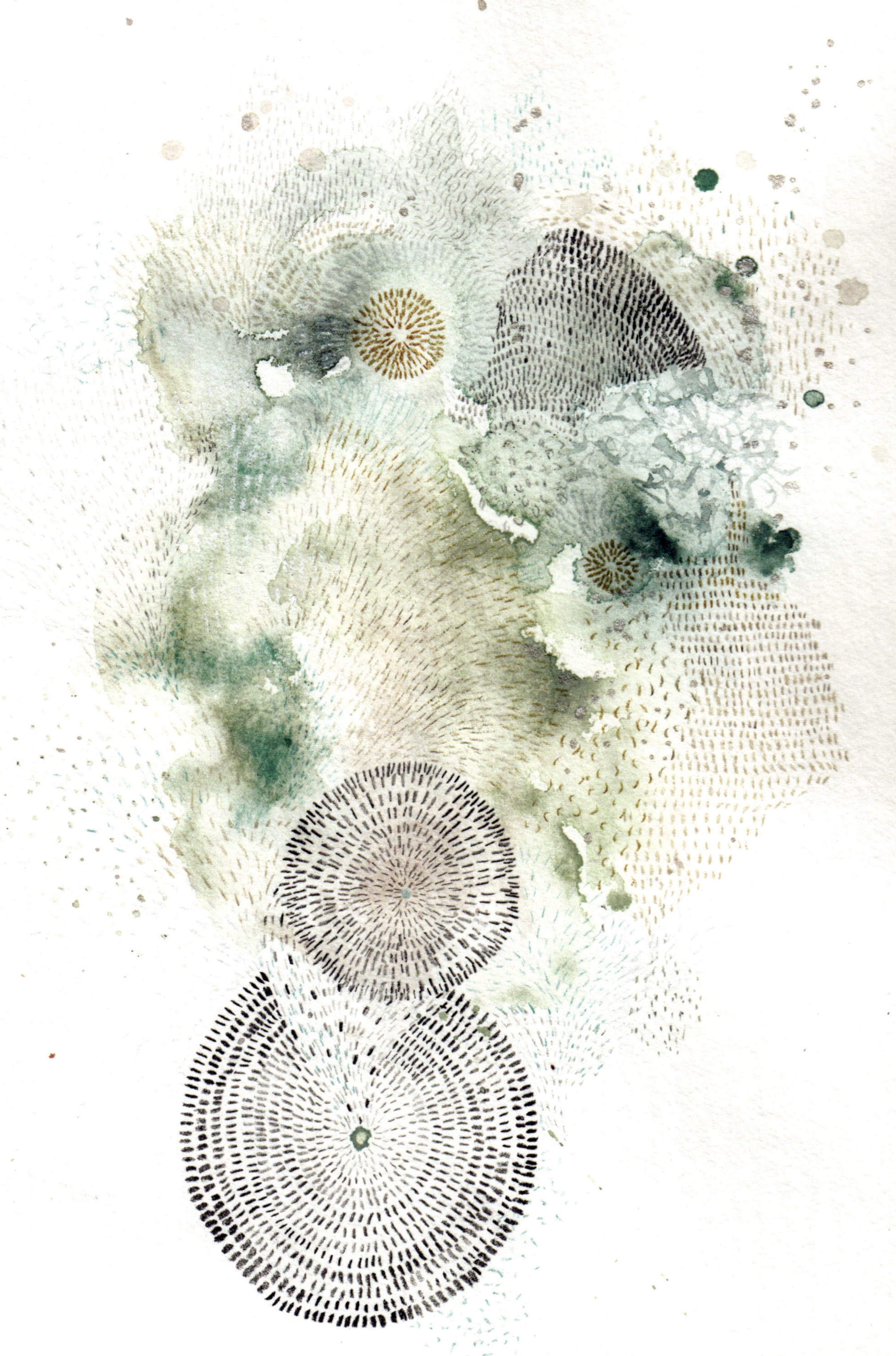

CONTENTS

INTRODUCTION

THE LESSONS

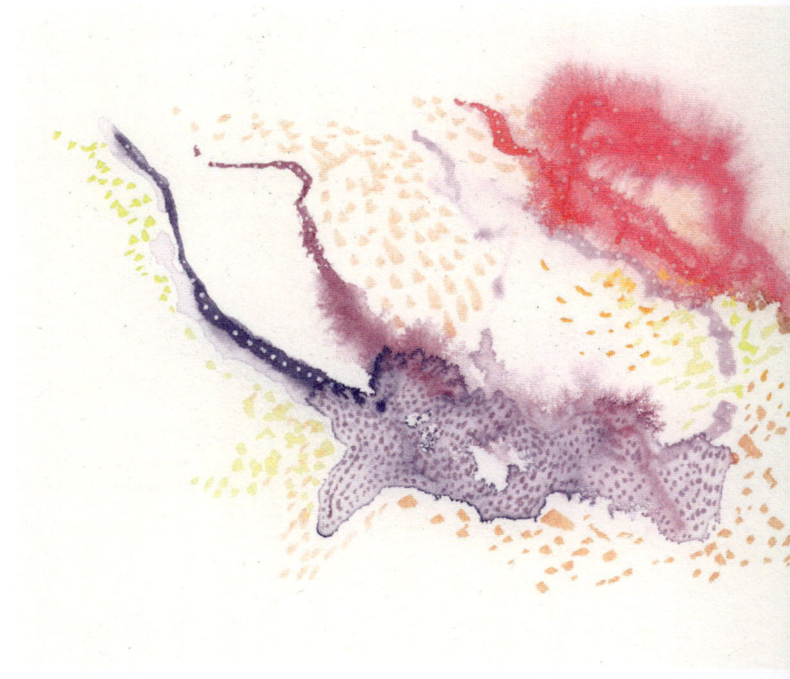

INTRODUCTION

A CREATIVE DRAWING PRACTICE FOR EVERYONE

Think back to the last time you watched a small child pick up a crayon to draw on paper. That tiny hand held the waxy stick, maybe even switched the crayon to the other hand, as the child moved it across the paper. She made her mark. She simply drew, without any preconceived idea of what would appear on the paper. There's immense joy in the act of putting those colorful marks down, and she certainly had no hesitation or fear of not being good enough. Hand an adult a crayon and a piece of paper, however, and you may see a person afraid to make a mark because it might not be good enough. "What if it doesn't look like anything? Why did I ever think I wanted to draw, anyway?"

At what point in the timeline of life does a drawing suddenly have to look like something? Why can't the simple tactile practice of dragging a colored pencil across a piece of paper bring joy and satisfaction? Somewhere along our path to adulthood, we lose that spontaneous, creative courage. My wish is to help you reclaim it.

In this book, we learn about two ways of drawing—the seeing-based representational way and the more expressive, abstract way. Both forms of drawing are much richer when we tap into our unique and intuitive way of mark making instead of following a step-by-step formula, which can lead to discouragement when what we draw doesn't measure up to our expectations of what we were trying to copy.

Seeing-based drawing is a way of documenting something tangible from the world around us by learning to slowly mark down the textures and shapes that our eyes see. It is meditative, calming, and accessible to anyone who can commit a few minutes a day to this invaluable practice. Every student I teach begins with seeing and drawing, and all are amazed at what they can create with this simple practice. There's no measuring, no perspective or foreshortening, and no fancy tools needed. We begin our lessons with a pencil and paper and learn to mark down what our eyes see in our unique way.

Once we build our mark-making vocabulary with pencil, we'll dive into the expressive world of color: colored pencils, markers, pens, and ink. With these tools, we can explore patterns, textures, and more abstract designs while continuing to hone our seeing-based drawing skills. Each lesson is simple to complete as shown, but also has unlimited possibilities for repeating with different results each time. At the end of each lesson, I offer inspiration on ways to make the project your own.

A bit of gentle advice as we begin: Leave your expectations and self-criticism at the door. As many of my students have discovered, we can be eternal beginners and find all the satisfying benefits and joy we could ever hope for in a creative practice. It's also good to know there is strong scientific evidence that those who enjoy a creative practice as a regular part of their lives also enjoy many benefits to their health and well-being, including a more positive outlook on life. This has certainly been true in my experience. My daily drawing practice has been a good and constant companion through many of my greatest struggles. It's the reason I began teaching. I want everyone to reap the same kind of benefits I receive from it.

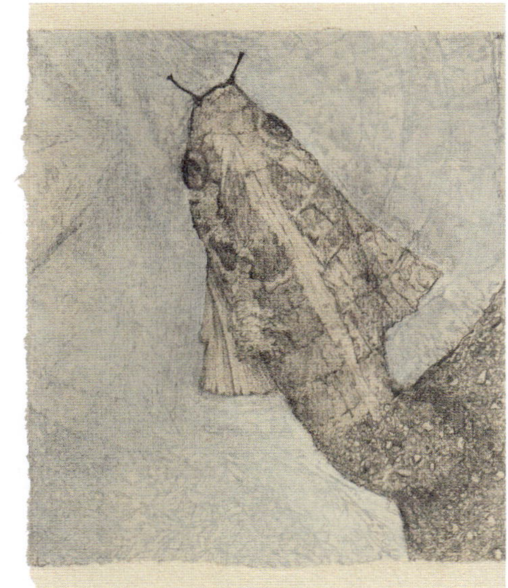

You may have arrived at these pages with a secret desire to unlock your creative potential. Perhaps you've always wanted to draw but were told you just didn't have the talent. Or, maybe you're a professional artist who feels your work has gone stale and methodical and are looking to tap into your intuition with fresh exercises. You could be someplace in between. Wherever you are on your journey, I welcome you to this space. The best place for any creative endeavor is in a beginner's mind. We are all beginners at something, and for the lessons held within this book, being a beginner is the best thing to be.

Welcome. Now, let's draw!

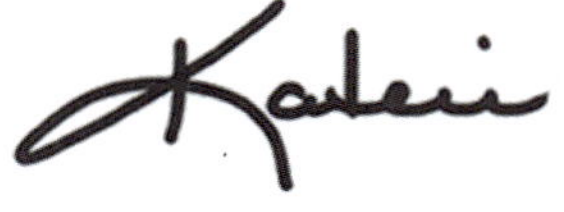

THE FOUR GUIDING PRINCIPLES OF A

CREATIVE DRAWING PRACTICE

ONE

Honor and Appreciate the Moment in Time and Your Tools and Materials

Our tools for a creative drawing practice are simple: an exquisite piece of paper, an assortment of drawing tools such as pencils, colored pencils, markers, and ink, and a few other miscellaneous supplies. This book is organized into three sections—Graphite, Colored Pencil, and Ink—of seven lessons each. At the beginning of each section is a thorough inventory of the tools you'll need and lots of advice on selecting the materials that will make your explorations fun and successful. No matter your budget, there are beautiful tools waiting to be discovered. In each section, we learn how to choose our tools and how to care for them, with this in mind: quality over quantity and less is more. Simplicity of and familiarity with our tools allow freedom of expression, without the confusion of wondering which materials to choose each time we sit down to create.

Over time, I've learned valuable lessons about where to spend a little more money and where I can be thriftier when it comes to art supplies. I'll share these tips with you! But, mostly, what I wish to impart is the idea that our tools are an extension of our head, hands, and heart. Each time we sit down to create, we can take a quiet moment to give thanks for the beautiful materials before us. It's also important to acknowledge the moment in time, to take a few deep, cleansing breaths, and to leave our expectations and stress behind. The time we spend drawing can be meditative and nourishing to our spirit. We must choose to be present and engaged in the act of using our beautiful materials to express something unique to each of us. We will learn more about this in each lesson along the way.

TWO

Show Up Every Day

Our creative practice has the potential to become a companion that can help us through many difficulties. It is a steadfast and intimate friend that will nurture us even if we only have a handful of minutes to spend each day. Some lessons can be completed in 15 minutes or less, while others can be worked on in small increments of time over several days. The magical part is, the less time we know that we need to commit, the more likely we are to stick with it. As days go on, we naturally find ourselves desiring more time in our daily lives for our creative practice. It feeds us in ways we never imagined. Art-making can become a vital component of our everyday lives, but only if we show up daily to take part in it.

So, let's keep it real and simple. I'm asking you to commit to at least 15 minutes a day as you work your

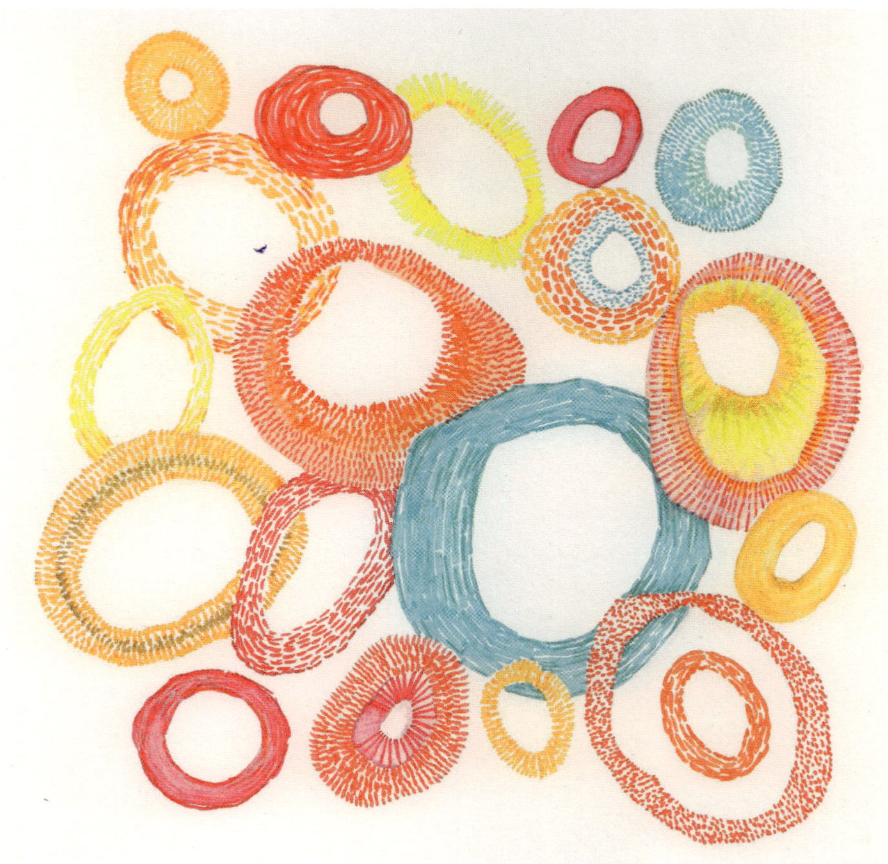

way through these lessons. If you have more time, great! When you have completed the twenty-one lessons in this book, you can begin again and attend to each lesson with new, more experienced eyes and hands. These lessons are meant to be fresh each time we engage in them. It's remarkable, really. I can teach these lessons to twenty-five people and there are never two results alike—and yet they are all beautiful and harmonious. Why is that?

Your unique way of seeing and experiencing the world and events around you is one of your most important, even sacred, possessions. These lessons are designed with that in mind. The colors you choose and the marks you create will be yours—and yours alone. There is no room to compare what you create to any specific example; my samples for each lesson are meant only as a guide to teach you techniques and process, not as something to copy. We each bring forth what is ours alone. This is the quality that makes art ART.

Give yourself plenty of time and space to begin again and again, if you choose. There are no mistakes when creating from these lessons. If you're like me, you'll have some lessons that feel amazing and some that feel average, but they're all immensely important as part of your creative journey. Each will have its own kind of gratification and will bring joy and a moment of respite and calm to your daily life.

One thing we must be aware of is our inner critic. As a teacher, I see many students make critical statements about their work and I gently remind them it's just one day among many, one lesson among many. We can choose to see our drawings with fresh, childlike eyes of wonder, or with the harsh eyes of our inner critic. I choose to see with wonder, and I hope you do the same.

THREE
Setting Your Intentions, Inspiration, and Two-Fold Joy

Every time we show up for our creative drawing practice, we have an opportunity to set our intention and take inspiration from a source of beauty. There are so many sources to choose from: art, guided meditations, inspirational literature, music, nature, poetry, and other beautiful art, such as decks like intuitive oracle cards, social media accounts of people that inspire you, and more.

The most important thing to inspire us, however, is right within our hearts: the capacity for two-fold joy. First is the joy we receive from the simple act of putting our mark to paper and watching the page bloom as we create something beautiful and unique. Second is the joy we give to someone else by sharing our creations or sending them to someone who might need a bit of joy, too. I liken two-fold joy to dandelions—a bright, cheerful flower that's prolific and shares its seeds freely on the wind. That's the spirit of sending out two-fold joy. We can think of these lessons as "Dandelion Lessons" to help us visualize this important component of our creative practice.

Let's talk about different sources of inspiration and how we might use them. At the beginning of each session, I unwrap my tools and arrange them on the table. Sometimes I light a candle; sometimes I dab a bit of aromatic oil on my fingertips and rub my hands together near my face while taking deep and calming breaths. Then, I sit for a moment and set my intentions for my practice. Almost always it's a simple, yet profound, wish for peace to all living things.

Depending on the day, I may have chosen a favorite book of poetry or another inspirational book with short pieces of writing within. I randomly open the book to a page and try to take away one word that depicts the essence my reading. I find that focusing on one word is a wonderful way to breathe more meaning into my practice and, often, I'll write that word somewhere on the finished drawing. Other days, I might play some music I love and let the sounds and rhythms carry my pen or pencil along, or I might enjoy a guided mediation. Sometimes I look at a beautiful book of artwork by an artist I admire, and sometimes I look at some treasures from the natural world I have brought home from a recent walk. Almost always I shuffle my deck of oracle cards and select one to flavor my session of intuitive painting. And some days I just close my eyes, take a few mind-clearing breaths, and simply begin to paint. These are just a few examples of things you might explore to center yourself and bring elements of inspiration to each lesson. They are optional, yet delightful, additions.

FOUR
Scatter Your Joy Far and Wide

After enjoying your creative practice for a while, you'll create a lovely stack of drawings and . . . you'll wonder what to do with them. Our natural desire is to share them with others, but we might feel shy to let anyone see our work. I have come to learn that this is unfounded; think of how you would feel if you received a hand-drawn postcard in the mail. It would make you feel special because someone thought of you and took the time to send you such a treasure.

A big part of these lessons is sending some of your work to others. You can either wrap it and give it as a gift or slip it into an envelope and send it in the mail. You can even send it anonymously. I have one student who sends her tiny paintings in a bundle to the local children's hospital to be given to children there who might need a smile.

This is one way we can share two-fold joy. Another way, and just as important, is sharing your creative practice with others by teaching them the benefits you have received and encouraging them to begin their practice. Can you imagine a world in which every person has the comfort and joy of art-making in their daily lives? I believe the world would be a kinder, gentler place if all people had the opportunity to create beauty and spread joy.

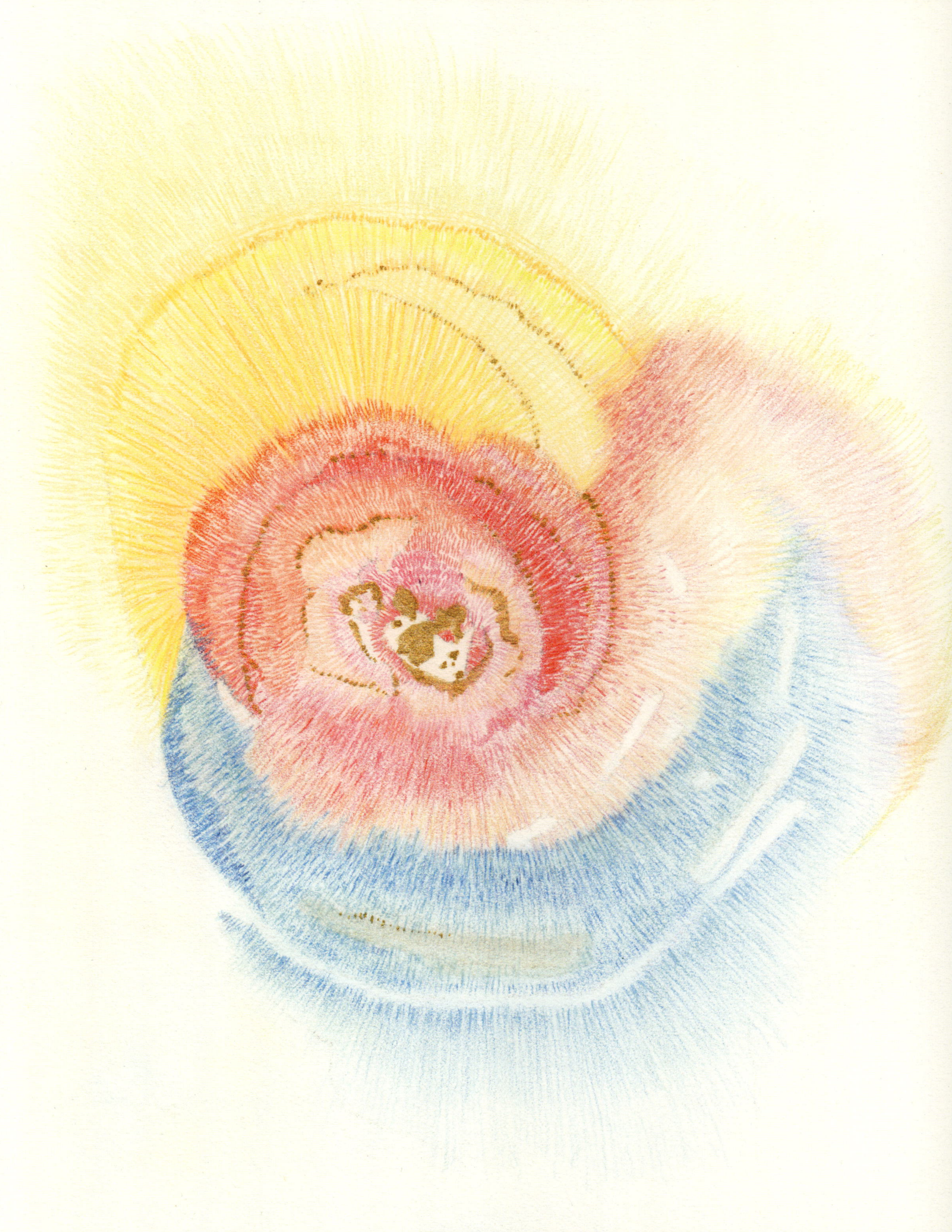

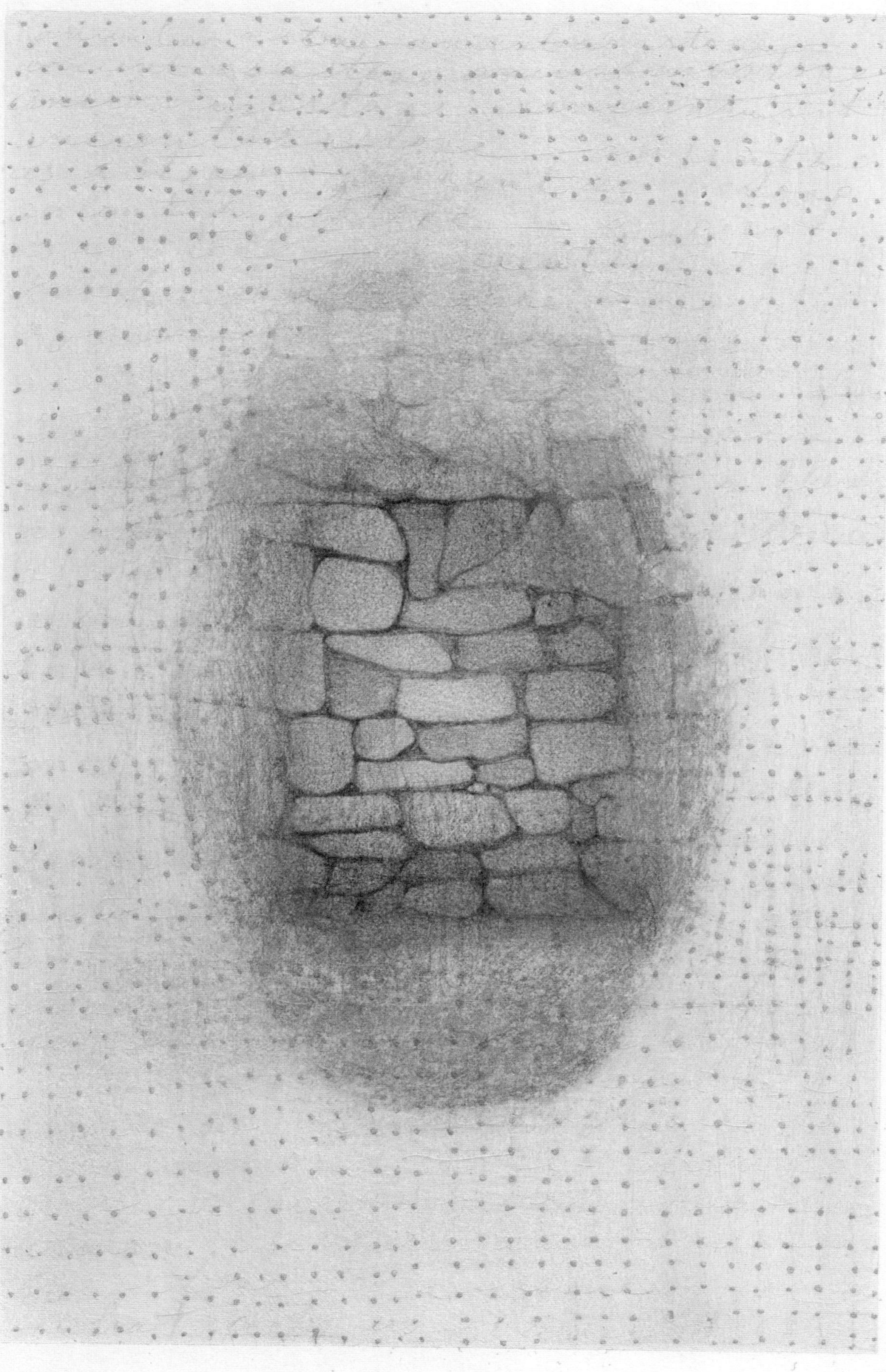

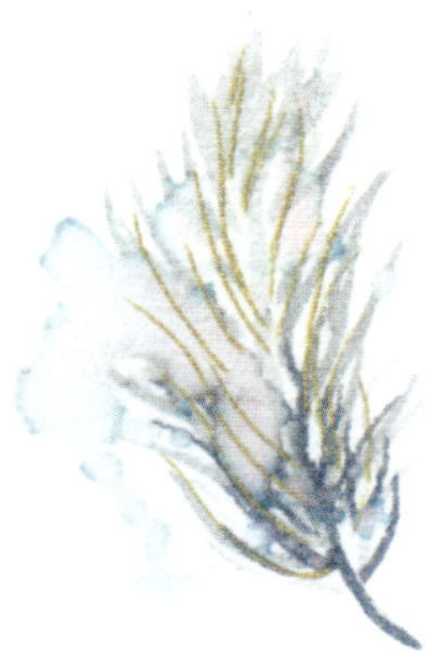

THE LESSONS

I like to think of the twenty-one lessons that follow as a map that will lead you to a magical place of creative discoveries. Each lesson provides a method for exploring a different drawing technique that leads to spontaneous play. The instructions are not as technical as you might find in other books about drawing, and they are introduced by philosophies and thoughts to help you open your head, hands, and heart to exciting new possibilities.

You can choose to explore the lessons in any order; however, I recommend starting your journey with the first lesson of each section. These openers help you develop the basic skills needed to progress with confidence. Remember, keep your time commitment short and your tools and materials simple while you are making your creative practice a regular part of everyday life. If you can complete these twenty-one lessons, I have no doubt you will have made your creative practice a daily habit and will soon be looking for more time, every day, to explore mark making in your unique way.

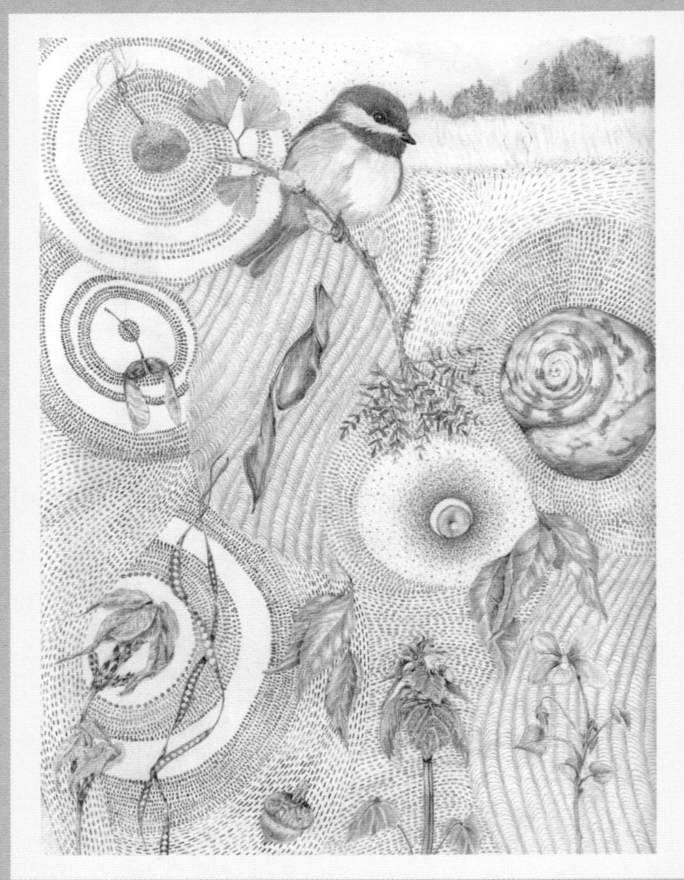

GRAPHITE

You might be wondering why it's called *graphite*, when it's just a pencil. There are many kinds of pencils available to artists—from charcoal pencils to colored pencils, even carbon pencils. All have their place, and hopefully one day you'll explore them. For now, we'll focus on graphite pencils.

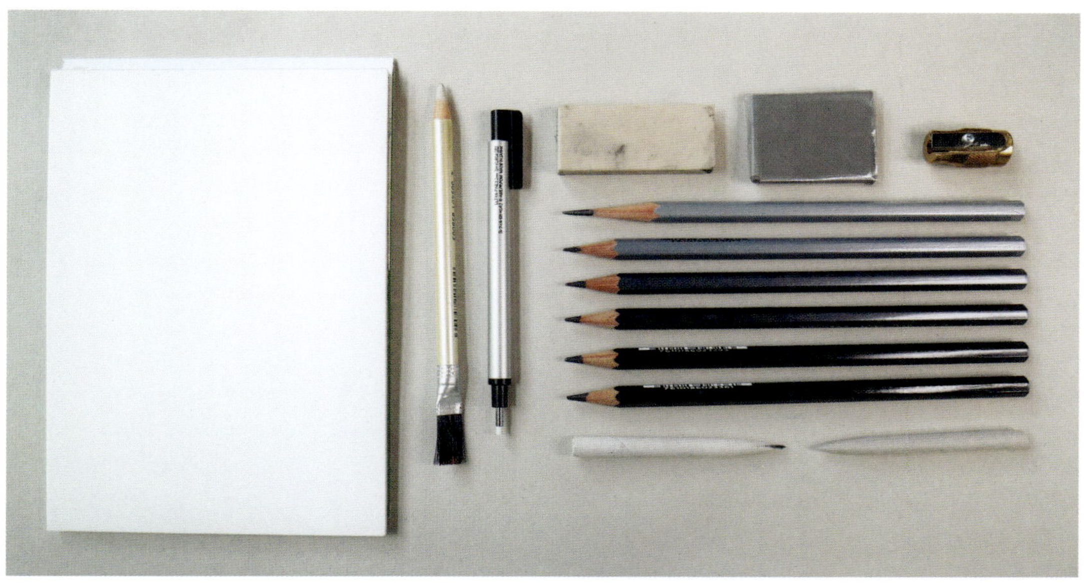

MATERIALS

Graphite is a gray, crystalline form of carbon with a metallic sheen; its name comes from the Greek *graphein* ("to write"). It's the humble material used to make the no. 2 pencils we have used since grade school, and it's also used to make the artist-grade pencils I hope you will try. Artist-grade graphite comes in varying degrees of hardness and softness. The hardest pencils, from H to 10H, create a paler, silvery, very defined line. The softest pencils, from B to 10B, create a smudgy, deep-gray line. HB is right in the middle of hardness and softness—the perfect balance—and is used to make the venerable no. 2 pencil.

For these lessons, I recommend a set of artist-grade pencils. A good variety of hardness and softness would be 2H, HB, 3B, 5B, 7B, and 9B.

You'll also need:

- **An eraser**, such as a kneaded (or putty) eraser, a stick eraser, or a white plastic eraser

- **A pencil sharpener.** Always keep a very sharp point on your pencils, even using a bit of sandpaper to refine the tip after sharpening

- **Paper blending sticks or tortillons**

- **Drawing paper.** I prefer at least 90# paper with a vellum finish. Cotton is nice, but buy what you can afford. We'll be using paper that's about 5 × 7 inches (13 × 18 cm) for all projects. You can buy larger sheets and cut them to size, or buy pads already cut to that size.

- **Feather or clean soft brush** to remove eraser dust and excess graphite from your paper

LESSONS

Our journey with graphite starts at the beginning: how to hold the pencil and put the material on the paper with a featherlight touch to give it the most beautiful appearance. Then, we explore the qualities of your individual mark and how that relates to seeing your subject and documenting what you see. We also explore the value (lightness and darkness) of your subject and the importance of capturing a three-dimensional object onto a two-dimensional piece of paper. Finally, we put all our learnings into practice in the last three graphite projects. Each lesson builds on the previous one and is meant to be further explored in your way.

Gather your materials, get those pencils sharpened, and let's begin!

LESSON ONE

THE TOUCH OF A FEATHER

Let's begin with the very foundation of drawing and the most important thing I can teach you—the feather touch. When we first begin to use a pencil or pen for drawing instead of writing, our natural tendency is to hold the writing implement as we do when writing our name. This can be handy when we need to be very precise, but in general, it forces us to use a firmer touch than desired.

When we see a beautiful drawing, some things we might notice are the fineness of the graphite application and the texture of the paper shining through. These contribute an element of lightness, of luminosity, no matter how dark in tone the marks may be. When we use too firm a touch with a pencil, it can hide that beautiful surface texture of the paper and create shine or reflective quality, which keeps our eyes from seeing the darker values.

TOOLS TO GATHER

- Selection of artist pencils in 2H, HB, 3B, 5B, 7B, and 9B
- Drawing paper, 5 × 7 inches (13 × 18 cm)
- Ruler
- Eraser

STEPS

1 - In this first exercise, we will use an HB pencil to layer graphite in darkening values. Using the most delicate touch you can, create 4 small swatches of graphite. *See A.* (This isn't easy! Give yourself time to practice this feather-touch technique.) Leave the first swatch as is. Build a second feather-touch layer on the next three. Add another layer to the last two and a final layer on the very last swatch.

Do you see how, by layering with this delicate touch, you can achieve darker values but still see the light and texture of the paper shining through? The fifth swatch is an example of pressing too hard with an HB pencil. It covers all the texture and light of the paper and creates a reflective sheen. This is what we'll work to avoid.

2 - Now that you know how to layer and create different values of light and dark with an HB pencil, let's make our job easier by using the varying shades of our artist's pencils, 2H through 9B.

Using the same feather touch as before, make a small swatch with each of these pencils, in order from light to dark, making sure to let the texture and light of the paper shine through. *See B.* This is the reason we have varying degrees of hardest and softness in graphite artist's pencils. It is much easier to choose a softer pencil when we need a darker value than to layer over and again using just one pencil.

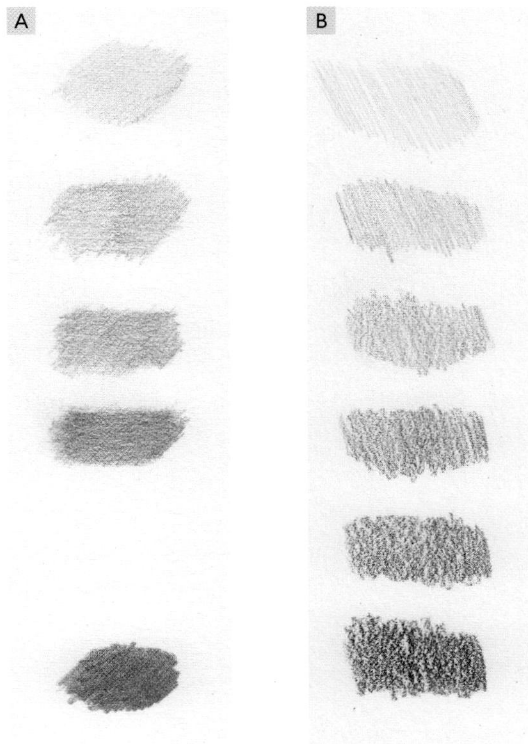

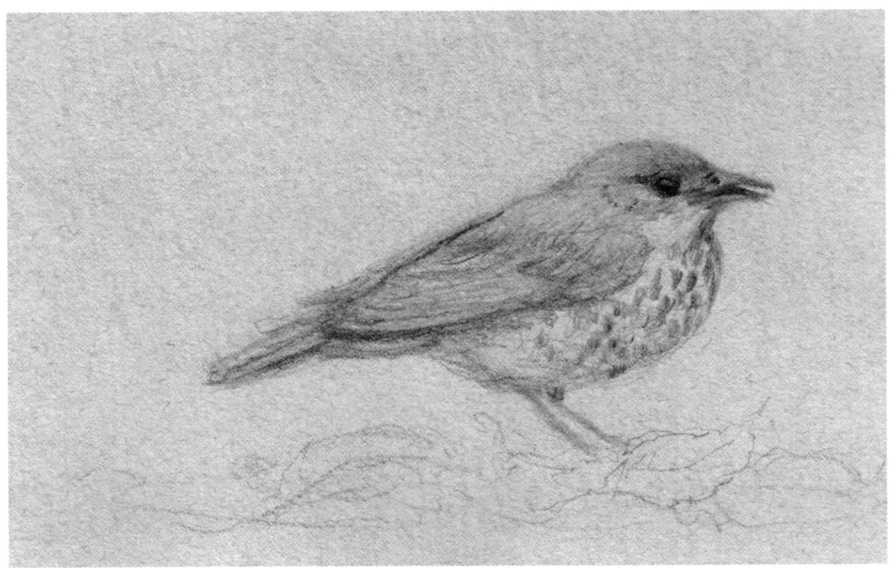

A delicate touch and an array of pencil hardnesses allow for a lovely drawing.

RULED VALUE SCALE

1 - For the next exercise, use a ruler to draw a rectangle, about 5 × 1½ inches (13 × 4 cm). Divide it into three 1-inch (2.5 cm) sections and leave the rest open. For the first section, use the 2H pencil in one direction, and fill the square as evenly as possible. *See C.*

2 - Fill the next square in the same manner using the HB pencil. Fill the third square with the 3B pencil. Then, evenly fill the final space with 5B, 7B, and 9B, in that order. *See D.* Use the lightest touch possible.

3 - Complete steps 1 and 2 again, filling in the spaces as directed but in another direction to create the most even tone possible. *See E.* If you've gone outside the lines of the rectangle, this is normal! It takes a lot of practice to control keeping the edges clean. The point of this exercise is to create a value scale using all your pencils and to practice achieving a smooth tone and texture with the light of the paper still shining through.

Repeat this exercise often over the next few weeks. Training our hands to use a delicate touch is so important. It helps us understand the varying values of our pencils and achieve an even tone using the feather-touch technique.

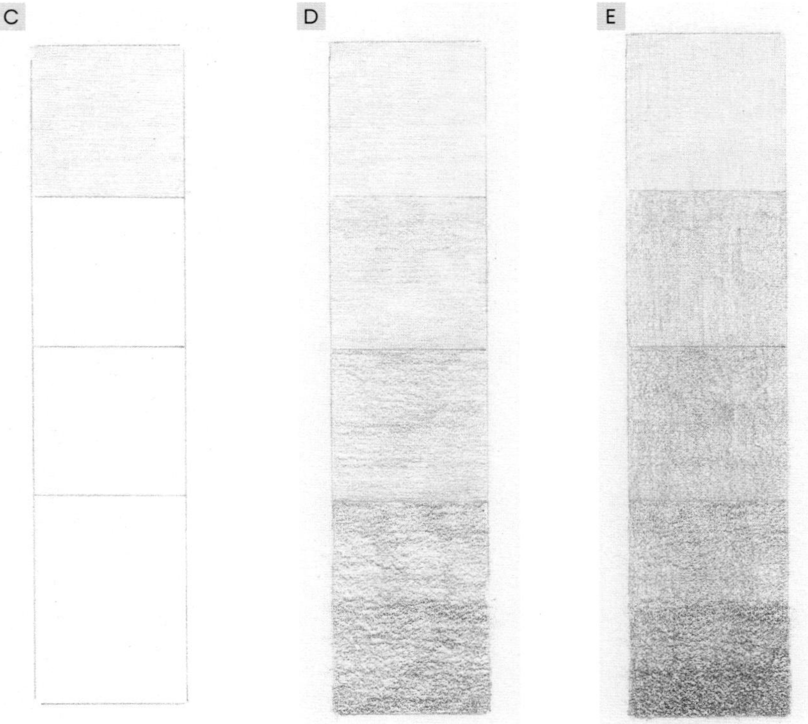

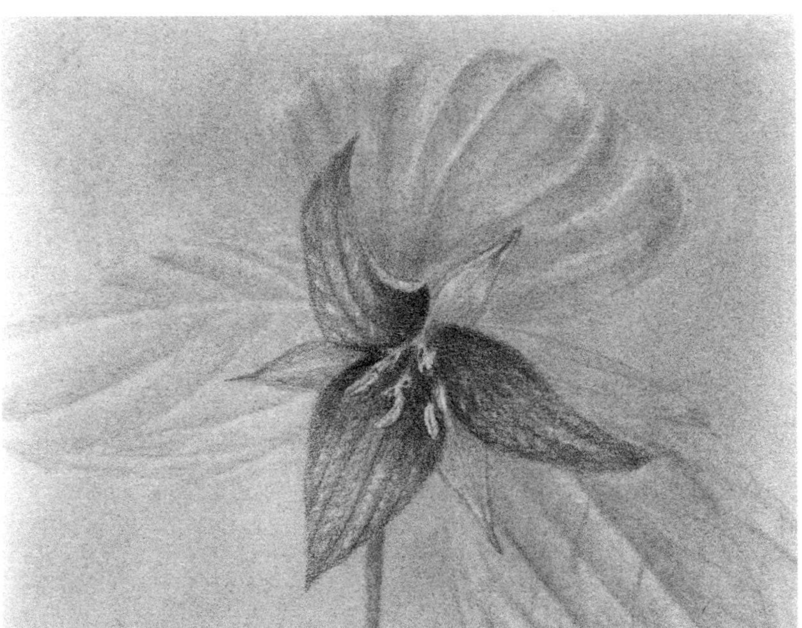

The feather touch is truly my secret to delicate, poetic drawings. Think of dragging a very sharp needle across the surface of very ripe tomato with tight skin. If you press too hard, you will break the skin. This is the image to keep in your mind when using a pencil on a paper.

LESSON TWO

LET'S MAKE MARKS

It's time to break the "I'm not sure what to draw" ice. For now, let's think about drawing as simply making marks on a piece of paper. In this lesson, we will create several designs using patterns of marks and then try our hand at putting them together to create a fun, expressive drawing.

TOOLS TO GATHER

- Pen, any color
- Ruler or straightedge, even an index card will do
- Larger piece of practice paper, about 9 ×12 inches (23 × 30 cm)
- Pencils in at least three different values, such as 2H, HB, and 3B
- Pencil sharpener, so you can keep those points sharp
- Blending stump or tortillon
- Eraser
- Piece of drawing paper about 5 × 7 inches (13 × 18 cm)

STEPS

1 - Using your pen and ruler, create 4 square boxes (see the examples for how to situate them), about 3 × 3 inches (7.5 × 7.5 cm), on your practice paper. Keep in mind that my examples are only examples. You do not have to copy the exact line placement—ever. *See A.*

- In the upper-left box, use the HB pencil to create a patterns of gently wavy vertical lines, as shown. I find it easiest to begin with a line down the middle and then proceed to draw lines between each pair of lines as you go.
- In the upper-right box, use the HB pencil to create vertical broken lines, as shown, and then fill in a few small circles, as shown.
- In the lower-left square, use a 3B pencil to draw random ovals in various directions, spread evenly throughout, as shown.
- In the lower-right box, use a 3B pencil to draw a slightly curved line that is thicker at the top and thinner at the bottom, as shown.

2 - *See B.*

- Use a 3B pencil to darken only the areas where the lines curve away from one other. Remember, use a delicate touch.

• Using a 2H pencil, fill in all the areas between the darker lines with more broken lines and a series of tiny dashes, as shown.

• Using a 2H pencil, fill in the areas between the ovals with delicate circles and ovals of varying sizes, shapes, and directions. They will not be complete shapes but, rather, will build one off the other. Follow my example for guidance.

• Using a 2H pencil, create a series of downward lines, like the markings on a feather, as shown.

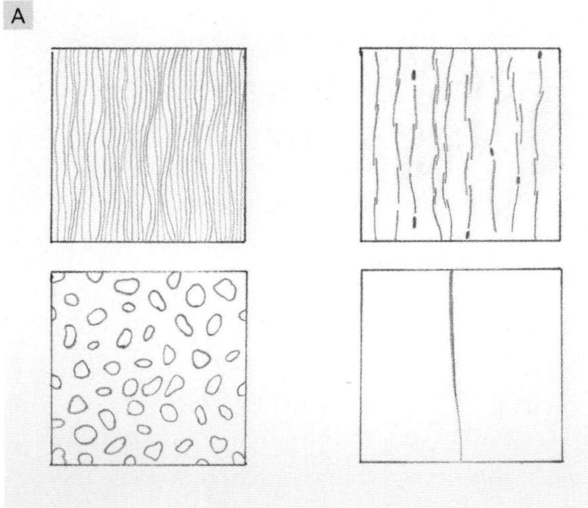
A

3 - *See C.*

• Time to use your blending stump! Gently use the tip of the stump to smudge the outline of the darker lines to fill them in, as shown. Notice how much this changes the appearance. Did you also notice how this pattern is like the ripples on water?

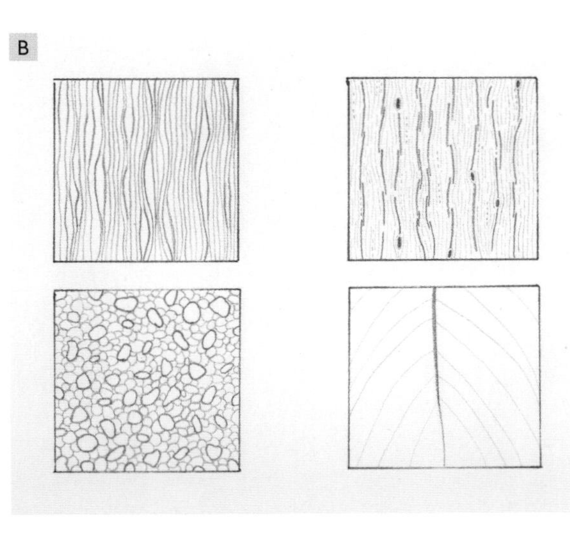
B

• Once again, use the blending stump to gently smudge the darker lines. See how it gives the illusion of a raised texture? That is the magic of shading. Does this pattern remind you of wood grain?

• You guessed it . . . blending stump again. But this time, use it to gently fill in the darker oval shapes and then to lightly fill in random lighter shapes, leaving most of them white. Wipe off the tip of the blending stick with a tissue if it starts to accumulate graphite build-up. Notice how this pattern looks a bit like pebbles?

• With your 2H pencil, create thin parallel lines between each of the thicker lines. Then, use your blending stump to gently smudge the dark, center line and each of the darker diagonal lines down the sides. Finally, use your eraser to create randomly placed circles, as shown. What does this remind you of? A bird's feather? A leaf that was lunch for a caterpillar?

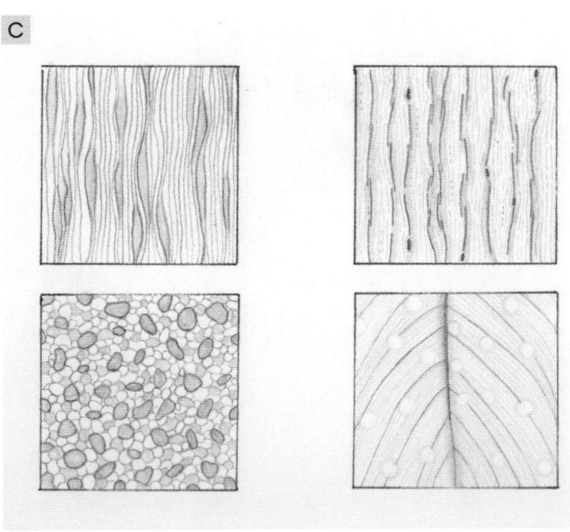
C

4 - Now that you have created several beautiful patterns, it's time to put them together into one drawing on your drawing paper. You can follow my example or use the patterns creatively to make your design. *See D.* Notice the tiny tick marks—like raindrops. These are one of my favorite ways to fill in spaces on expressive drawings—and are so easy to do! Use the full value range of your pencils. See how I use the broken-lines technique to create something that looks like a tree stump in the middle? Be fearless here. See how many different marks you can create from the patterns we have learned. It's for your eyes only. This is practice, and this is fun!

5 - Use your blending stump to give your drawing some dimension and contrast. I even lightly pressed my eraser on the tick marks randomly to create some interest. *See E.*

Your first creative drawing is complete! I'm proud of you.

D

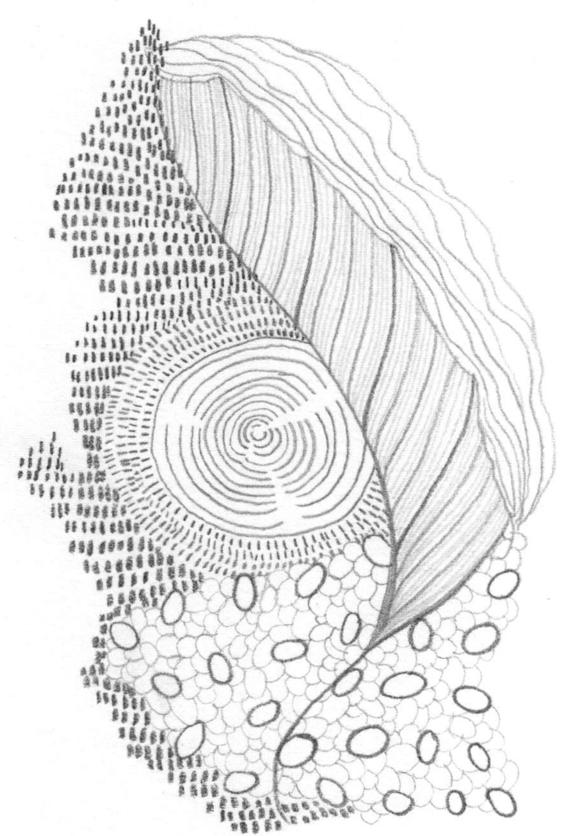

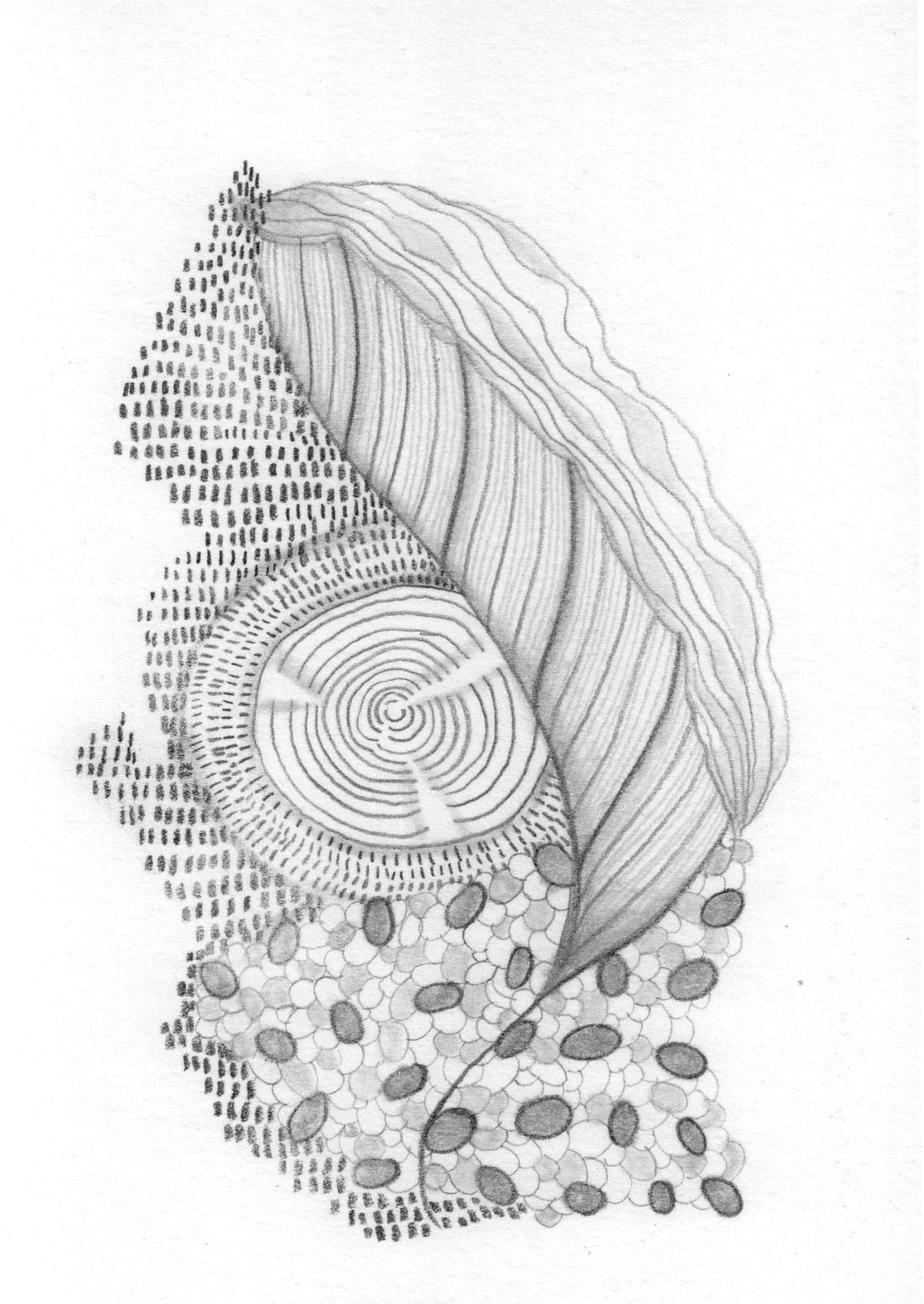

LESSON THREE

HYDRANGEA IN SHADES OF GRAY

How do you feel when you see the finished image in this lesson? Does it make you worry it may be too hard for you? Or, are you excited to try something you didn't think was possible with the skills you have right now? Well, it's very possible! So, let's do this.

In this lesson, we will build a complex-looking flower, step by step, using patterns of repetitive marks, just like we did in Lesson 2 (page 20). The difference is, this time we will work to create something recognizable, such as a hydrangea flower. Put your doubts aside and let's draw this together, step by step.

TOOLS TO GATHER

- Drawing paper, about 5 × 7 inches (13 × 18 cm) or larger
- Pencils in 2H, HB, 3B, and 7B
- Blending stump or tortillon
- Eraser

STEPS

1 - Just to the upper right of the center of the paper, use an HB pencil to draw a tiny circle. Switch to a 2H pencil and draw 4 petal shapes. *See A.* This is the basic pattern for the flower head.

2 - Use the HB pencil to draw another tiny circle just to the upper left of the first one, as shown. Repeat the same petal pattern using the 2H pencil, but *notice* the way one petal goes underneath the first flower. When this happens, just draw the parts that are visible and do not go underneath. *See B.*

3 - Fill out the remainder of your flower by repeating step 2 until you have created a roundish shape of petals that is pleasing to you. You may use my example as your guide. Remember, all the petals do not need to be the same and can vary in size and direction (with smaller flowers toward the edges). Notice how the center circles are evenly spaced but in a random way. *See C.*

A

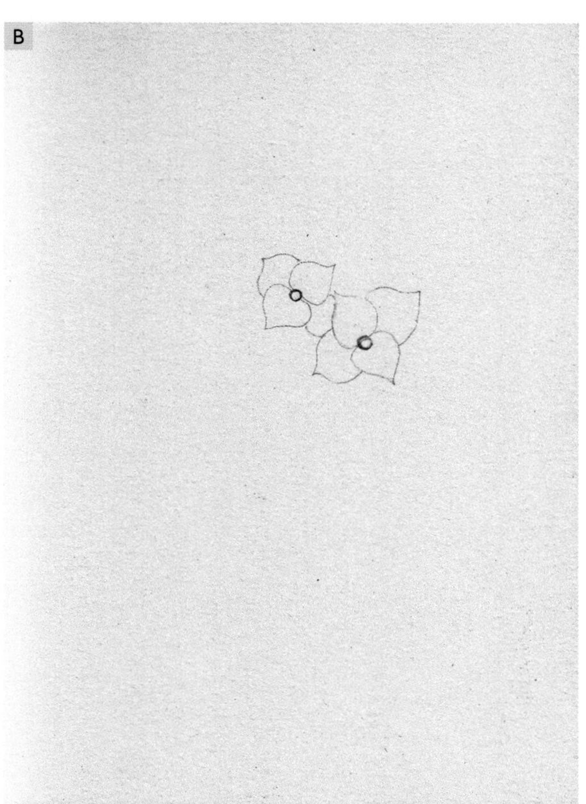
B

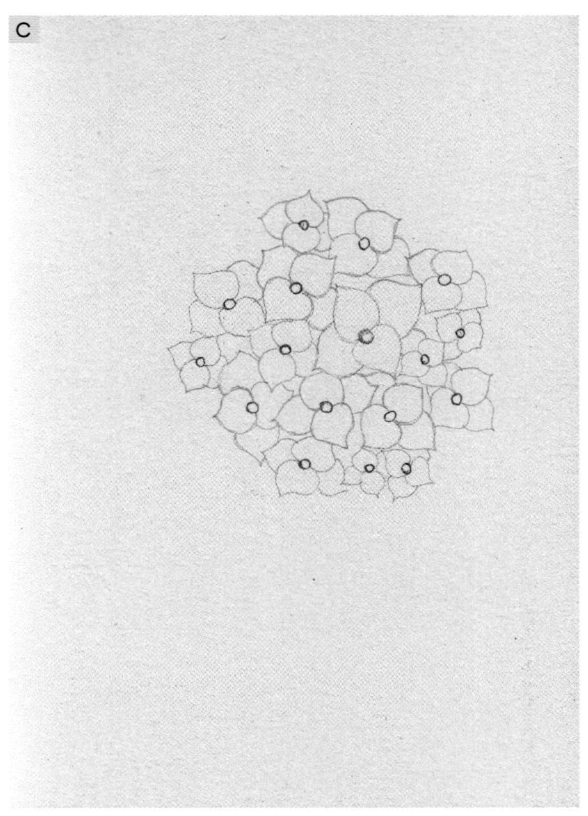
C

4 - Use the HB pencil to fill in the tiny spaces between the petals, as shown. Take your time with this and look carefully. *See D.* Remember, use your feather touch!

5 - Time to add some simple leaf shapes. This is not too different from one of the patterns we created in Lesson 1 (page 16). With an HB pencil, lightly draw 5 leaf shapes around the outer edge of the flower. Use the example here as a guide. Then, add a stem with another leaf coming off the stem, as shown. I draw the leaf shape first, add the center vein, and then add the secondary veins. *See E.*

6 - With your 3B pencil, fill in the lower section of each of the tiny spaces from step 4. Begin to fill in the right side of each of the 3 larger leaf shapes, leaving a tiny sliver of white paper below each secondary vein line, as shown. I turn my paper as needed so my hand is in a comfortable position and I am not smearing previous marks where I rest my hand. Draw a line down the right side of the stem. *See F.*

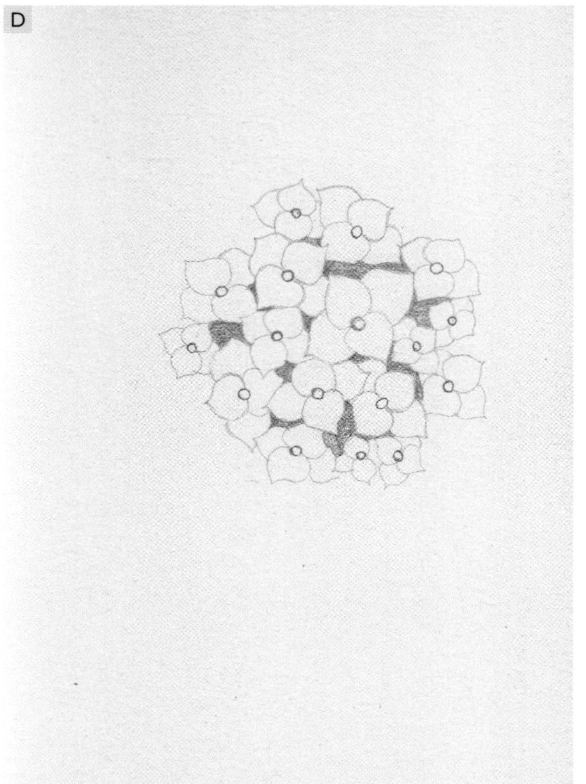

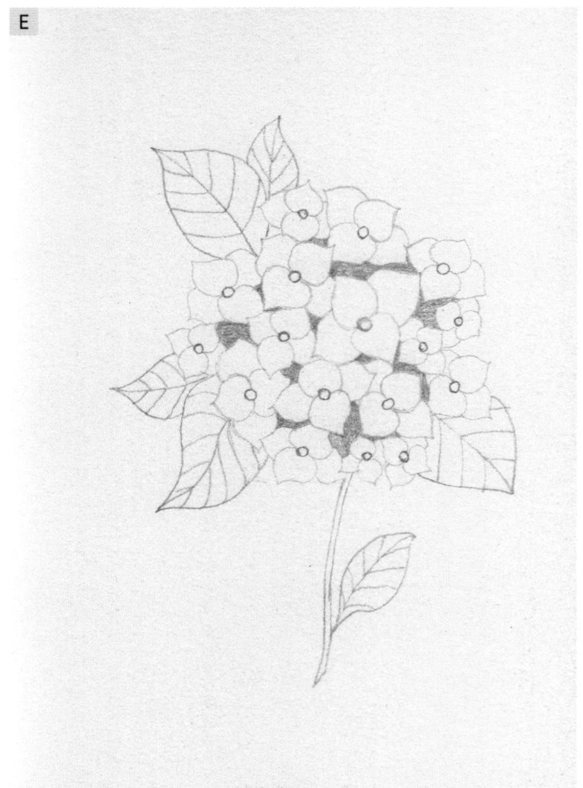

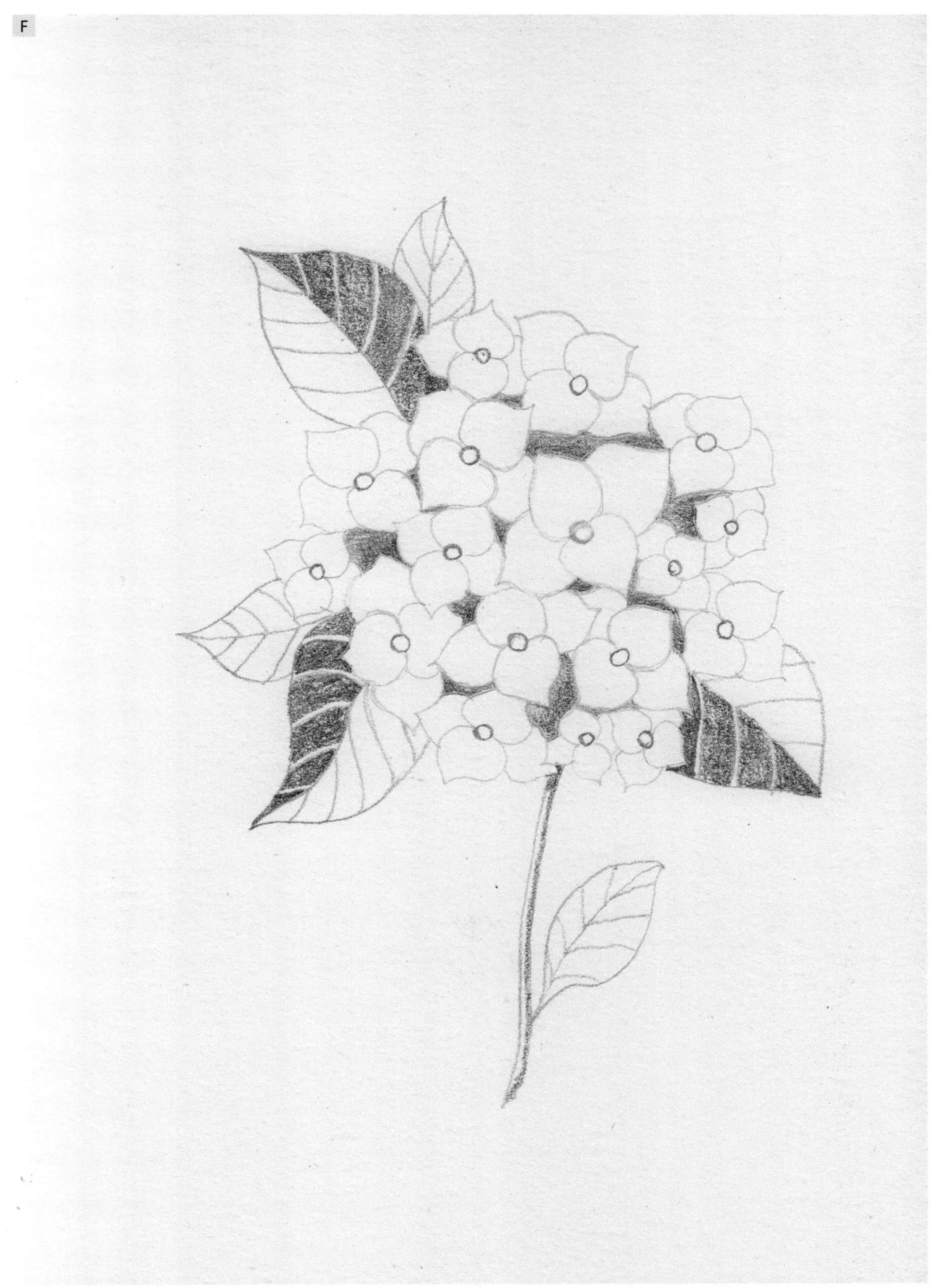
F

7 - Continue to fill in the left-hand side of each leaf while leaving a thin sliver of white paper at the center rib as well as below each secondary vein line. With an HB pencil, repeat steps 6 and 7 for the 3 smaller leaf shapes. *See G.*

8 - Now that the drawing is complete, let's use the blending stick to put the finishing touches on our flower. Remember, use a feather touch and do not press the point of the blending stick or flatten it. Wipe the point clean with a tissue every now and then to keep it clean of excess graphite. *See H.*

- Use the tip to smudge the center tiny circle of each floret.

- Smudge the area on each floret where the top 2 petals overlap the bottom 2 petals, as shown.

- Use the tip of the blending stick to draw a soft line from the center of each "top" petal to the tip of it, as shown.

- Use the tip to smudge the right side of the stem toward the left side, so it softly blends from dark to light.

- Use the tip to smudge the areas of each leaf that border the white petals or another leaf, as shown. Also, smudge the bottom of each leaf to slightly darken it.

Sit back and admire your beautiful hydrangea!

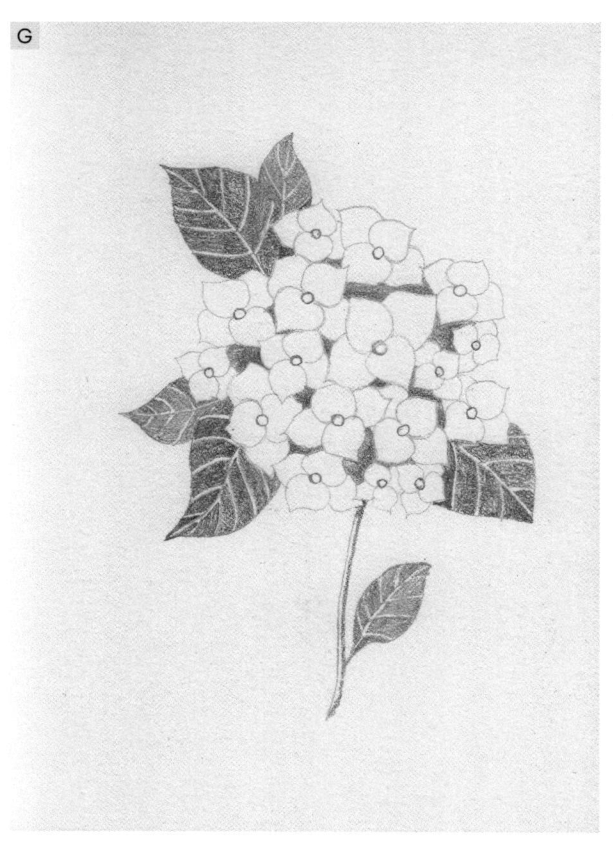

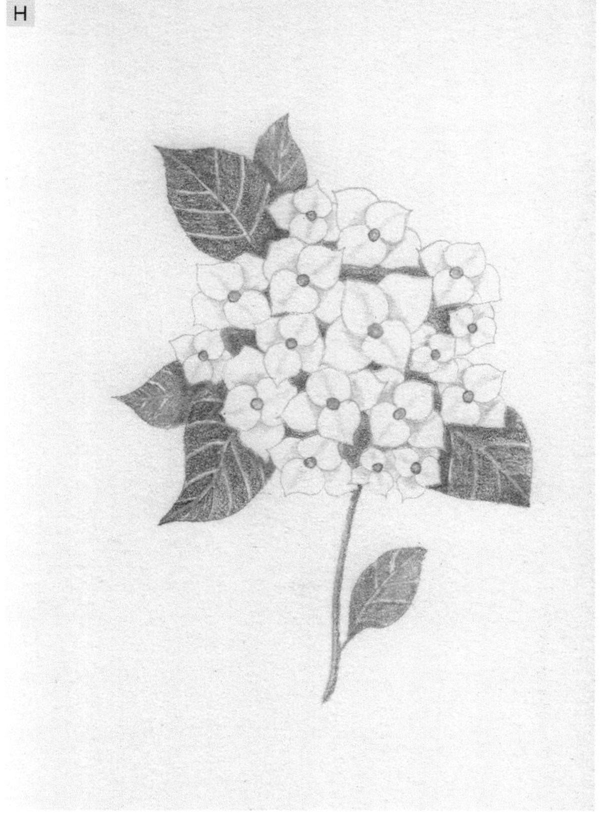

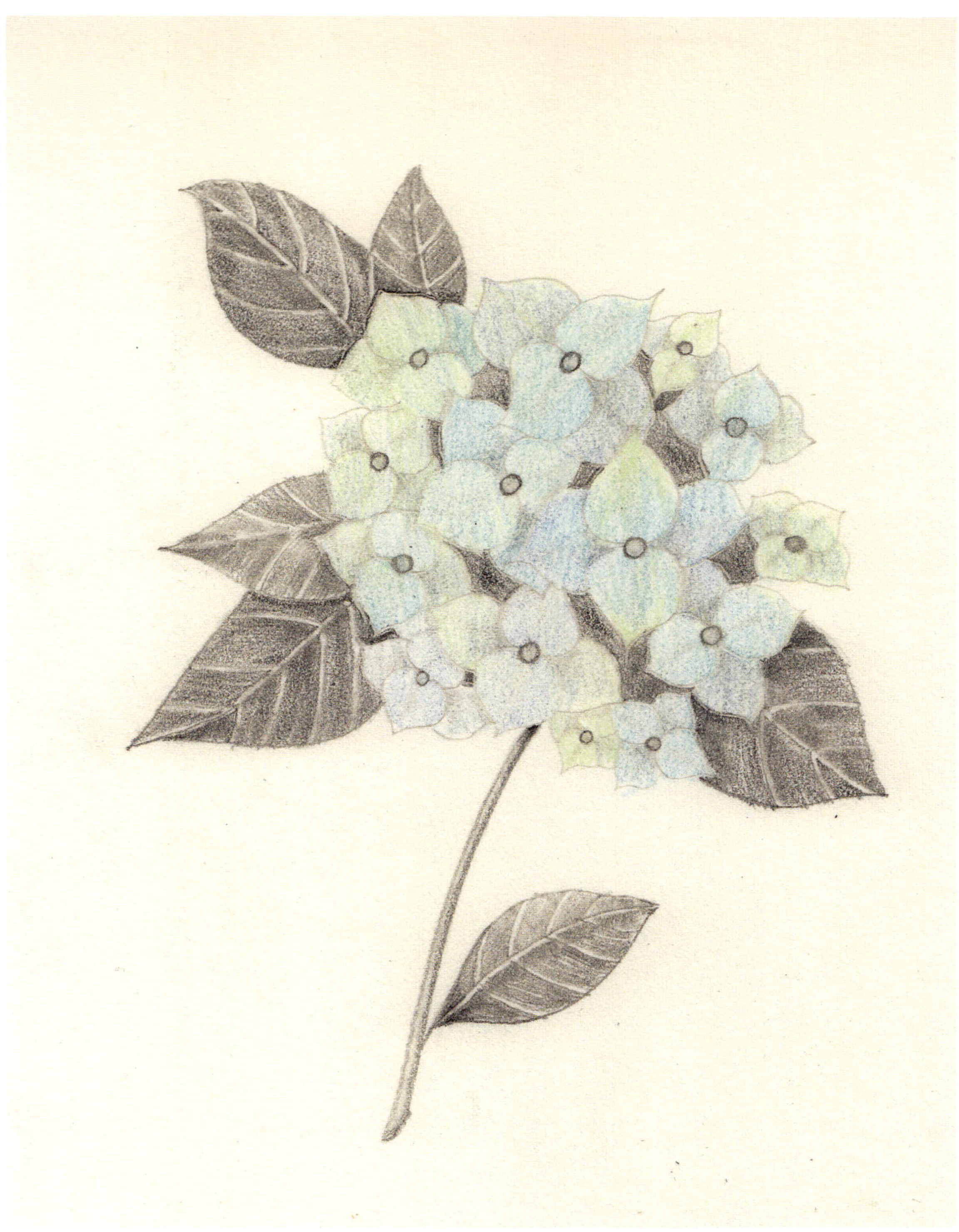

What if you used colored pencils to shade the petals of the flower? What if you drew the entire flower in colored pencil? What if you created an entire bouquet of hydrangeas? What other flowers could you break down into similar steps using different shapes?

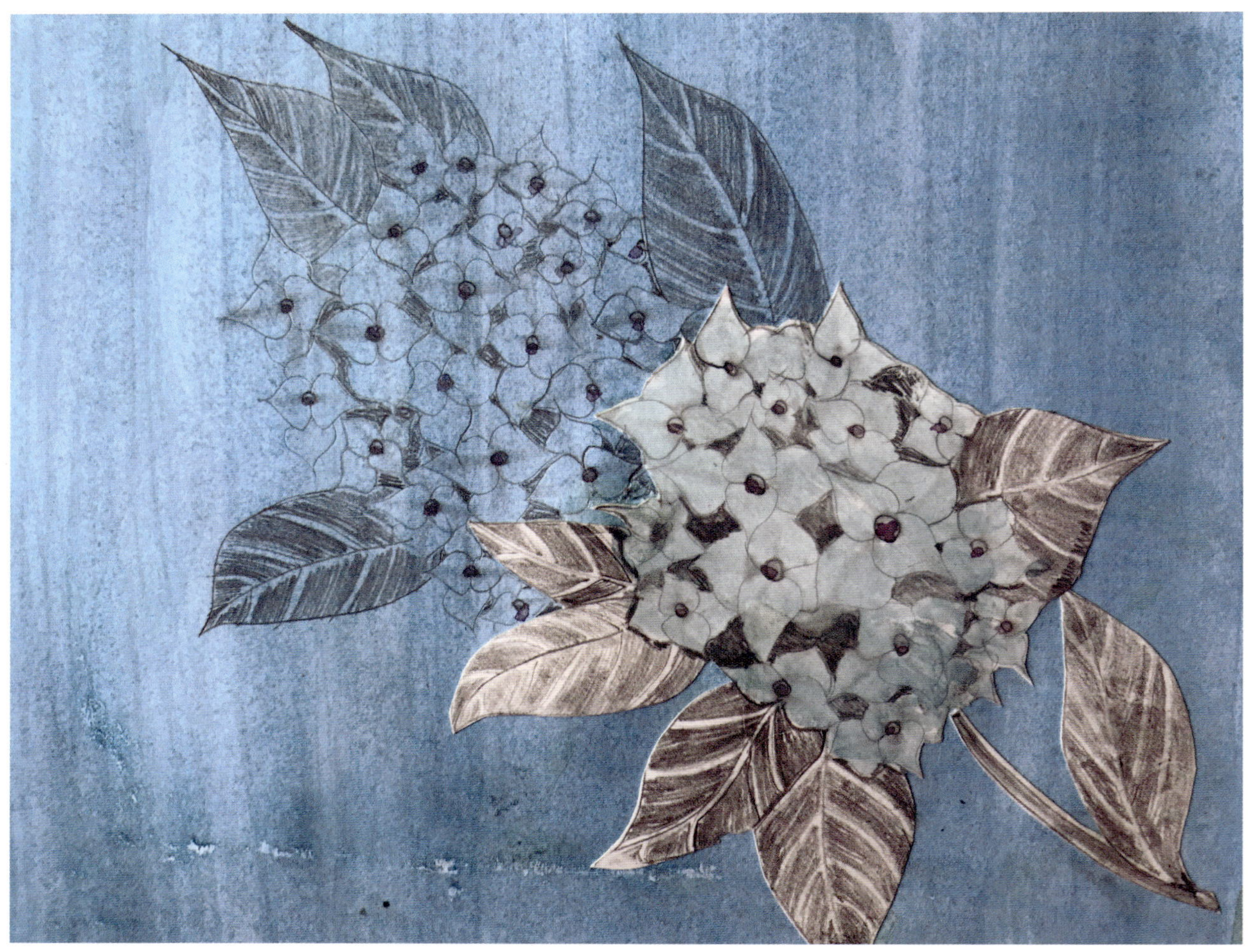

Mary Dowson

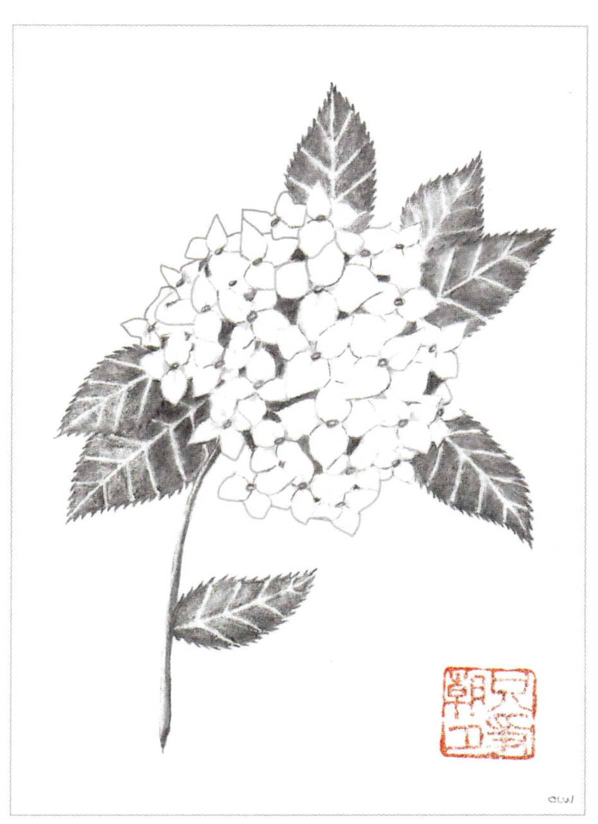

Carol Williamson

Jane Woker

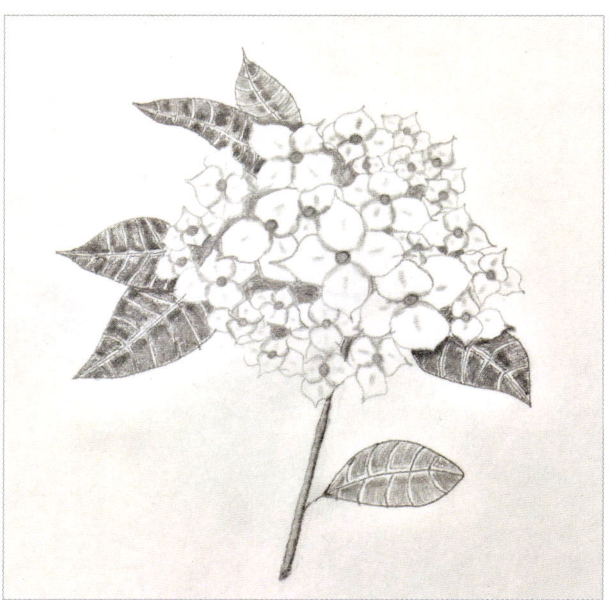

Lina Card

LESSON FOUR

THE SEEING AND DRAWING PRACTICE

Now it's time to get representational with our new drawing skills. All this means is that what we draw has a likeness to a real subject we are looking at as we make our marks; it is not simply from memory or imagination. Our first projects were more freeform and imaginative, or based on technical skills. Now, it's time to look closely at a simple subject and use our pencils to make marks based on what we see. I call this Seeing and Drawing Practice, and it is the way I taught myself to draw real, tangible things from everyday life. There is no measuring, no rulers or perspective or foreshortening. Instead, we rely on the way our eyes perceive something, line, light, and shadow, and we make intuitive marks in our own way.

Every time I lead a group of beginners in a seeing and drawing lesson, people are amazed at their results. "I had no idea I could do this!" is something I hear commonly. So, let's get started on our first subject—a lettuce leaf.

TOOLS TO GATHER

- Pencils in 2H, HB, and 5B
- Drawing paper, about 5 × 7 inches (13 × 18 cm) or larger
- Eraser
- Blending stump or tortillon

STEPS

1- We will practice our seeing and drawing skills with the leaf in the center of the reference image, but I hope you continue this practice by trying all the leaves! Begin by using an HB pencil to create a simple outline of the leaf shape. Start anywhere it feels natural and slowly create a light outline of the leaf shape you see. Don't be afraid to start and stop; use your eraser, but don't get too hung up on perfection. We are not trying to create a photocopy, but a tender drawing of how our eyes perceive this lovely lettuce leaf. Use the sample image as a guide. Remember, do not press too hard with your pencil—keep that feather touch. *See A.*

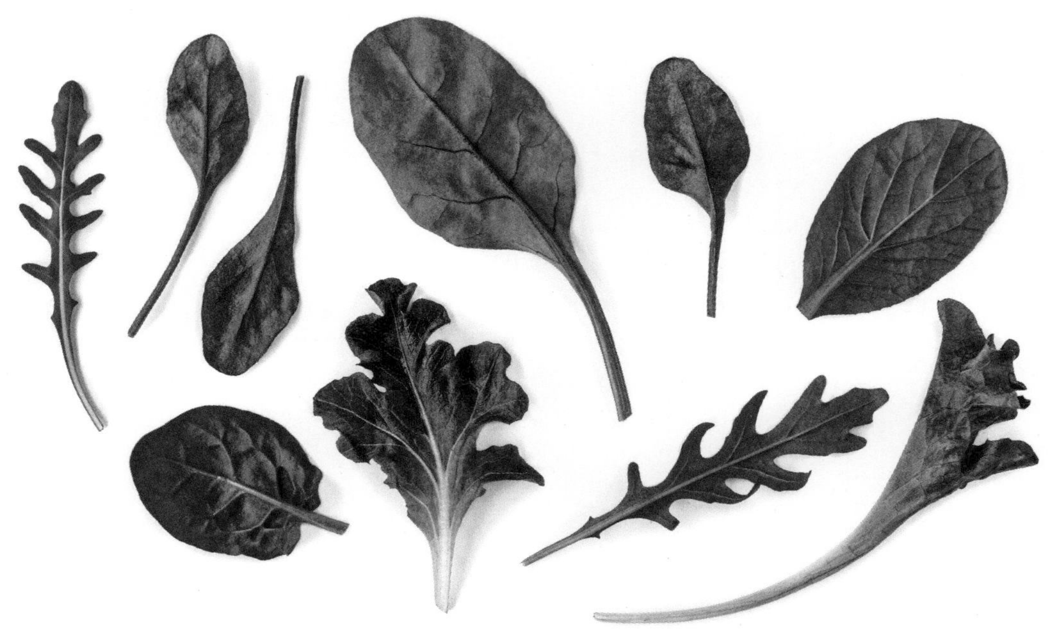

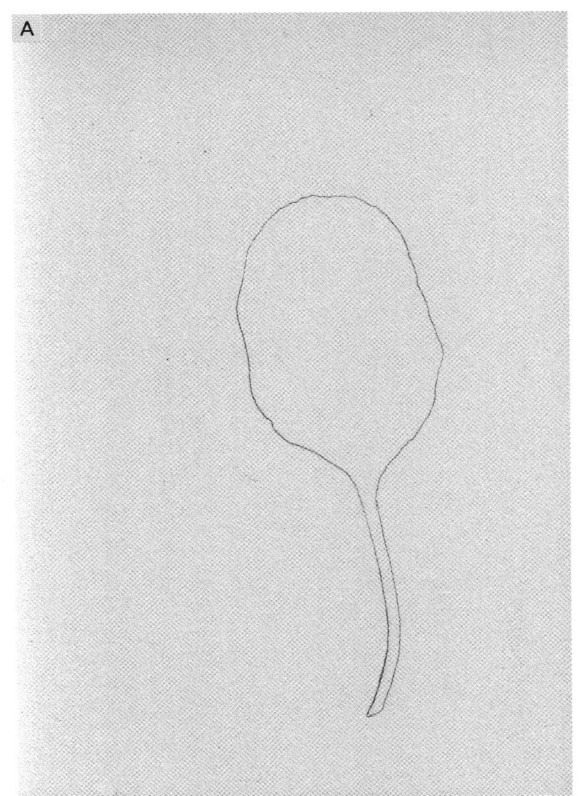
A

2 - With the HB pencil, start at the top of the leaf and create a soft shading mark to form the center rib. Notice how it starts out very thin and gradually becomes as wide as the stem at the bottom of the leaf. Fill in the stem with gentle shading marks, smoothly moving the pencil in small strokes as evenly as possible. Then, use the same technique to create the side veins, as shown. Look at the reference image, not the sample drawing, as you create your marks. The sample is just a guide to show you which parts of the subject we are working on. *See B.*

3 - Switch to the 2H pencil. Paying close attention to the reference image, lightly fill in the leaf where you see the darkest areas. Let your marks move in the same direction that you notice on the subject. Study the sample image as an example, but also look directly at the subject when making your marks. Again, feather touch. It should be a lighter gray than the HB pencil marks. *See C.*

4 - Finally, switch to the 5B pencil. Notice the places on the stem, center rib, and veins that are darker in value. Use your 5B pencil lightly to create these small areas of darkness. Sometimes these final dark areas are very small, but their impact makes a big difference. *See D.*

How did that feel? I recommend trying this exercise three times: first for learning, second for practicing what you learned, and a third time when you will not be so worried about the steps and can relax and really see and draw what you notice. Remember, do not get too rigid about creating an exact likeness; that is not our goal. Now, try some of the other leaves, starting with the flatter varieties and working your way to the curly lettuces.

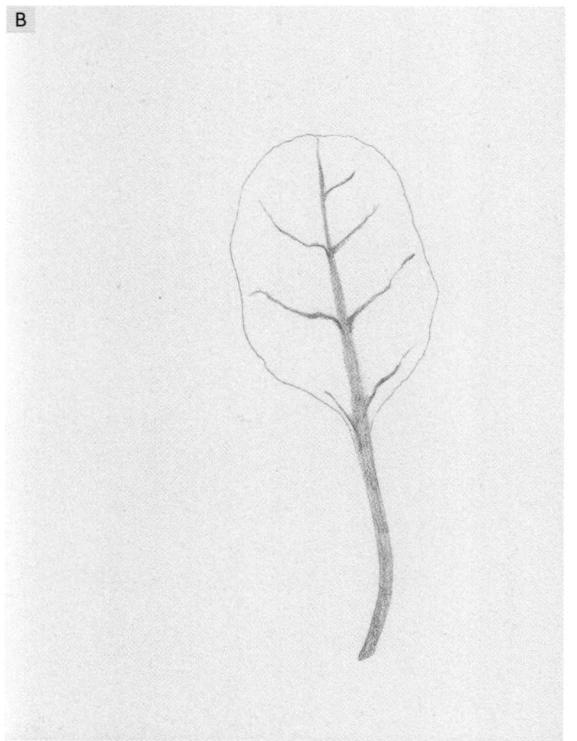

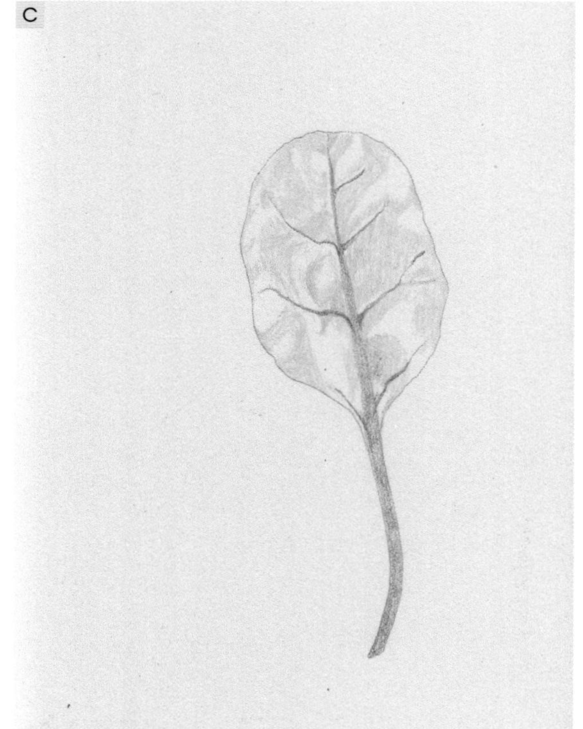

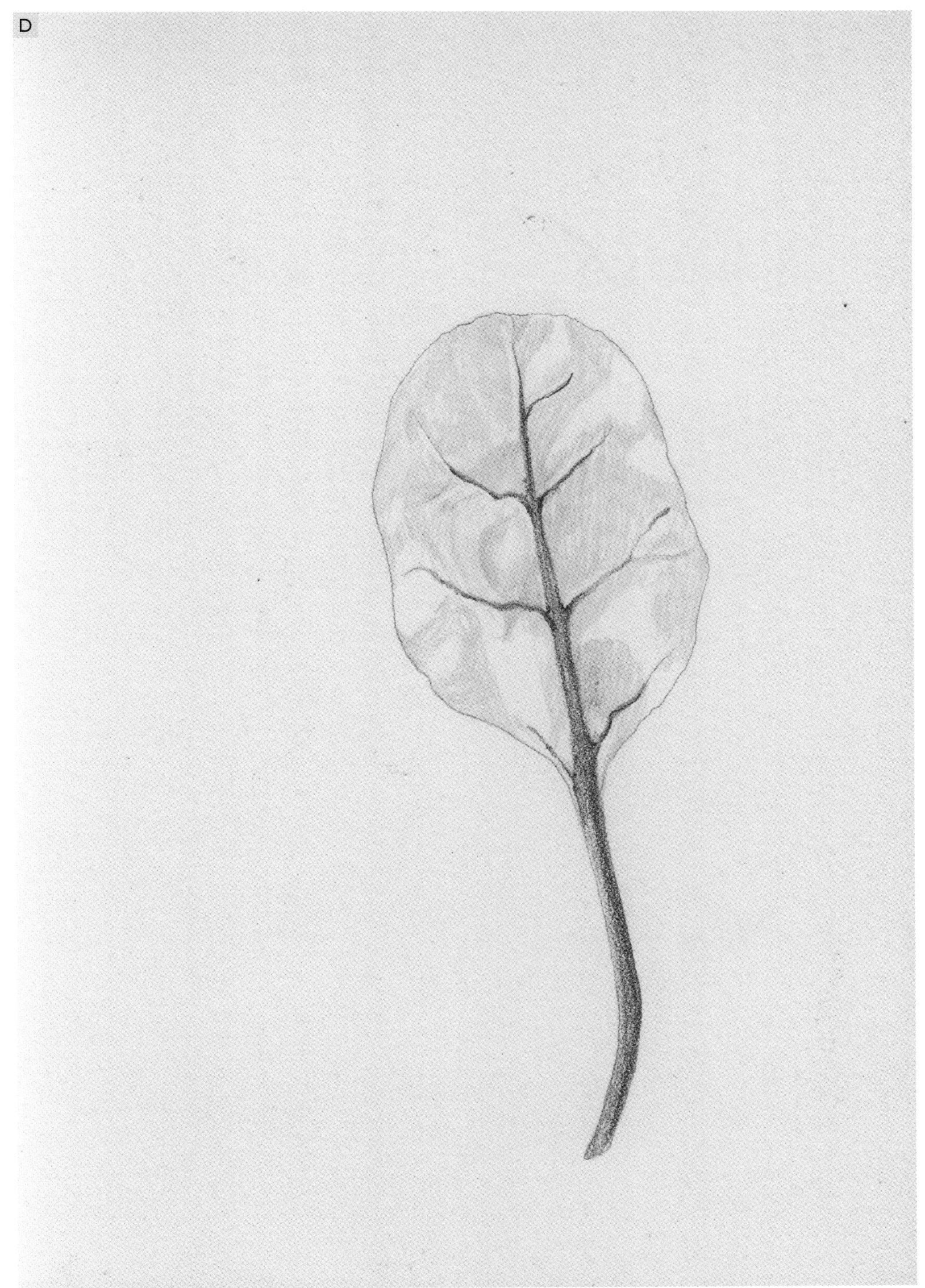
D

LESSON FIVE

TO DRAW A STONE

In the winter of 1856, John Ruskin, artist and famous art critic, wrote in his book, *The Elements of Drawing*:

> *Now if you can draw that stone, you can draw anything; I mean, anything that is drawable. Many things (sea foam, for instance) cannot be drawn at all, only the idea of them more or less suggested; but if you can draw the stone rightly, everything within reach of art is also within yours.*
>
> *For all drawing depends, primarily, on your power of representing Roundness. If you can once do that, all the rest is easy and straightforward.*

This idea of learning to represent roundness by drawing a stone is the subject of this lesson. In Lesson 4 (page 32), we drew a fairly flat subject, a lettuce leaf. Now, we will build on what we have learned by drawing a more three-dimensional object—a smooth stone. To make any subject appear three-dimensional on a flat piece of paper, we must learn to see and depict contrast and shadow, the lights and darks of our subject, and the smoothness of transitions between them, as our eyes see them. Although we will use a reference image of a stone, I hope you will continue this lesson with a real stone to further explore the technique. At the end of this lesson are stones drawn from life by other beginner artists. This lesson requires your attention and time, but the results are remarkable and will give you the confidence to try many other subjects you wish to draw—the principles are the same no matter the subject.

TOOLS TO GATHER

- Pencils in 2H, HB, 3B, and 7B
- Drawing paper, about 5 × 7 inches (13 × 18 cm) or larger
- Kneaded eraser
- Blending stump or tortillon

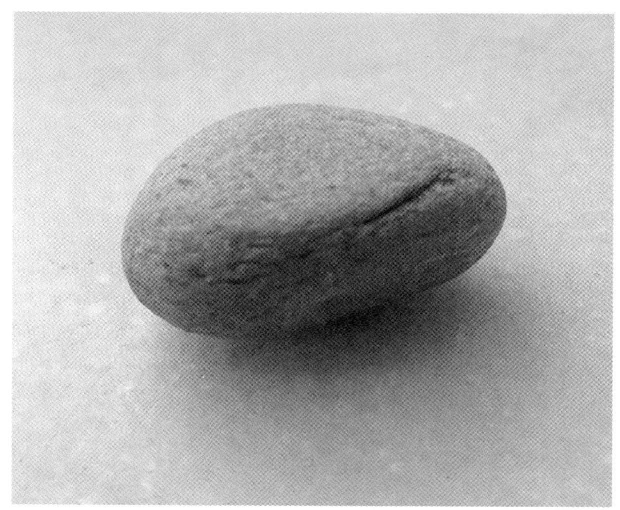

STEPS

1 - With an HB pencil, take your time to create a line drawing of the outline of the stone on your paper. Use an eraser to make adjustments, if needed.

2 - Continuing with the HB pencil and a feather touch, make small marks to shade the inside of the stone, paying attention to the direction of form of your marks. Instead of simply making random back-and-forth marks in one direction, direction of form follows the contour of the subject. Study the sample image in comparison to the reference image for how this is achieved. And remember, we all see things differently, so yours will be different from the sample. Using this technique to fill in a shape gives us the start of the illusion of roundness.

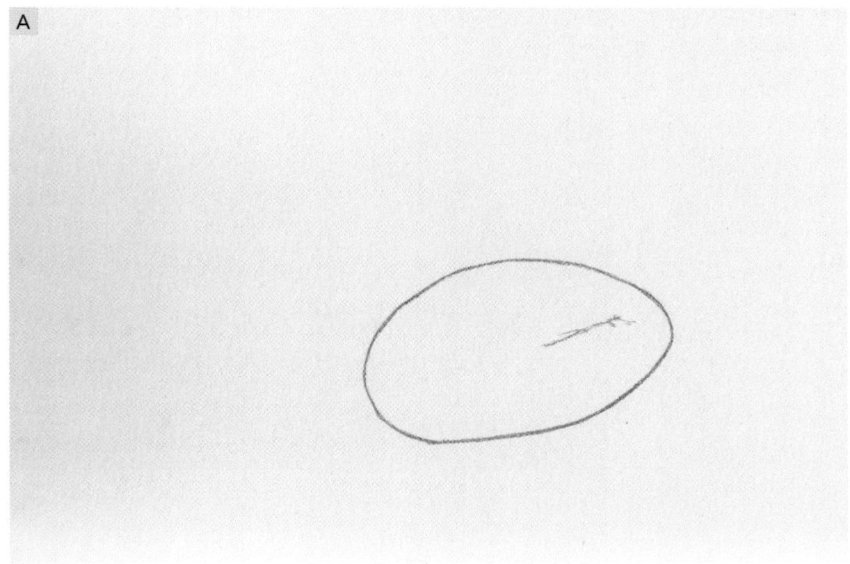
A

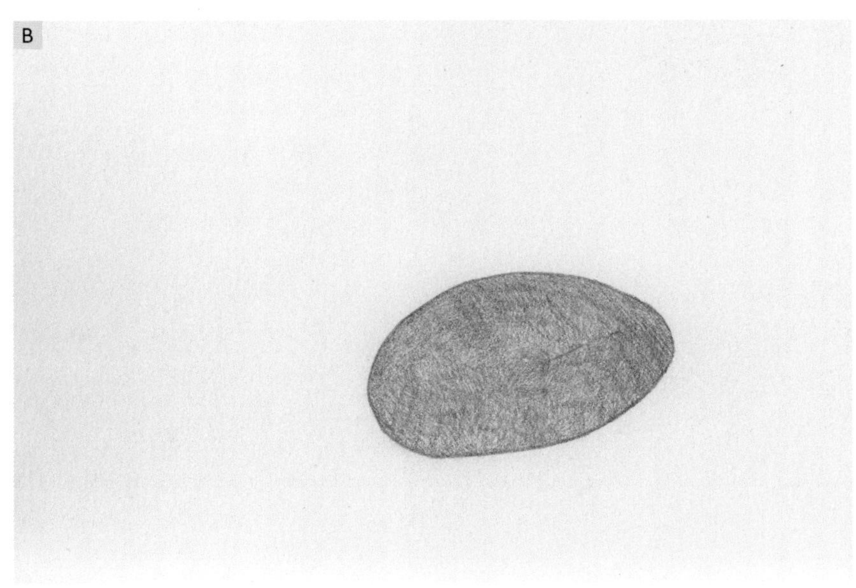
B

3 - Use your kneaded eraser to lift off some of the graphite in areas where the reference stone is lighter in value—gently press and lift the flattened section of the eraser. Pay attention to anywhere the stone seems lighter to your eye. Use the sample image as a guide, but always do your work directly from the reference image or actual subject. *See C.*

4 - Use the 2H pencil to create marks that mimic the textural details your eyes see. Let your eyes comb the entire surface of the rock as you add these delicate markings. Pay attention to the area where the lighter section that you erased meets the darker section. Use the 2H pencil to blend these areas with small, short marks. *See D.*

5 - Use your 3B pencil to put a fine layer of graphite over the lower half of the stone that is in shadow. Remember, use the feather touch so you do not disturb the layers and textures already there. Then, use the same pencil to create the cast shadow, noticing where the darkest areas begin and end. Use the sample as a guide. *See E.*

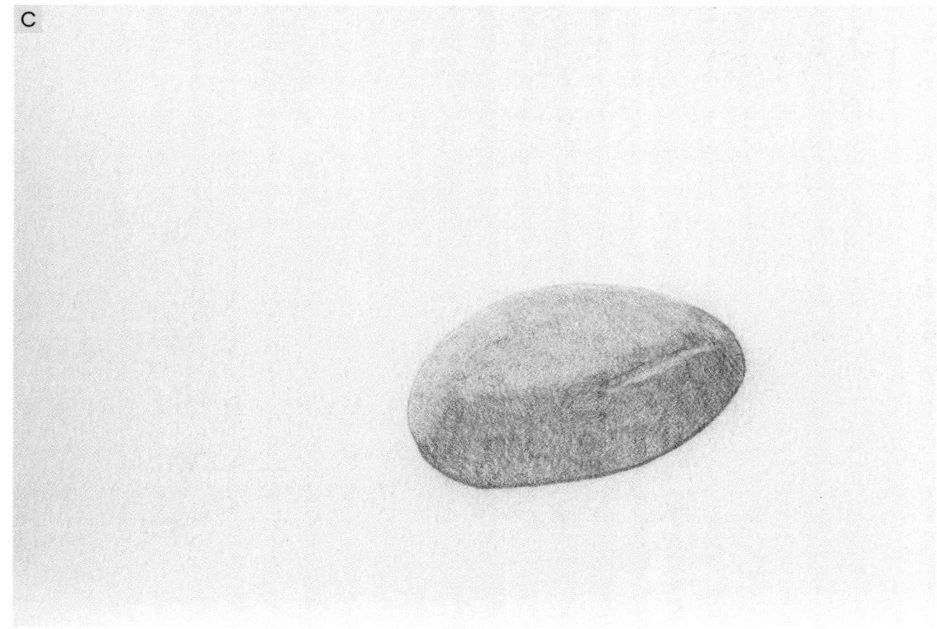

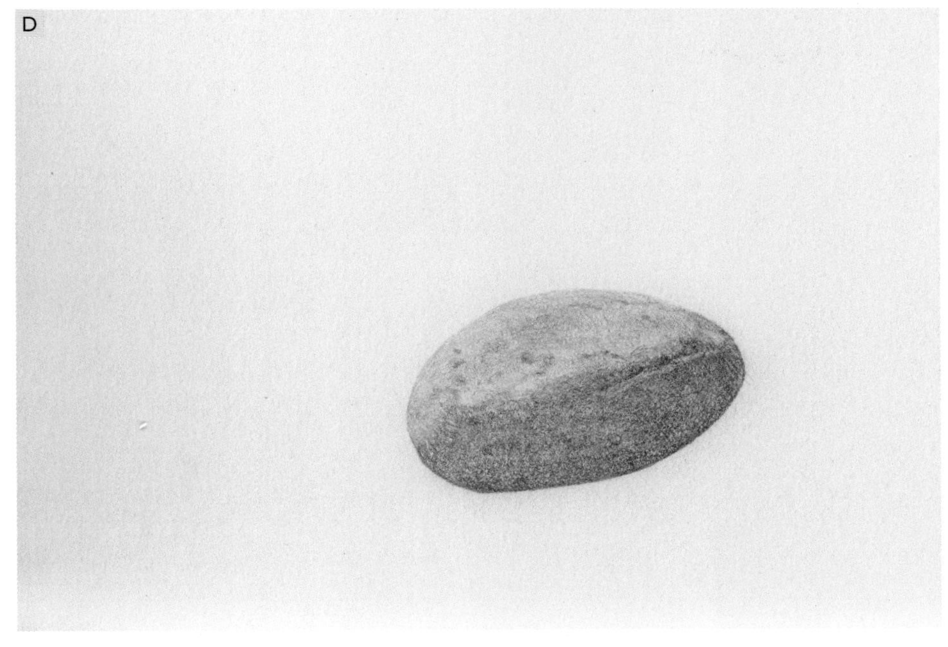
D

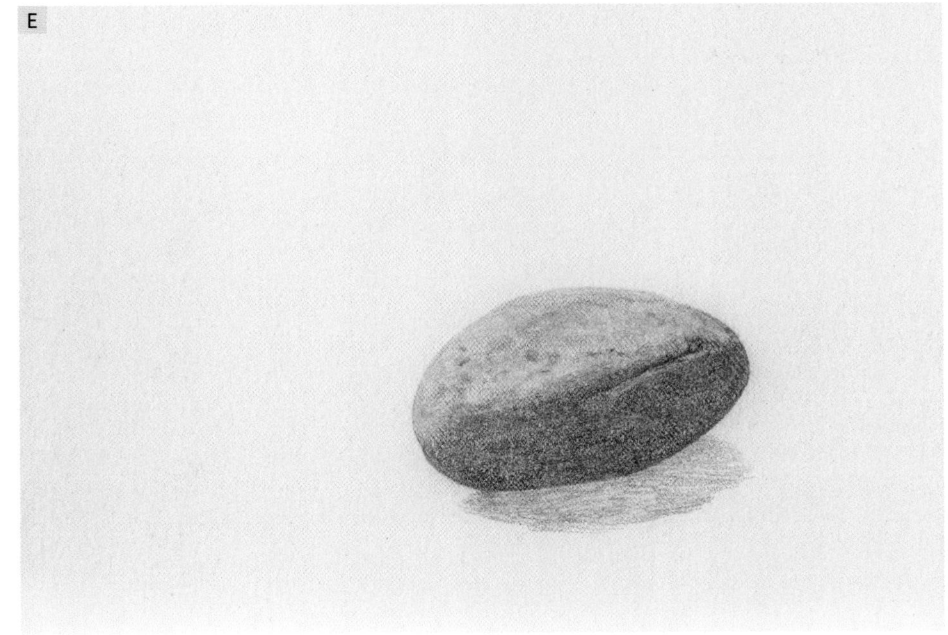
E

6 - Use the 7B pencil to add tiny dark contrast marks to the center of some of the textural marks on the stone, as shown. Then, create an inner layer of darkest cast shadow under the stone. *See F.*

7 - Finally, use your tortillon to lightly blend and soften the cast shadow underneath the stone. Use your eraser to further soften this, if needed. *See G.*

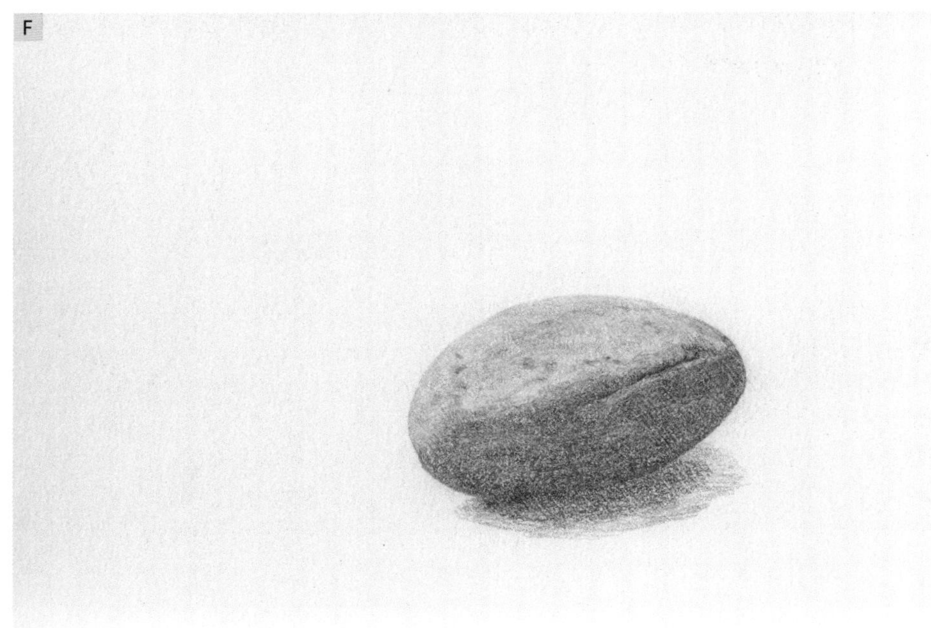
F

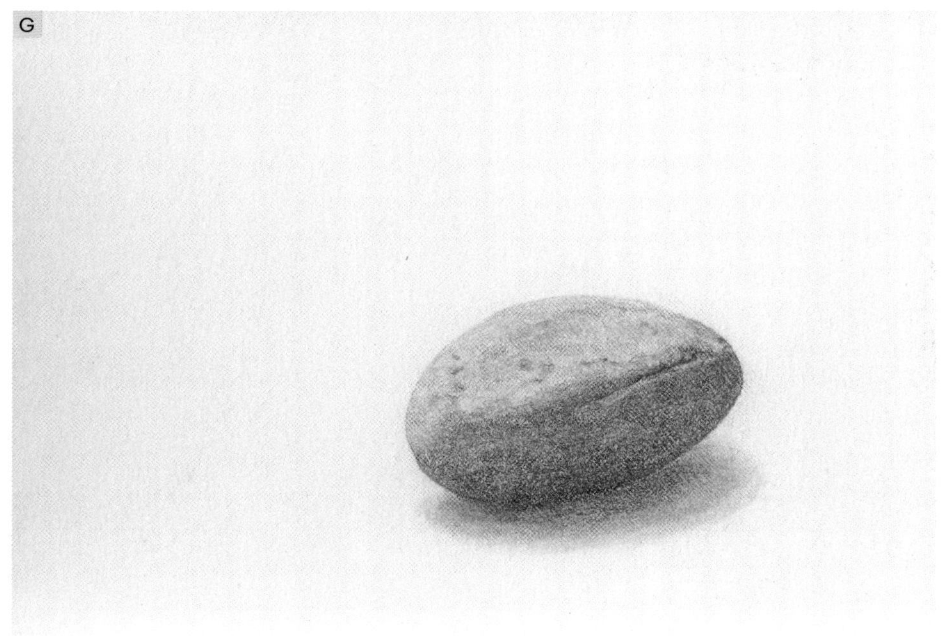
G

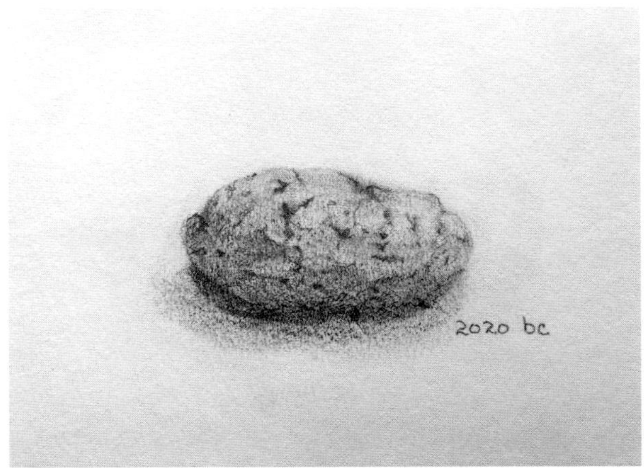

Beverly Eddy

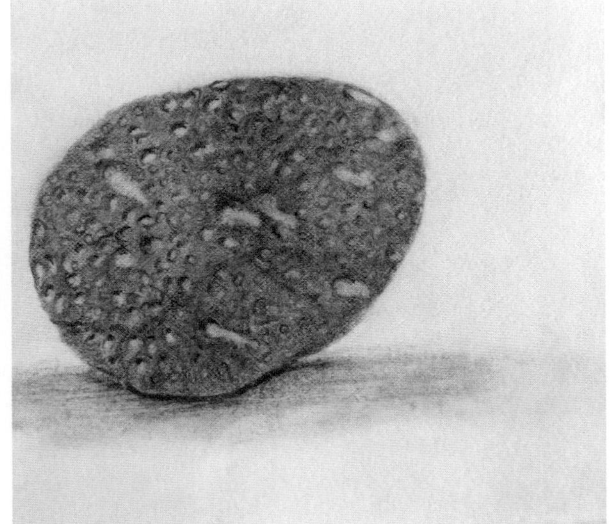

Liz Gamelin

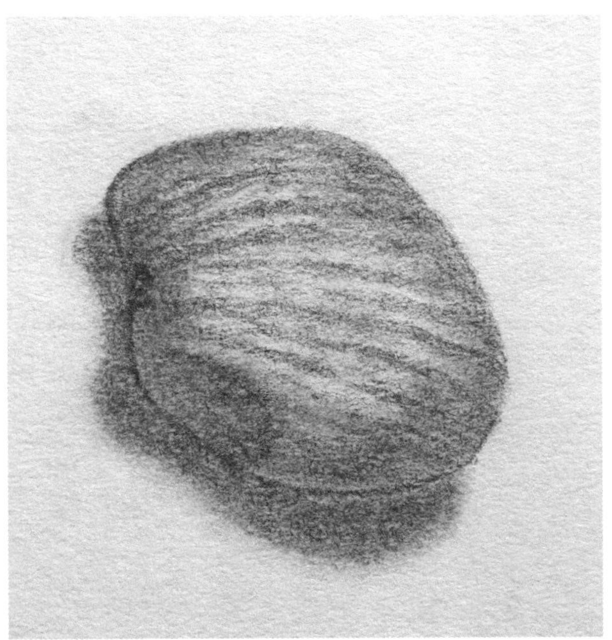

Nathalie Bélanger

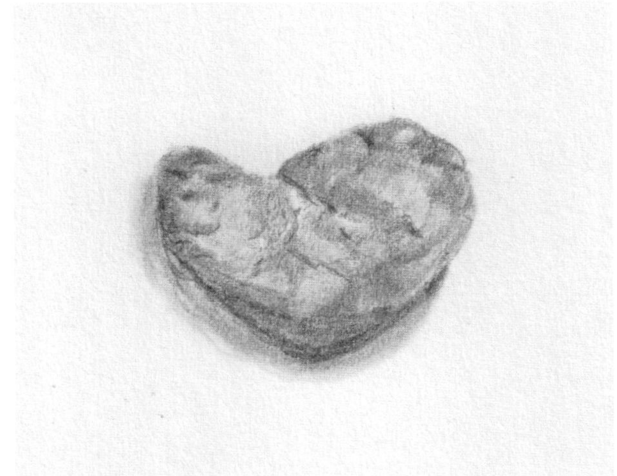

Lisa Hoffman

LESSON SIX

LEAVES AND DIRECTION OF FORM

If the feather touch is the first most important tip I can share with you for making beautiful drawings, the concept of direction of form is a close second. It can be a tricky concept at first, but this lesson will surely set you on your way to using it in every drawing you create. The best example I can think of to help demonstrate this is drawings of leaves. The reference images for this lesson will provide the plant you practice from, but for now, look at the leaf on the far right, middle row. Notice how it is curled and has real dimension.

Now, look at the example below and notice that although it is the same leaf shape, it looks flat, even with shading added in the same places. This is because the lines that fill in example A simply go back and forth, instead of following the curvature of the different parts of the leaf. Look again at the reference image leaf and notice how the lines follow the shape and curvature of the form. This, in a nutshell, is direction of form. Shading alone can make a difference, but it will not prove nearly as successful as making our marks and filling objects in with direction of form.

Let's try two examples of leaves, each from a different angle, to practice direction of form.

TOOLS TO GATHER

- Pencils in HB and 5B
- Drawing paper, about 5 × 7 inches (13 × 18 cm) or larger
- Kneaded eraser
- Blending stump or tortillon

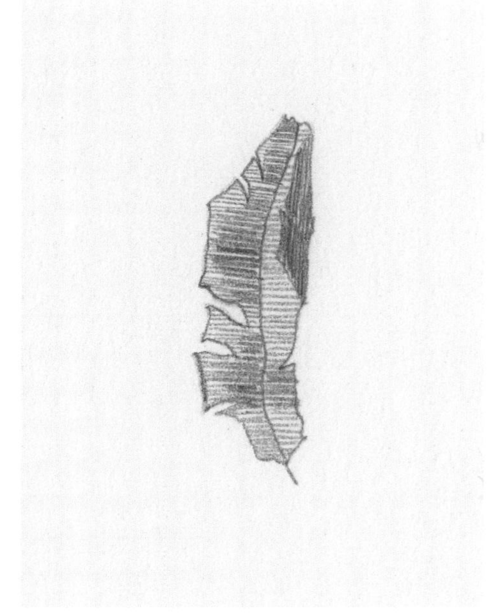

STEPS

1 - With an HB pencil, create a simple outline drawing with a center vein for each of the two leaves, as shown. Do not worry if they do not match exactly. The techniques will work regardless of precision. And remember, you have an eraser, if needed! *See A.*

2 - Draw lines from the outer edge, diagonally, to the center rib, as shown. Even if you change the angle a bit, it will still work. All leaves are different! We are simply aiming to create a sense of dimension. *See B.*

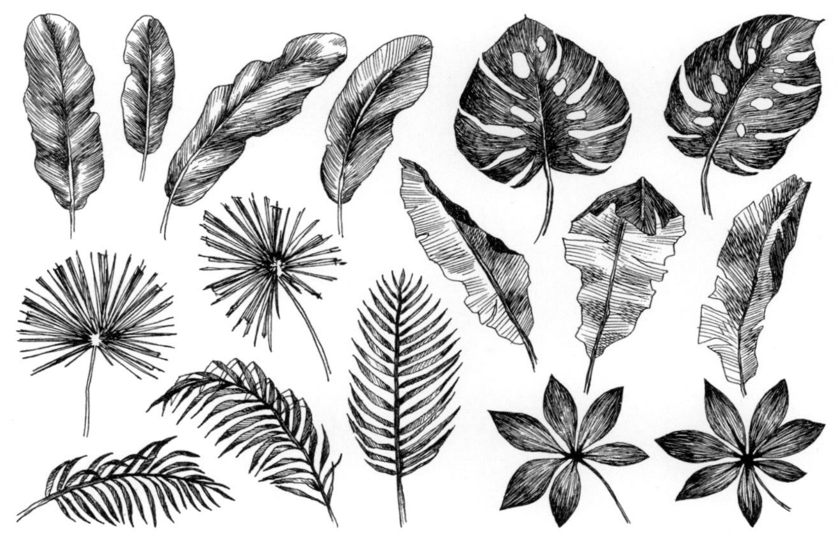

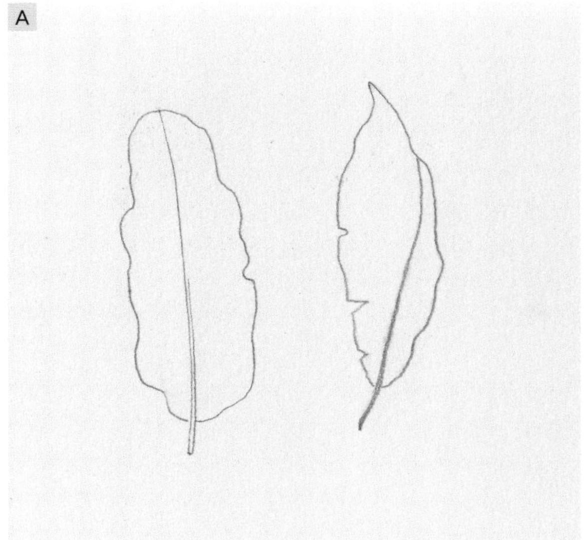

A

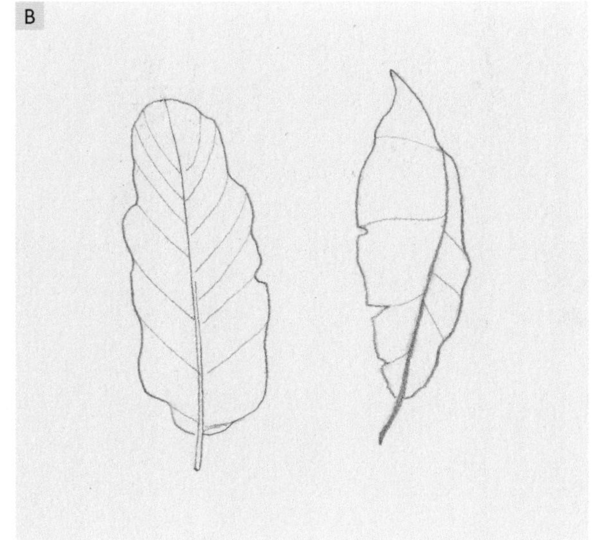

B

3 - Continue to fill in more lines, following the direction of form, as shown. *See C.*

4 - Using a blending stump or tortillon, also in direction of form, lightly blend the graphite. *See D.*

5 - Using an eraser, lift out some areas of light. Use the reference image of leaves as an example of where light might be seen on similarly shaped leaves or follow the sample image. Then, use the 5B pencil to lightly add some darker shading where it might be darker. Follow either the reference image or the sample drawing. *See E.* You do not have to be exact. Having areas of contrast—light and dark—is what matters most. See how the leaves don't look flat, but have dimension to them? That is the illusion that contrast and direction of form help create.

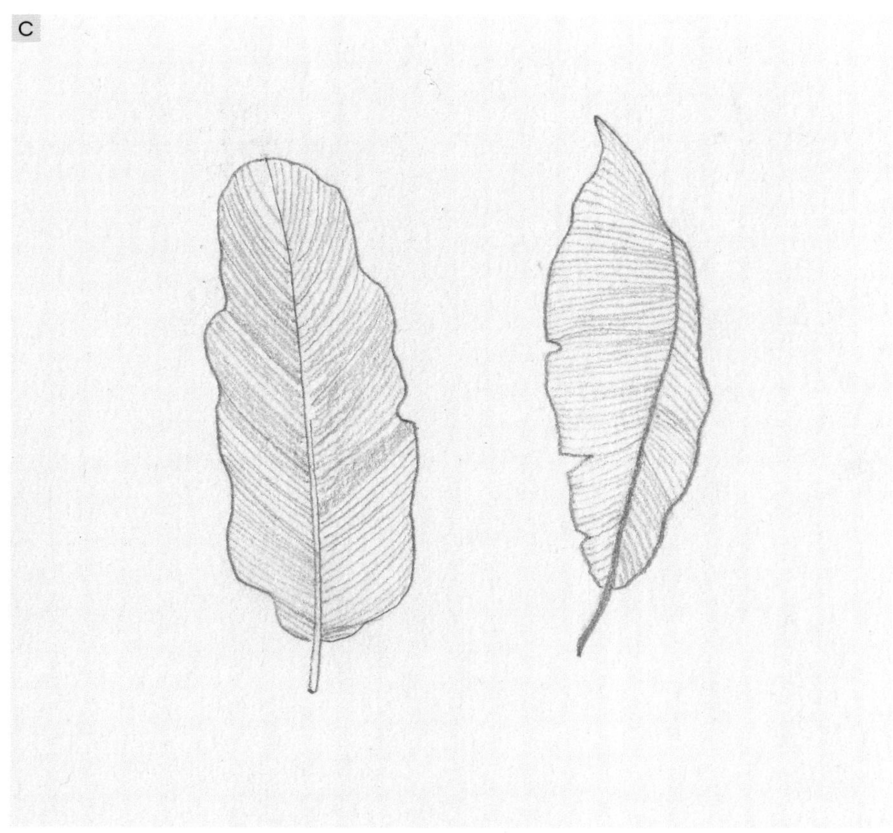

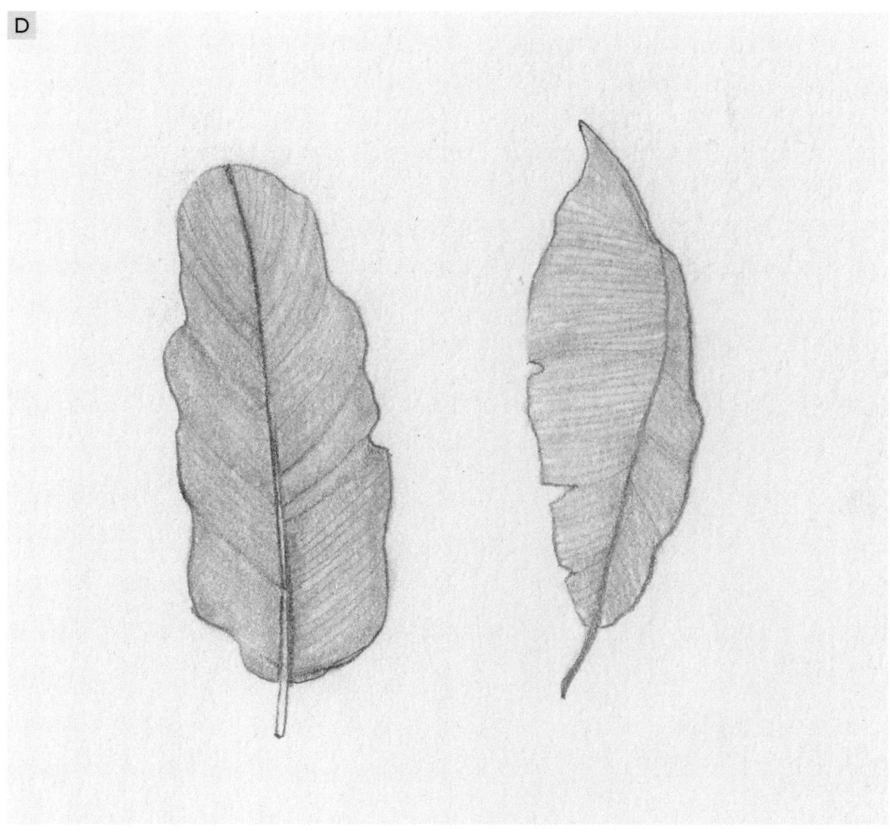
D

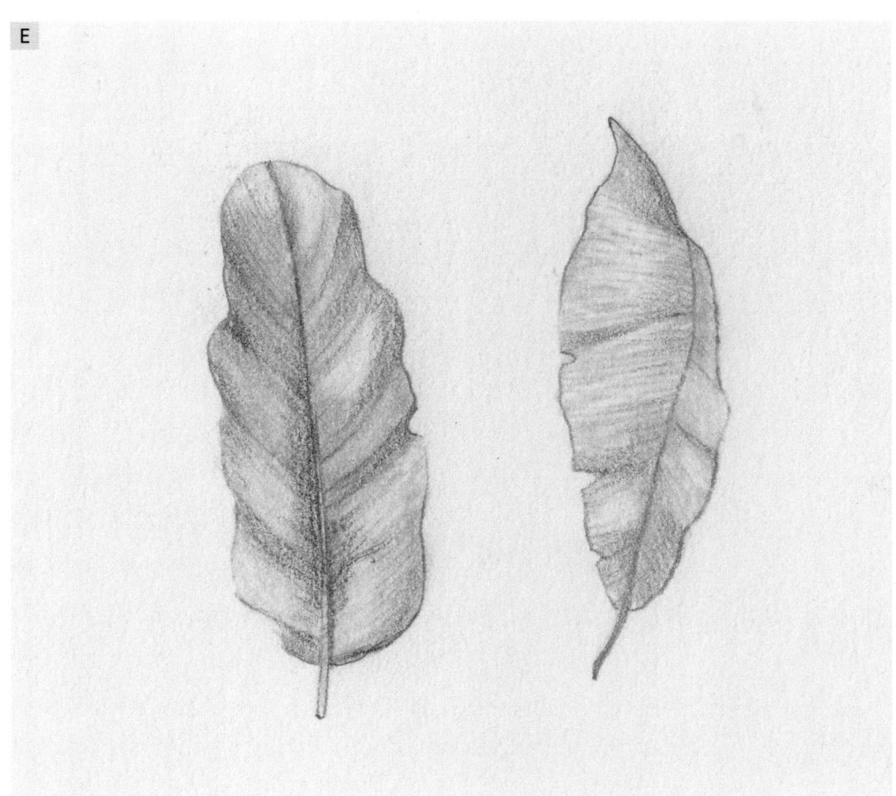
E

TAKE IT FURTHER

1 - Now, choose other leaves from the reference image as examples on which to practice these same steps. I chose one from the bottom right *(see F)* and followed steps 1 through 5 on the previous pages. Notice how my leaf isn't exactly like either of the two shown in the reference but still has the same qualities and is full of dimension. *See G.*

2 - Finally, draw some real leaves using this technique. *See H and I.* Once you get the basic outline shape, pay close attention to direction of form and contrast—there is really nothing you cannot draw.

F

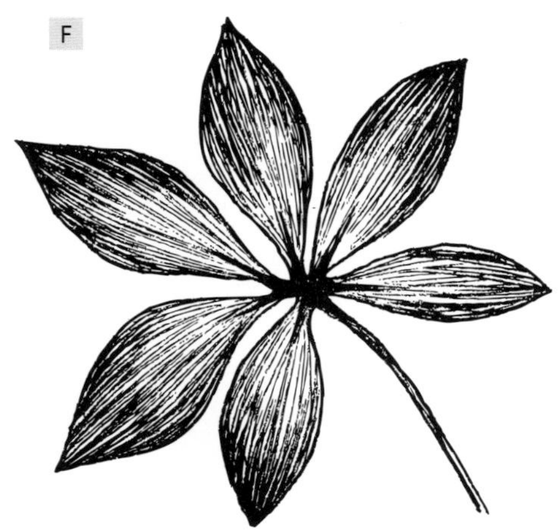

G

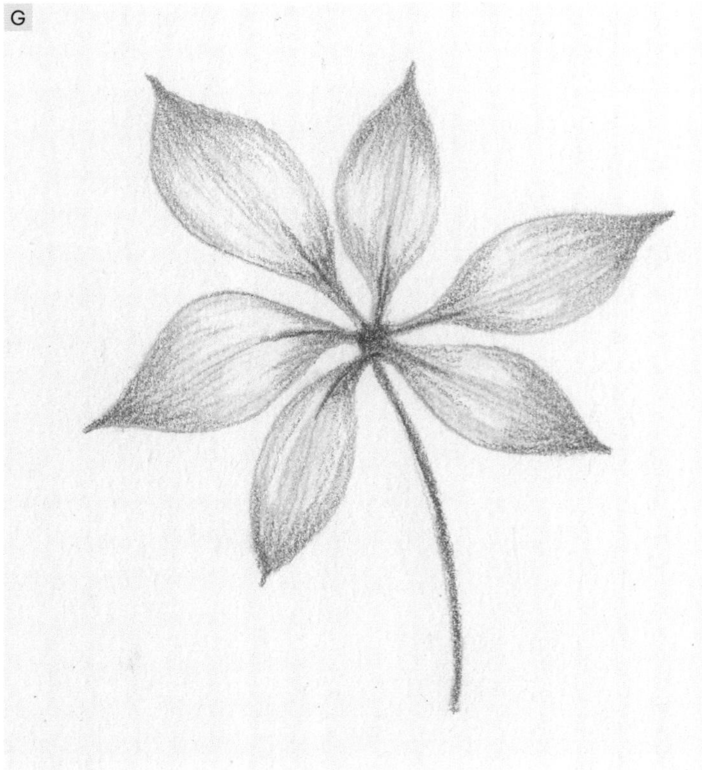

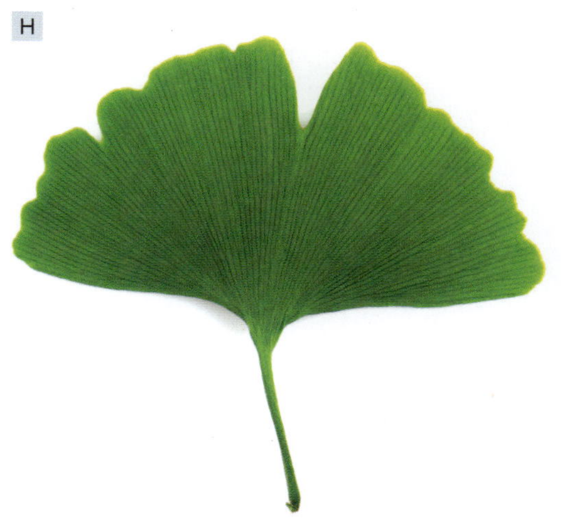
H

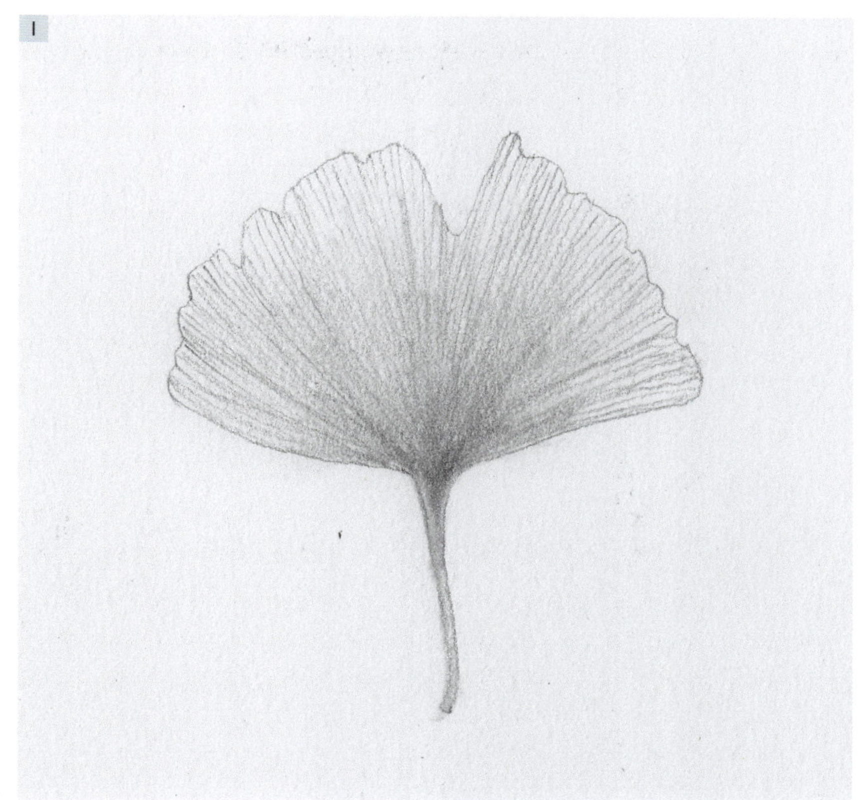
I

LESSON SEVEN

POCKET TREASURE COLLAGE

Now, it's time to create a piece of artwork that brings together all the elements we have learned so far. I like to think of these drawings as pocket treasure collages because, often, they are created from random assortments of acorns, seeds, leaves, rocks, flowers, bits of bark, and the like that I collect in my pockets while out on walks. These drawings can also include landscapes or birds, a special cloud formation, etc., and always include random mark making to fill the spaces between the objects I've drawn. It's a great mix of intuitive expressive work and representational work.

At right is an example of a collage I made; see page 53 for another. Notice how intricate they can become. The more you practice, the more elements you can add to them. The possibilities are endless! For this lesson, let's keep it simple using images from the reference photos we have used so far, as well as the mark making we have been practicing. Follow along for some good fun!

TOOLS TO GATHER

- Pencils in 2H, HB, 3B, 5B, and 7B
- Drawing paper, about 5 × 7 inches (13 × 18 cm) or larger
- Blending stump or tortillon
- Kneaded eraser
- Reference images from previous lessons and this lesson
- Workable fixative (optional)

To prevent smudging the graphite, feel free to use a workable fixative between steps, if you tend to rest your hand on the paper while you draw. You can also rest another piece of paper under your hand to prevent accidental smearing as you work.

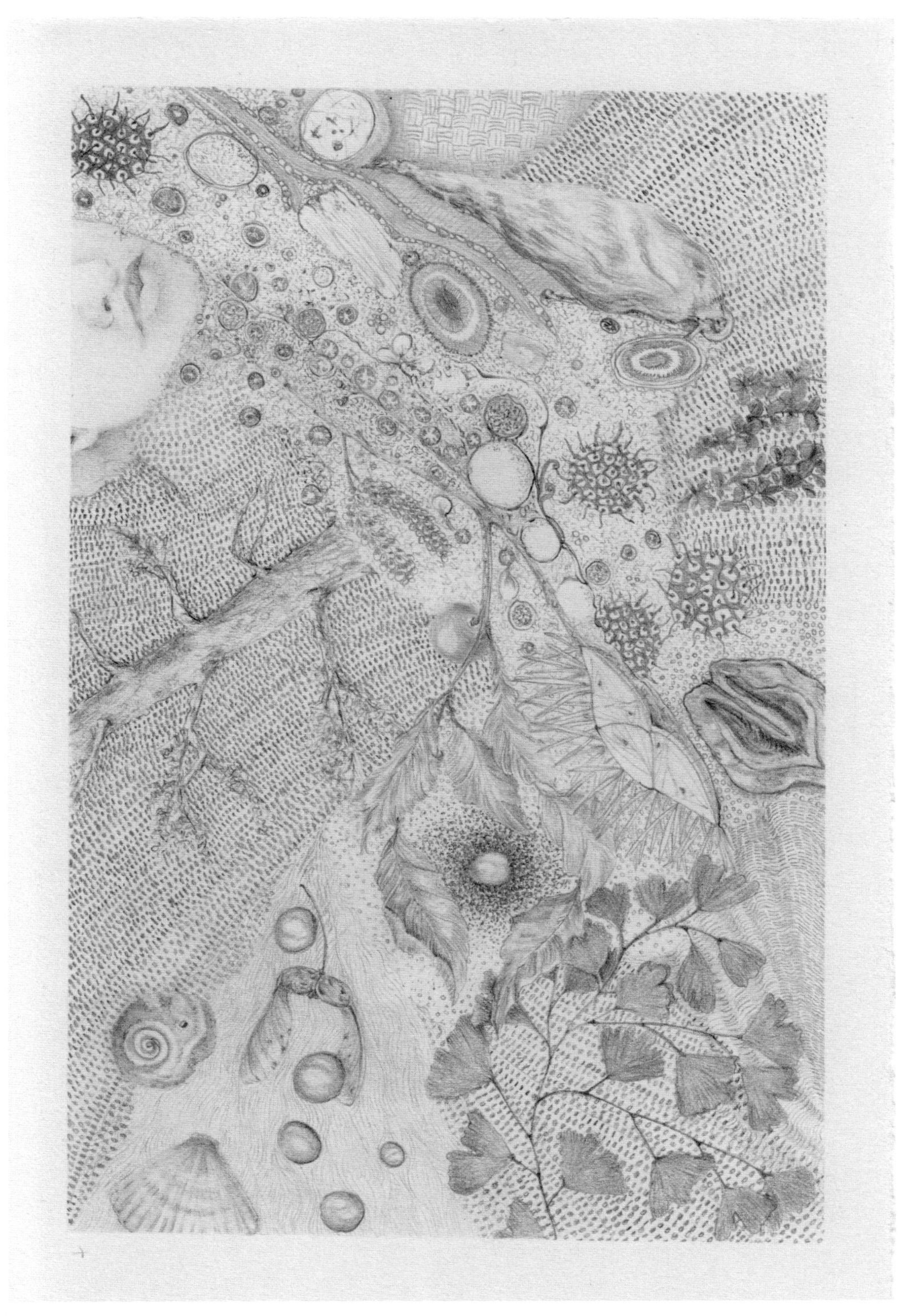

STEPS

1 - Begin by drawing the outline and direction of form markings of the acorn, as shown. Place it toward the center right of your paper. *See A.*

2 - Finish the acorn in the same way we created the leaves in Lesson 6 (page 42). Then, create a drawing of the piece of bark in the same way. You can choose other subjects in the reference image if they appeal to you more. Make an outline drawing of another leaf between the first two subjects using images from the reference photos, as shown. *See B.*

3 - Finish the leaf, and then add the line drawing for a smaller version of the hydrangea we created in Lesson 3. *See C.* Revisit any previous lessons for refreshers on how to create these drawings.

4 - Finish the hydrangea, and then fill out the rest of the page in a balanced way, with more line drawings of subjects from the reference images. *See D.* They don't have to be exact. Use the references on page 43 as a guide.

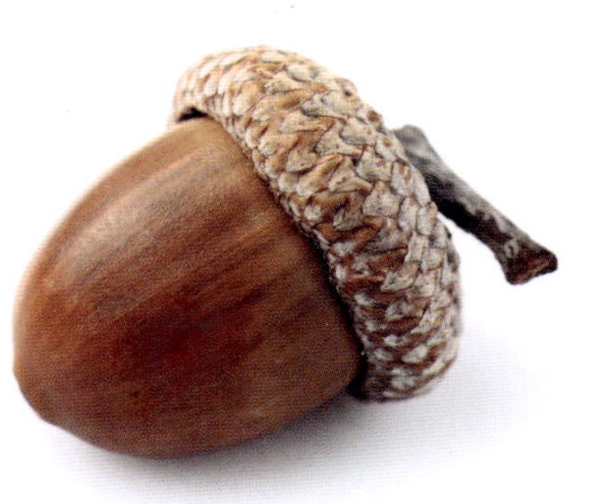

A

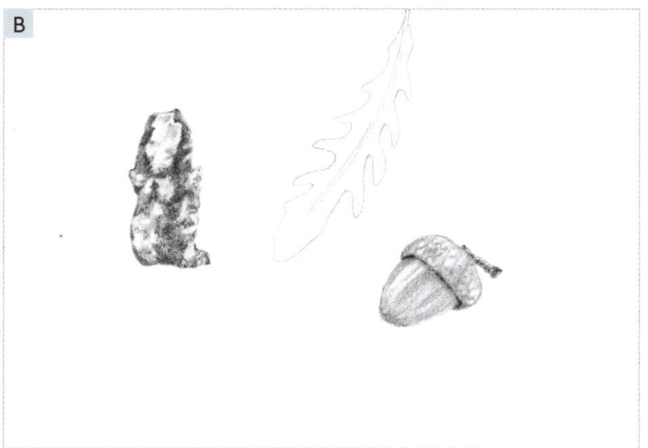

B

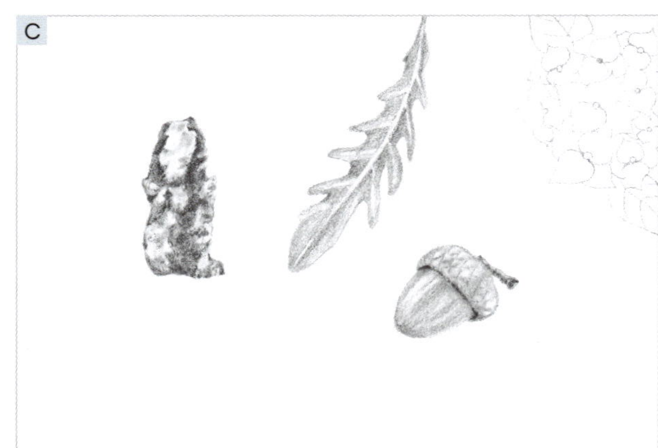

C

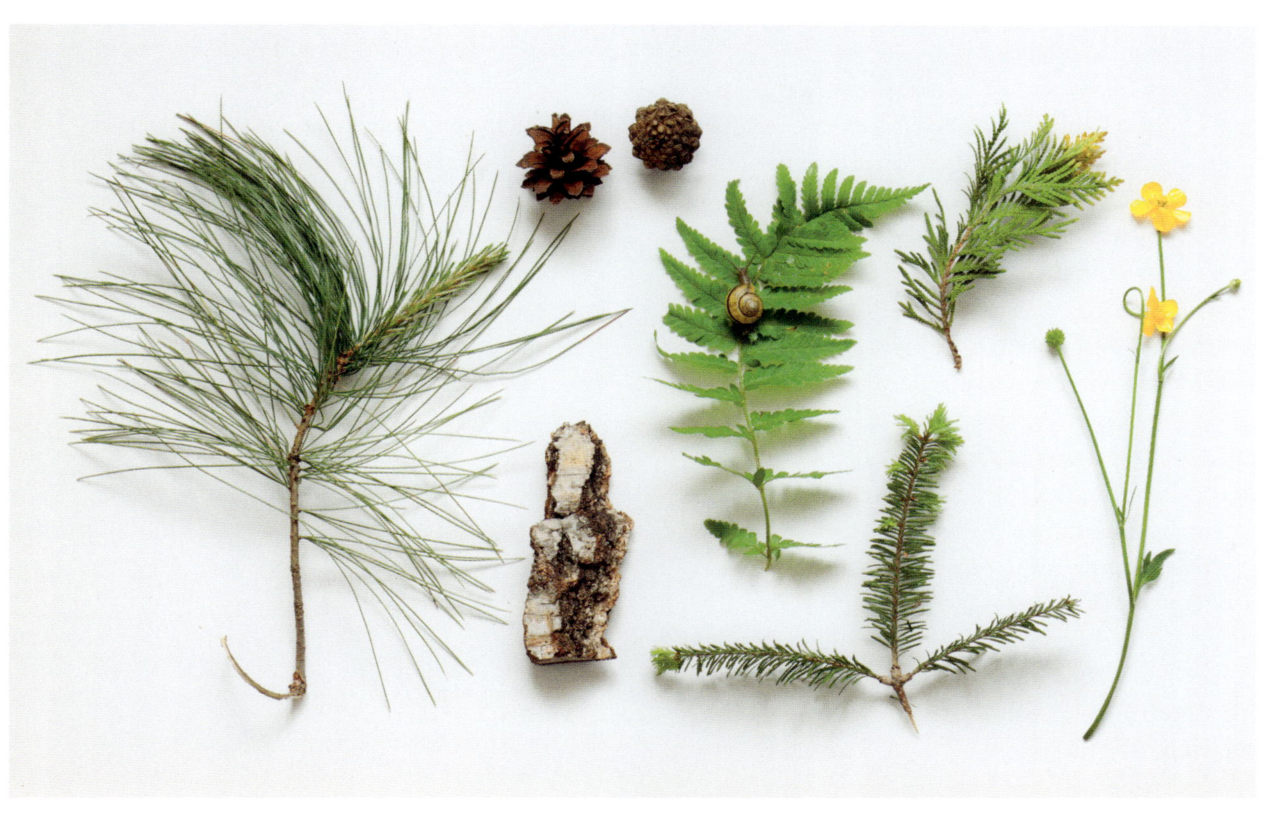

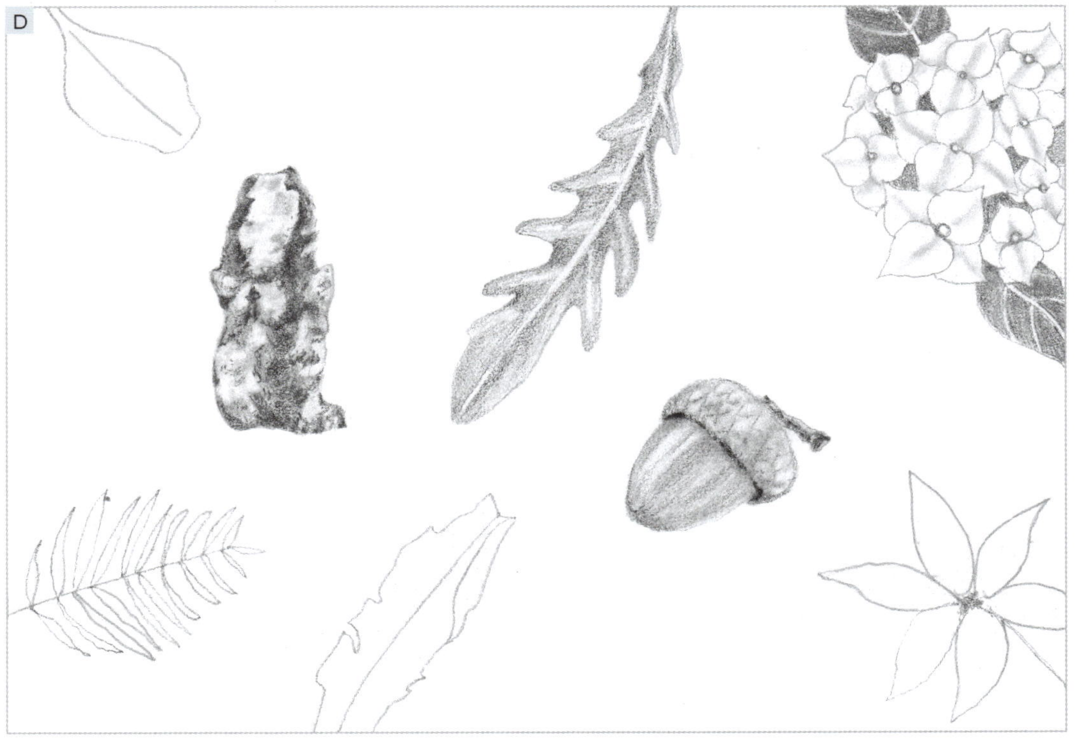
D

5 - Finish the drawings of the leaves you began in step 4, and then begin to create a circular pattern of the tiny tick marks we used in Lessons 2 and 4. Use different pencils to achieve different shades of gray to bring interest to the pattern. Spray your drawing with fixative (if using), if your hand is smudging the pencil marks on the paper. Finally, use an HB pencil to draw in some dividing lines lightly, as shown.

6 - Use the sample as a guide to suggest ways to fill in each section with tiny marks. You can also experiment with your mark making in these sections. Be creative and free, using different pencils to create a variety of marks and shades of gray. Notice the technique in progress, filling in the long sections with curved lines. When this is complete, use your blending stump to gently smudge along each long line, as shown in step 7.

7 - The finished drawing is a feast for the eyes—many natural treasures surrounded by energetic, expressive mark making.

Try this lesson using different objects you might find throughout the year. Frame a few to give as gifts, personalizing the objects for the recipient. People love these intricate-looking pieces of art.

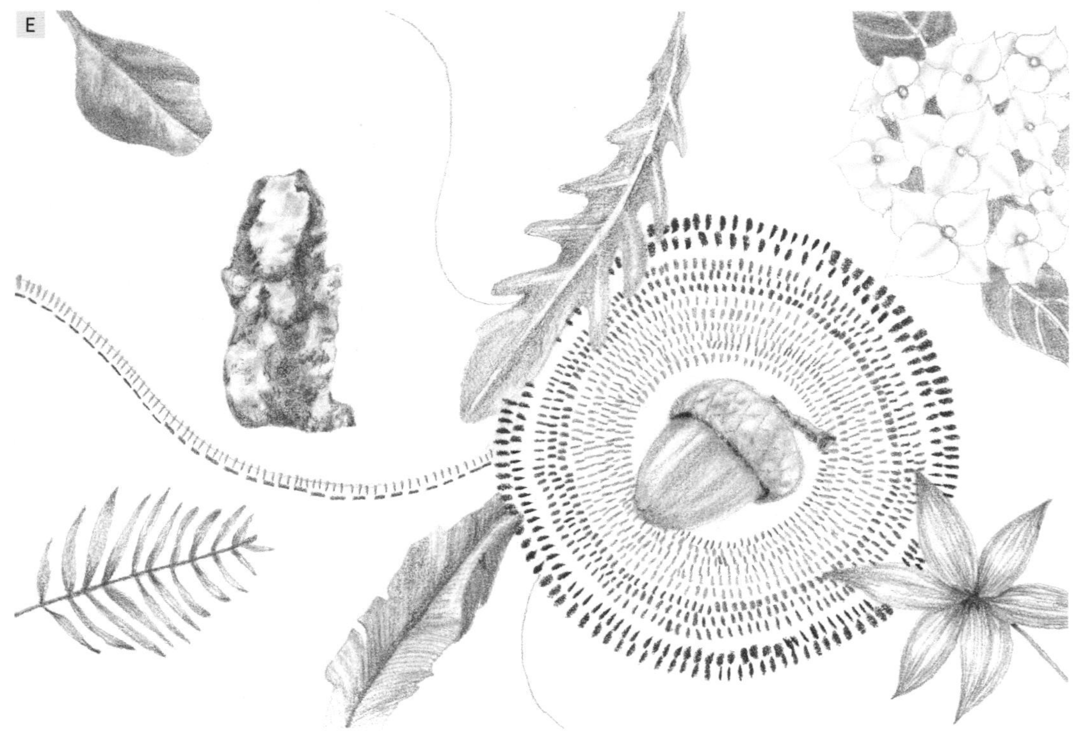

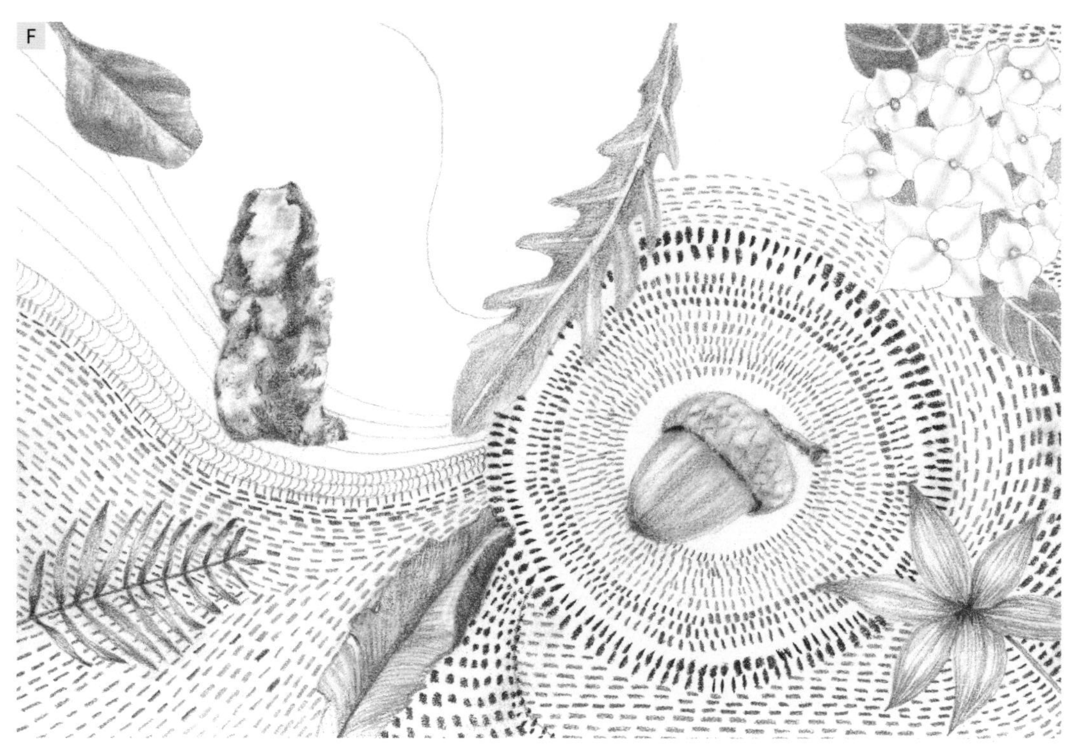
F

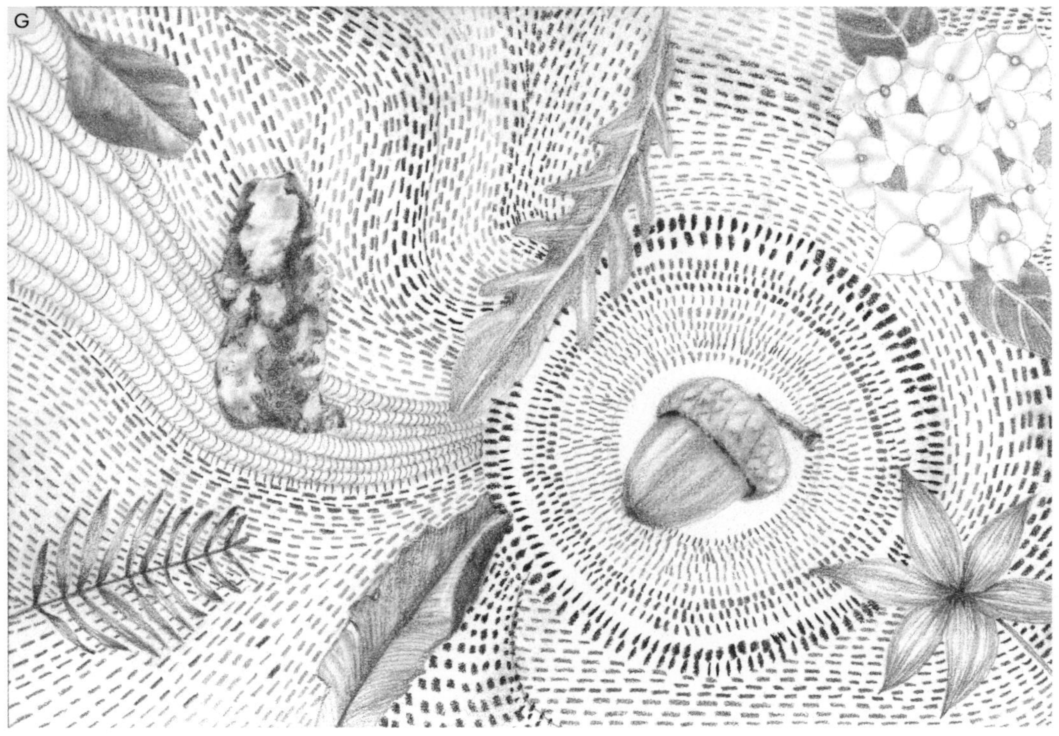
G

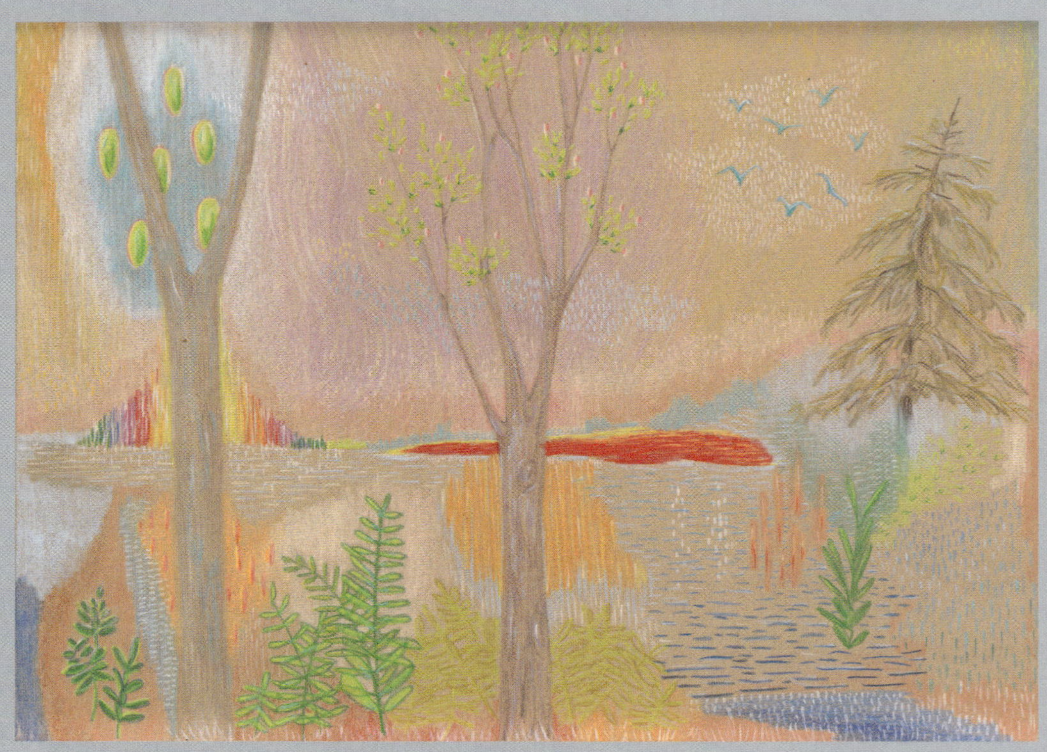

COLORED PENCIL

Oh, the pleasures of color. It can lift our spirits, soothe our anxiety, and bring energy to our days. The world loves color, and color brings the world to life. Although graphite can give us elegant monochromatic drawings of grays, colored pencil brings our efforts into full-spectrum beauty.

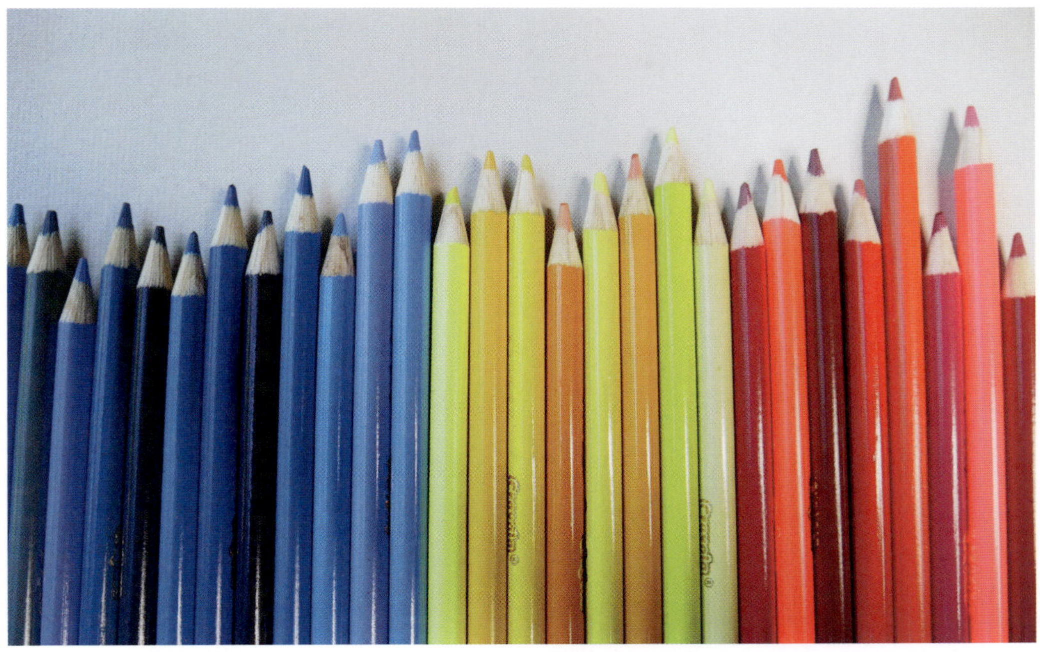

MATERIALS

Colored pencil can be used a lot like graphite, and we will build on the graphite techniques we have already learned—the same feather touch, shading, and mark-making techniques. One big difference between the two materials is that most colored pencil is difficult to erase, except brands made to be erased. Just like graphite pencils, the colored variety come in both student grade and professional grade. Some are wax-based, and they are a bit easier to erase, and some are oil-based and so a bit softer, allowing for creamier blending techniques.

The good news is, for our purposes, any colored pencils will do. My only suggestion is to buy a set with lots of colors, at least 24, with a good selection of grays and neutral tones. Even the large sets of 120 available for children are great. I use a variety of student- and professional-grade pencils, and list my favorite brands in the Resources section (see page 124) at the end of this book.

Our materials for these lessons are simple:

- A set of colored pencils in a wide range of colors
- A good handheld pencil sharpener (see Resources, page 124)
- Drawing paper in white or a variety of pastel colors, about 5 × 7 inches (13 × 18 cm)

LESSONS

Our lessons with colored pencils will take us through a few simple application exercises and mark-making techniques to build a foundation, and then we will apply our new skills to some beautiful color-rich projects you will be proud to frame or share.

LESSON EIGHT

A SWATCH OF MANY COLORS

It's time to add some color to our drawings! This lesson introduces the colored pencil and is a foundational exercise in how to use a feather touch while creating a smooth application that allows for layering to create new hues. Colored pencil can quickly build up, so further layers are not as affective and luminous. Just as with graphite pencil, using the lightest touch with color helps us keep the light of the paper shining through, so we don't saturate the paper's texture.

We will begin by selecting all the primary colors in our colored pencil set—the reds, yellows, and blues. As we create an interwoven mix of rectangular shapes, we will see new color hues appear where the different hues overlap. Not only is this an instructive exercise, but it also results in a lovely drawing that is a work of art by itself.

TOOLS TO GATHER

- Selection of red, yellow, and blue colored pencils
- Piece of drawing paper, about 5 × 7 inches (13 × 18 cm)

STEPS

1 - Beginning with a yellow pencil, draw a small square, as shown, toward the center of the paper. Fill it in as evenly as possible, using your feather touch. Then, use a red pencil to create another rectangular shape overlapping the yellow just a bit, as shown. Finally, use a blue pencil to create another shape overlapping both the other shapes. *See A.*

2 - Continue by using a different yellow, then red, and then blue pencil to create overlapping shapes, one after the other, moving around the shapes created, as shown. It's up to you how big the shapes are, what shape they take, and where they overlap. Use my example as a guide, remembering to use a light touch to fill in the shapes as evenly as possible. Notice how the overlapping areas create new colors. *See B.*

3 - Continue in this manner until you have used all your red, yellow, and blue pencils, creating a pleasing composition as you go. *See C.*

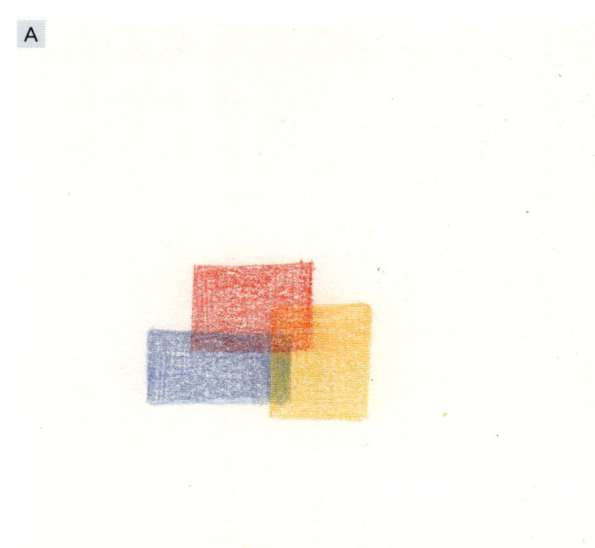
A

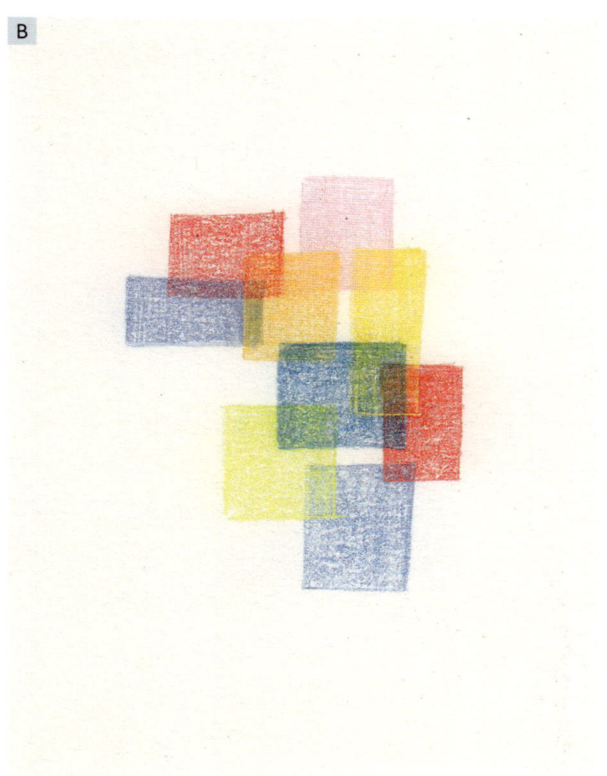
B

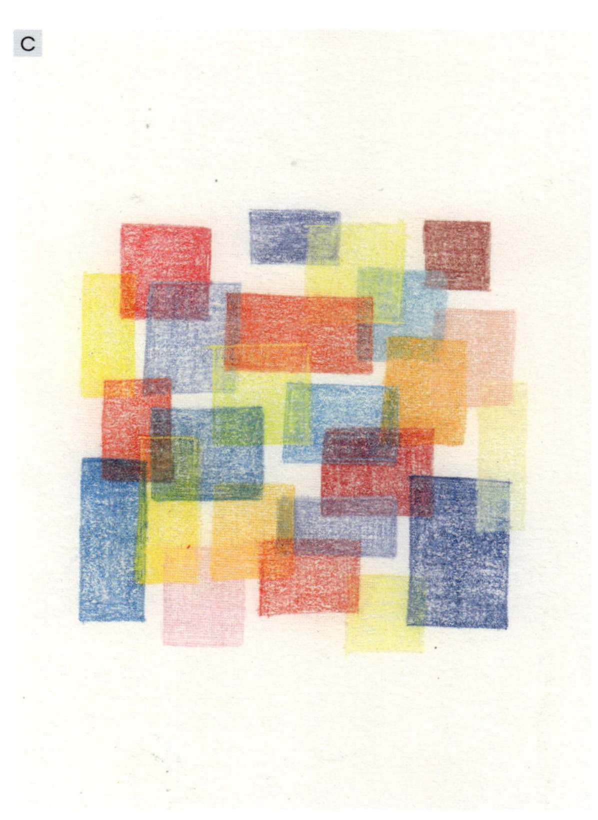
C

USE YOUR CREATIVITY

Try this exercise several times.

• What if you used every color of the rainbow to fill the entire page? *See D.*

• What if you made circles instead of rectangular shapes and limited your palette to various shades of two colors? What if you made a second ring of color around a few of those shapes? *See E.*

• What if you used a selection of pastel or muted tones in the same color family? *See F.* Or, maybe only very dark colors? How about the colors of your garden, the forest, or the seaside? Or, how about various shapes of many hues of one color, such as blue?

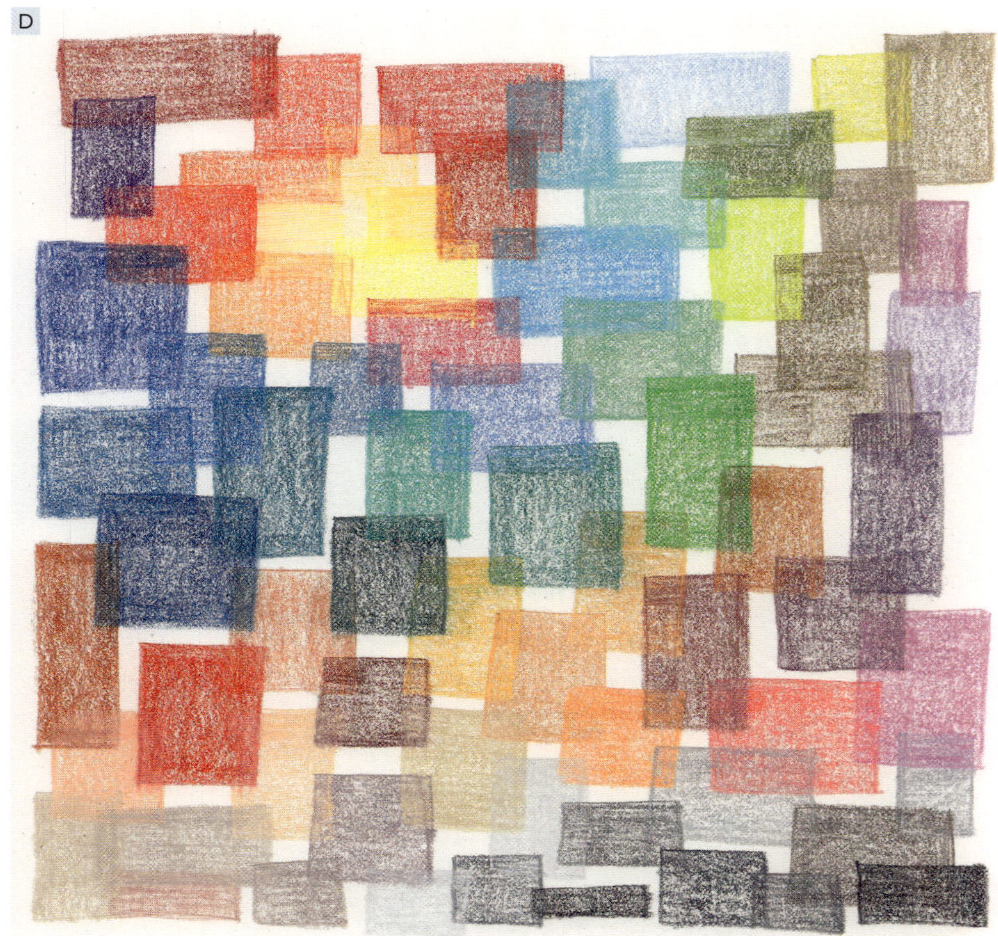

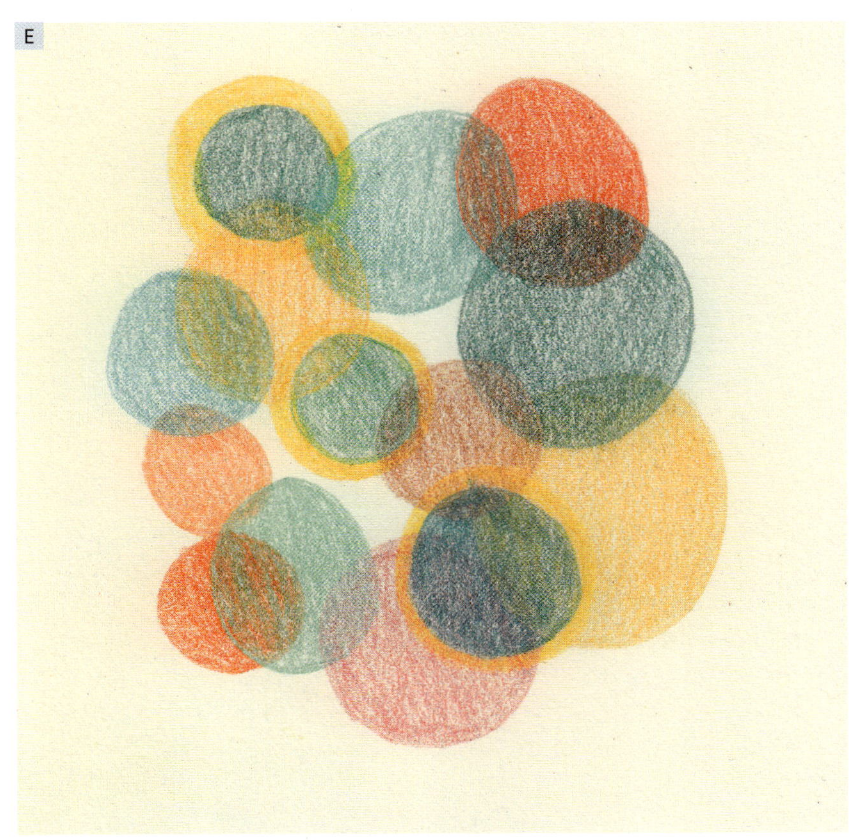
E

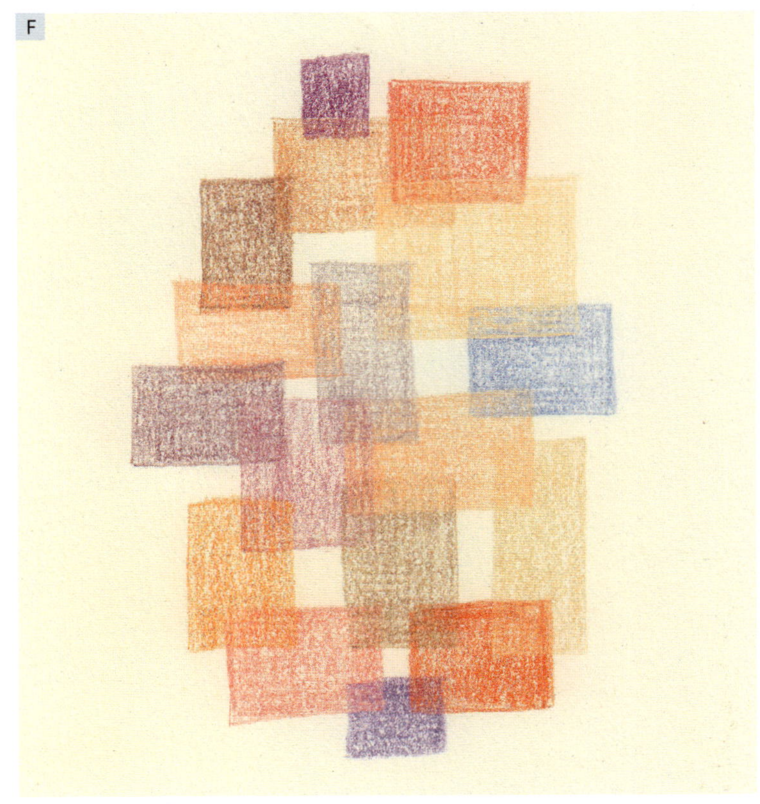
F

LESSON NINE

RAIN SHOWERS AND SWIRLING WIND

Now that we have learned how to smoothly apply and layer colored pencil on paper, it's time to begin mark making. This lesson teaches us how to create curved and linear patterns of line that echo one another. It also teaches us to be random in our mark making, which brings more life and personality to our drawings. This lesson may seem simple, but it should be approached slowly and with control. The techniques here are reminiscent of the paintings and drawings of Vincent van Gogh. Once you have practiced the steps here, try your hand at drawing this image of a Van Gogh painting using the same kinds of marks. We will come back to this technique in future lessons.

TOOLS TO GATHER

- Colored pencils in shades of gray and blue
- Piece of drawing paper, about 5 × 7 inches (13 × 18 cm)

STEPS

1 - Choose a medium-gray colored pencil and begin by drawing 4 directional swirls. *See A.*

2 - Choose a lighter gray pencil and create 10 or so more directional swirls that branch off from the original. *See B.*

3 - Switch to yet another shade of gray. Using a slow and steady hand, draw a line that mimics the curve and shape of each of the previous swirls. *See C.*

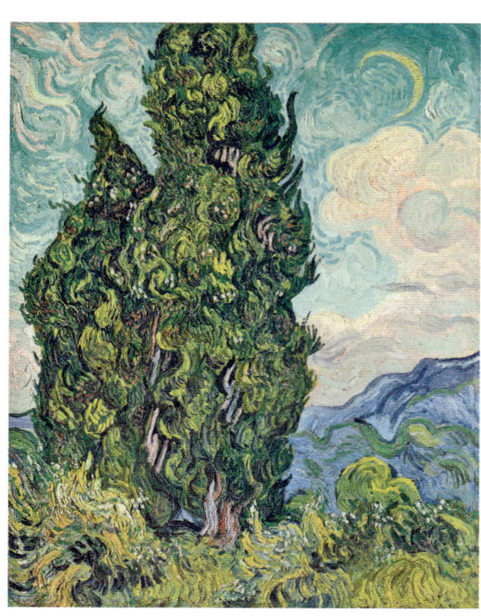

Cypresses. Vincent Van Gogh, 1889.

A

B

C

4 - Repeat step 3 using various shades of gray until the section is completely filled in. *See D.*

5 - Switch to the blue pencils. Begin by drawing randomly dashed lines from the swirls to the bottom of the paper, spaced evenly apart, across the page. Switch colors and draw randomly dashed lines between each previous pair of lines. *See E.*

6 - Repeat step 5, using various shades of blue, until the section is completely filled in, making sure the spacing and length of the dashes are random. Fill in some of the areas between the swirls with shades of light blue. *See F.*

USE YOUR CREATIVITY

• What if you changed the shapes of the original lines to diamond shapes or concentric circles? What if you used rainbow hues and various line thicknesses?

• Now, try to recreate the below image, reminiscent of a Van Gogh painting, to see how this simple technique can be stretched and reimagined into many scenes and subjects. Could you draw a sunflower using this technique? Could you recreate the Van Gogh painting of the cypress shown at the beginning of this lesson?

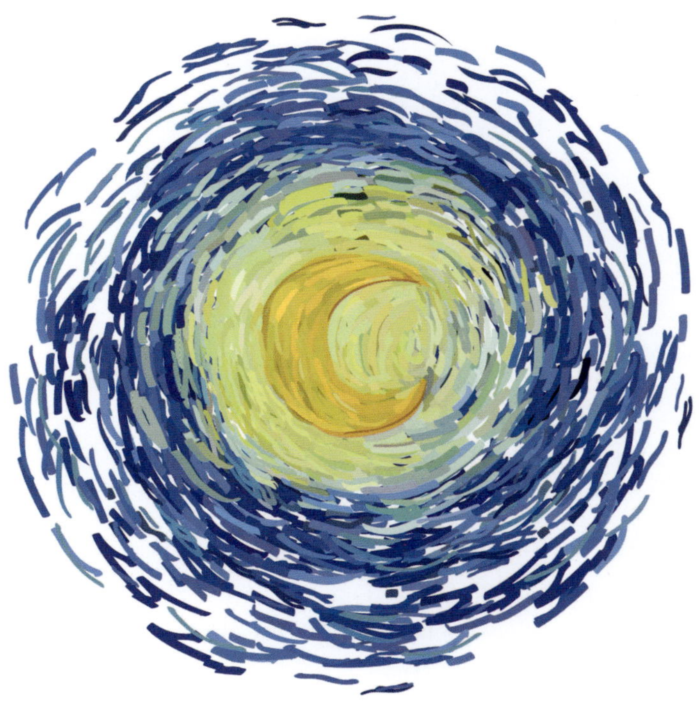

LESSON TEN

WORD PLAY

When my daughter was 10, she made a beautiful drawing of the word *ponder*, filled with all sorts of patterns and designs using colored pencils. I framed it, hung it on our living room wall, and treasure it still today. We all have special words, or even names of people we love, that we could draw on a piece of paper and embellish to give as a gift or frame to hang in our home.

This lesson is all about finding a word that's meaningful to you and decorating it using some of the patterns we have learned in previous lessons. I have chosen the word *peace* as our first example. Once you have tried this lesson, I hope you will choose other words to draw and embellish, too. At the end of this lesson, you will find samples from my students demonstrating that the possibilities are endless. Choose your rainbow selection of colored pencils and follow along with me!

TOOLS TO GATHER

- Graphite pencil
- Drawing paper, 5 × 7 inches (13 × 18 cm; I used a cream-colored paper)
- Permanent fine-tip black marker
- Eraser
- Colored pencils in a variety of rainbow hues

STEPS

1 - Using a graphite pencil, draw the word *peace*, as shown. You can trace the letters as shown in this image or draw them freehand. Then, trace over the letters with the black marker. Let the ink dry completely, and then use the eraser to remove any pencil line you can still see. *See A.*

2 - Using shades of yellow and orange, create a sun with rays, as shown in the letter C. *See B.*

3 - Using shades of green, make tiny dashes to create a grasslike effect, as shown in the letter E. *See C.*

4 - Choose hues of red and pink to create half-moon shapes around the edge of the letter A, and then fill in the rest with radiating lines. *See D.*

5 - Using shades of violet and dark blue, make a pattern of vertical lines, as shown in the letter E. *See E.*

A

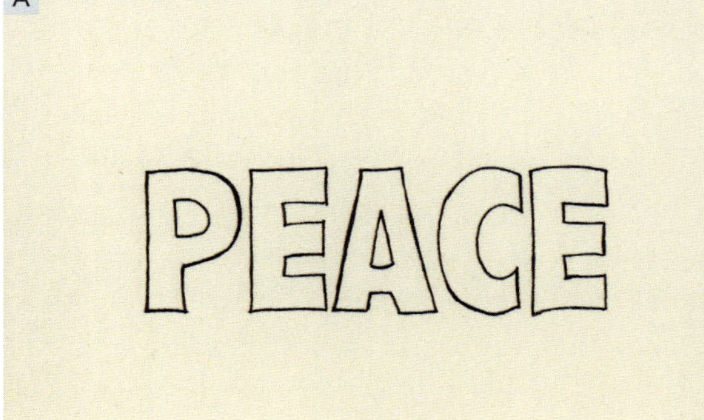

B

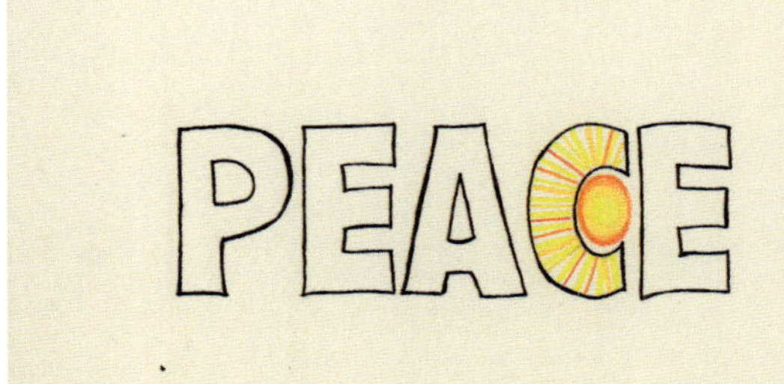

C

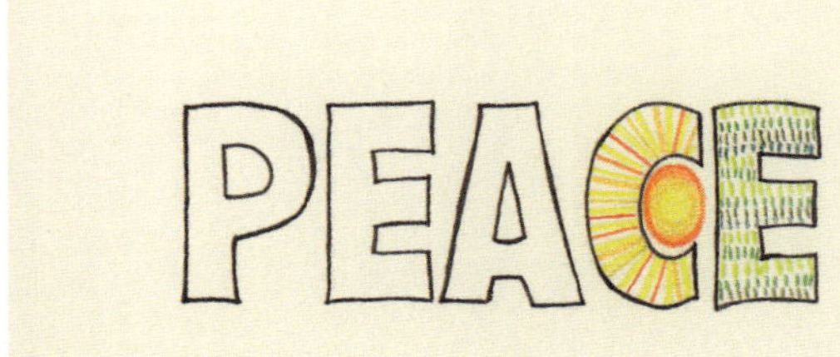

D

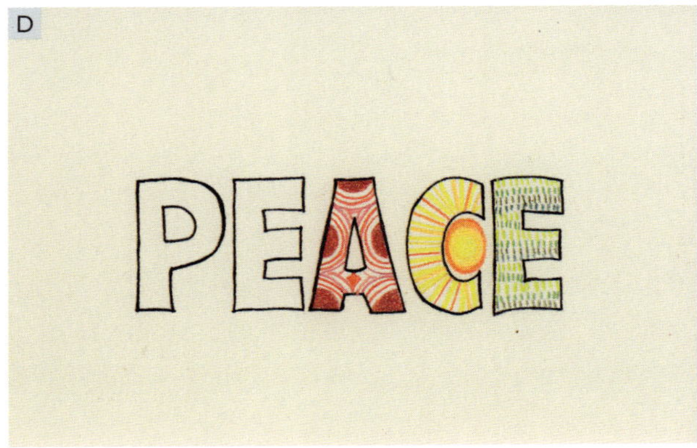

E

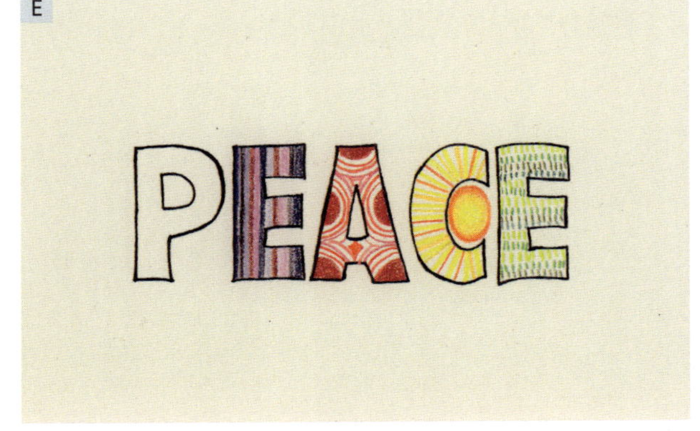

6 - Using shades of blue and turquoise, make random circles, and then fill in the spaces with echoing lines, as shown in the letter P. *See F.*

USE YOUR CREATIVITY

The examples of student work on the right show other possibilities for colors and patterns.

What other words could you create with? How about your family surname, or the names of your children or grandchildren? Can you think of other colorful patterns that are appropriate for your chosen word? What would happen if you made your designs surrounding the letters instead of inside of them? Let your imagination run wild with Word Play.

F

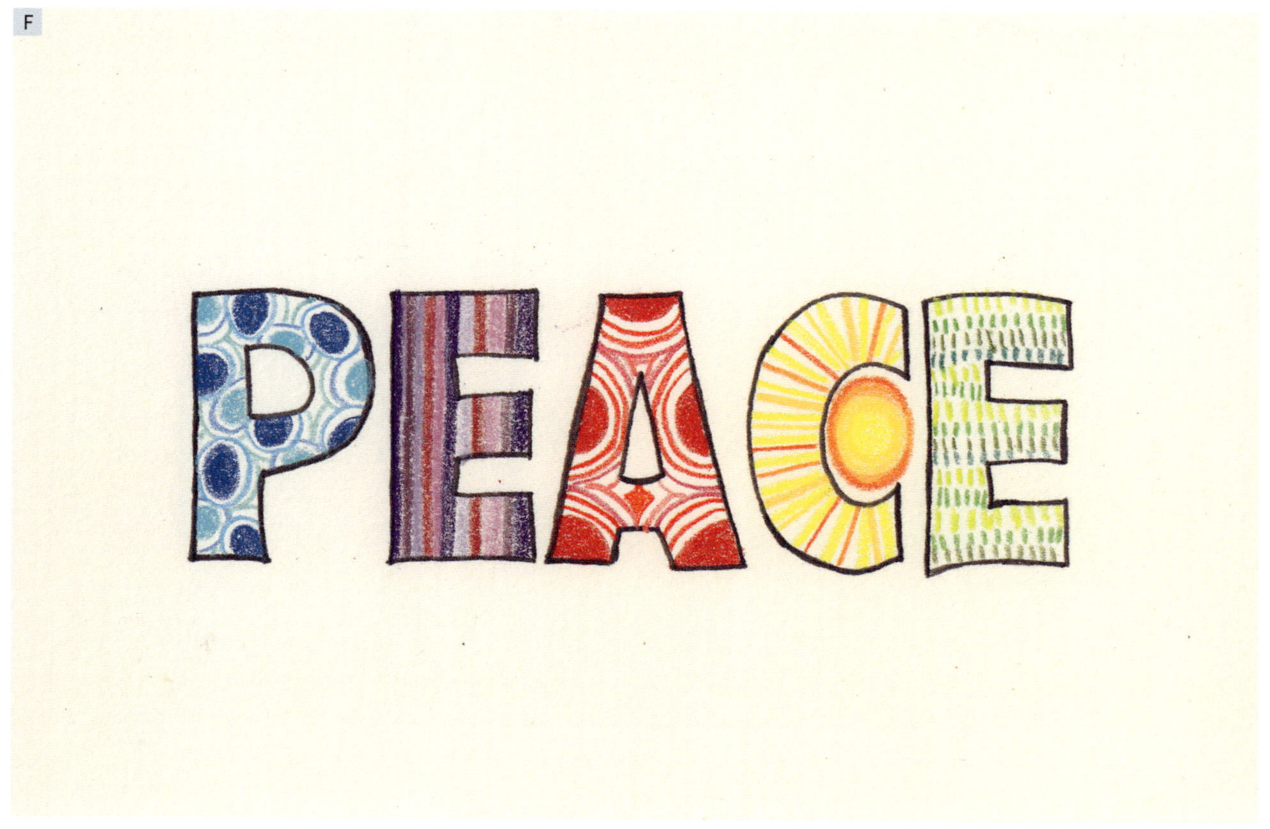

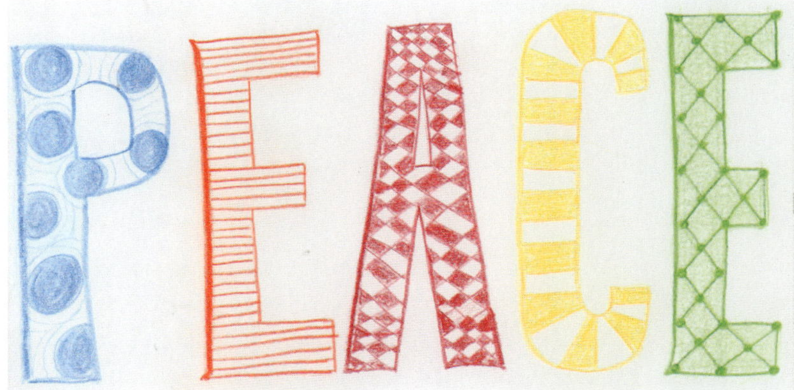

Mary Dowsa

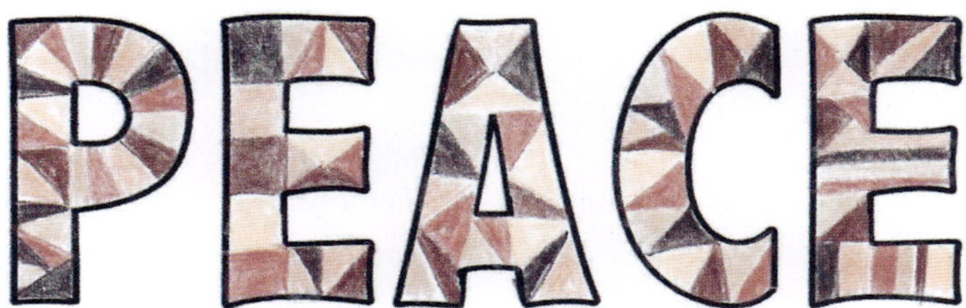

Liz Tobosa

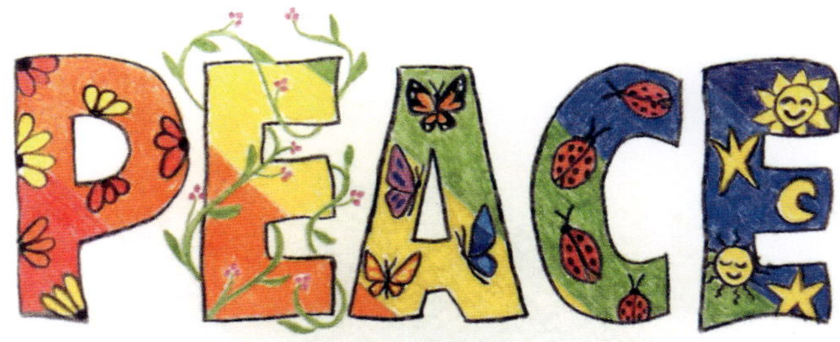

Lizabeth Craig

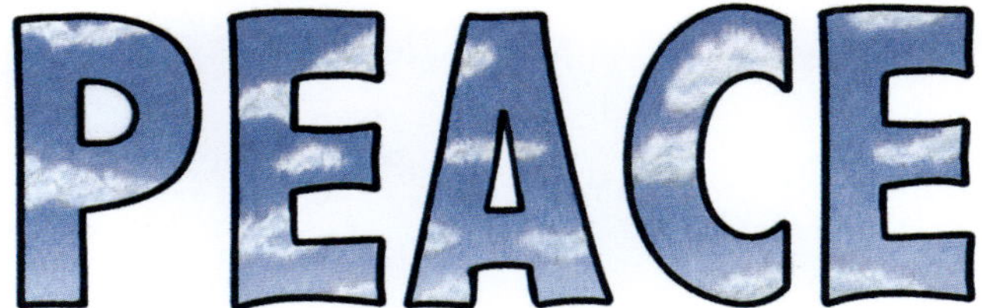

Jon Pedersen

LESSON ELEVEN

SKY | WATER | EARTH

Some of my favorite colors can be found in the hues of sky, water, and earth. These are the hues that soothe us naturally. In this lesson, we will create a drawing with a stained-glass effect—smooth washes of color outlined in black ink or colored pencil—that suggest a distant mountain range near the sea.

We have done basic mark making and color layering with our colored pencils. Now, it's time to practice laying down double layers of color and blending several colors in one larger area. Then, we will have the option to use a colored pencil blender that further blends and makes everything more brilliant.

TOOLS TO GATHER

- 1-inch (2.5 cm) masking tape or paper craft (washi) tape for clean borders (optional)
- Drawing paper, 5 × 7 inches (13 × 18 cm; I used a cream-colored paper)
- Graphite pencil
- Eraser (just in case)
- Colored pencils in a variety of blues, blue greens (turquoise), greens, golds, and earth tones
- Medium- or brush-tip black marker, black pen, or black colored pencil
- Colorless blender pencil (optional; my favorites are by Prismacolor and Caran d'Ache Luminance)

STEPS

1 - As an optional step as I have done here, apply the tape around the edges of the paper to protect the borders, so you can color more freely while still staying within the lines. If you choose not to use the tape, you can take the color all the way to the edge of the paper.

2 - Using a graphite pencil, draw horizontal lines on the paper from top to bottom, as shown, depicting the layers of sky, earth, and water. Use an eraser to correct any mistakes. *See A.*

3 - With shades of blue, color in each section using a feather touch, filling in the space in one direction and then going over it again in another direction to evenly fill each space. Start with the darker blues at the top and gradually shift to the lighter blues as you near the bottom layers of sky. The center "eye" shape can be left white with a subtle later of very light blue or gray to suggest shadow toward the right side. *See B.*

4 - Switch to earth-tone colors for the mountains. Use the lightest shade, such as golden brown, for the mountaintops, gradually shifting to medium shades and then darker shades of brown. Color in one direction, then another, to evenly fill the spaces. *See C.*

5 - Using golden yellows in two shades, make vertical lines across the section directly beneath the mountains. Then, use these golden shades to make horizontal shading marks across the top, divided, section of earth, following with shades of green for the bottom, divided, section of earth. *See D.*

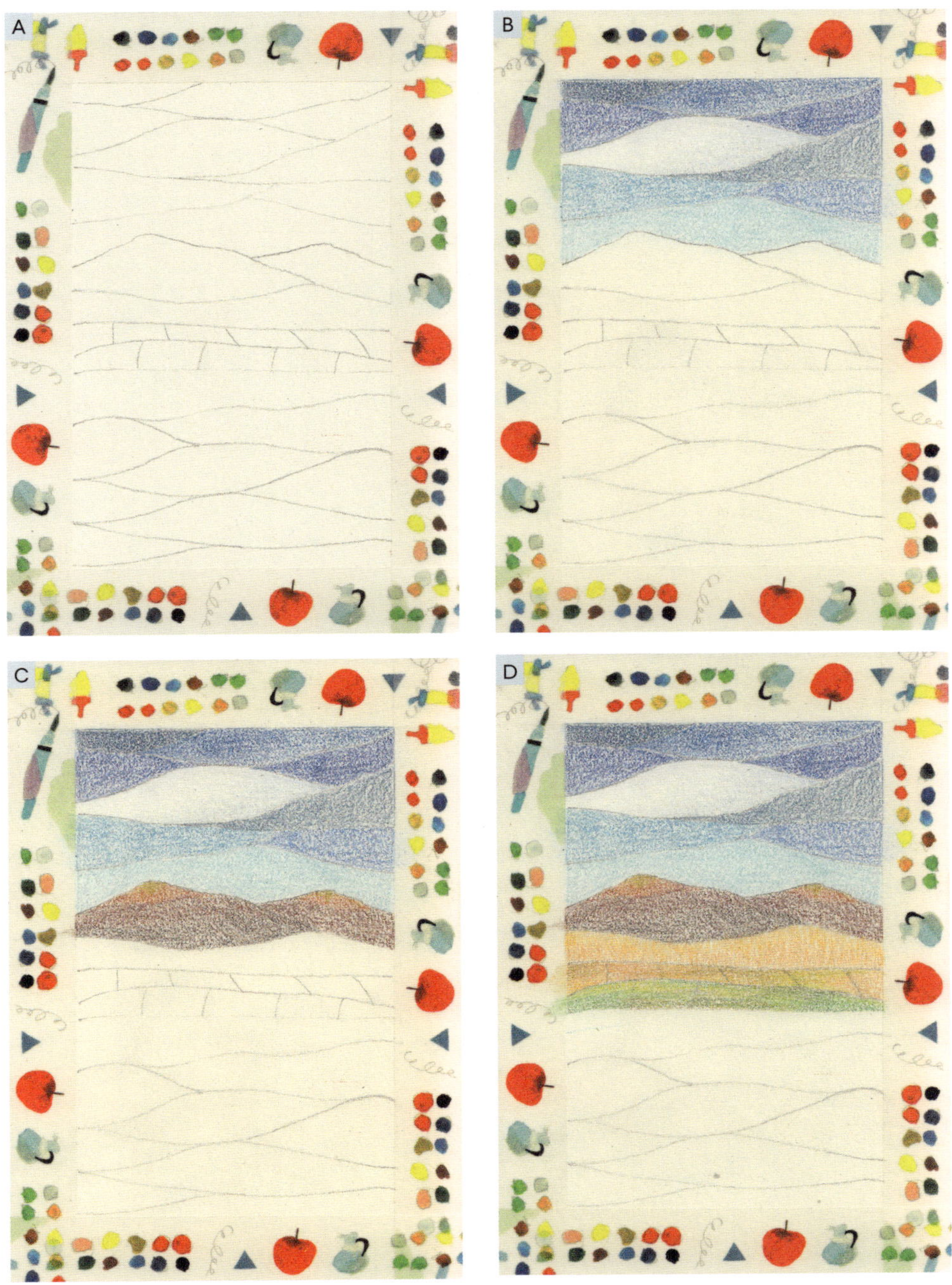

6 - Use the blue-green and turquoise pencils to fill in the lower sections of water, beginning with the lightest colors, gradually getting darker, as you reach the bottom sections. *See E.*

7 - Use a black marker, pen, or colored pencil to draw over the dividing lines, as shown. I used a black brush pen to achieve random line weights. If you use pen, let the ink dry completely, and then remove the tape to reveal the clean border. Your drawing can be complete at this stage; if you have a blender, complete step 7. *See F.*

8 - To use the blender, lightly go over each section of color with gentle pressure. Notice how the colors come to life, becoming richer and more jewel-like, and how the variations in color blend even more. *See G.*

USE YOUR CREATIVITY

What other scenes can you dream up using simple lines and a stained-glass technique? How about a sunrise or sunset over the ocean, or the undulating grasses of a prairie? What about a simple still life? You can even find images of stained glass you love and recreate them with colored pencils and a black pen. The sky is the limit!

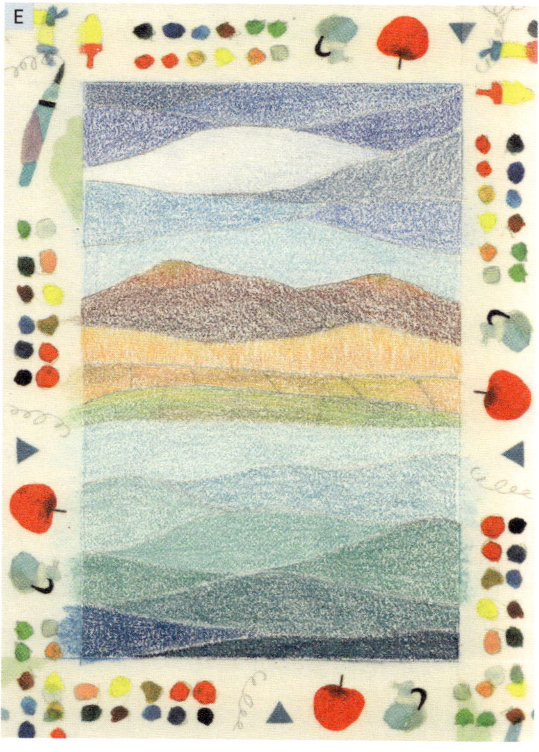
E

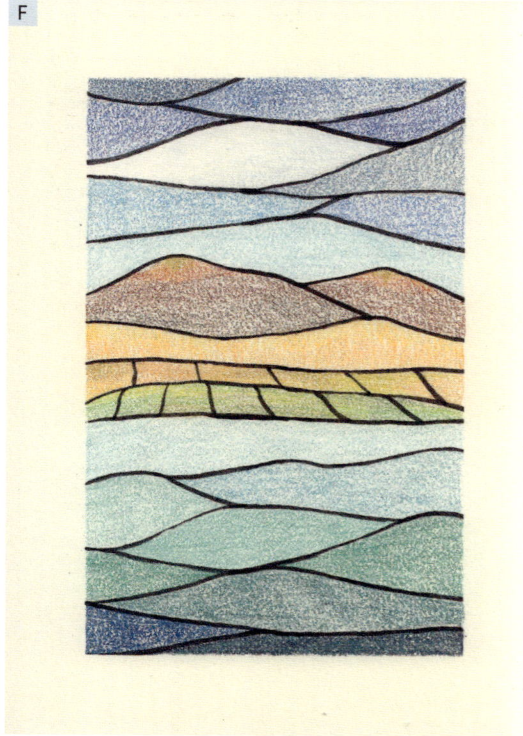
F

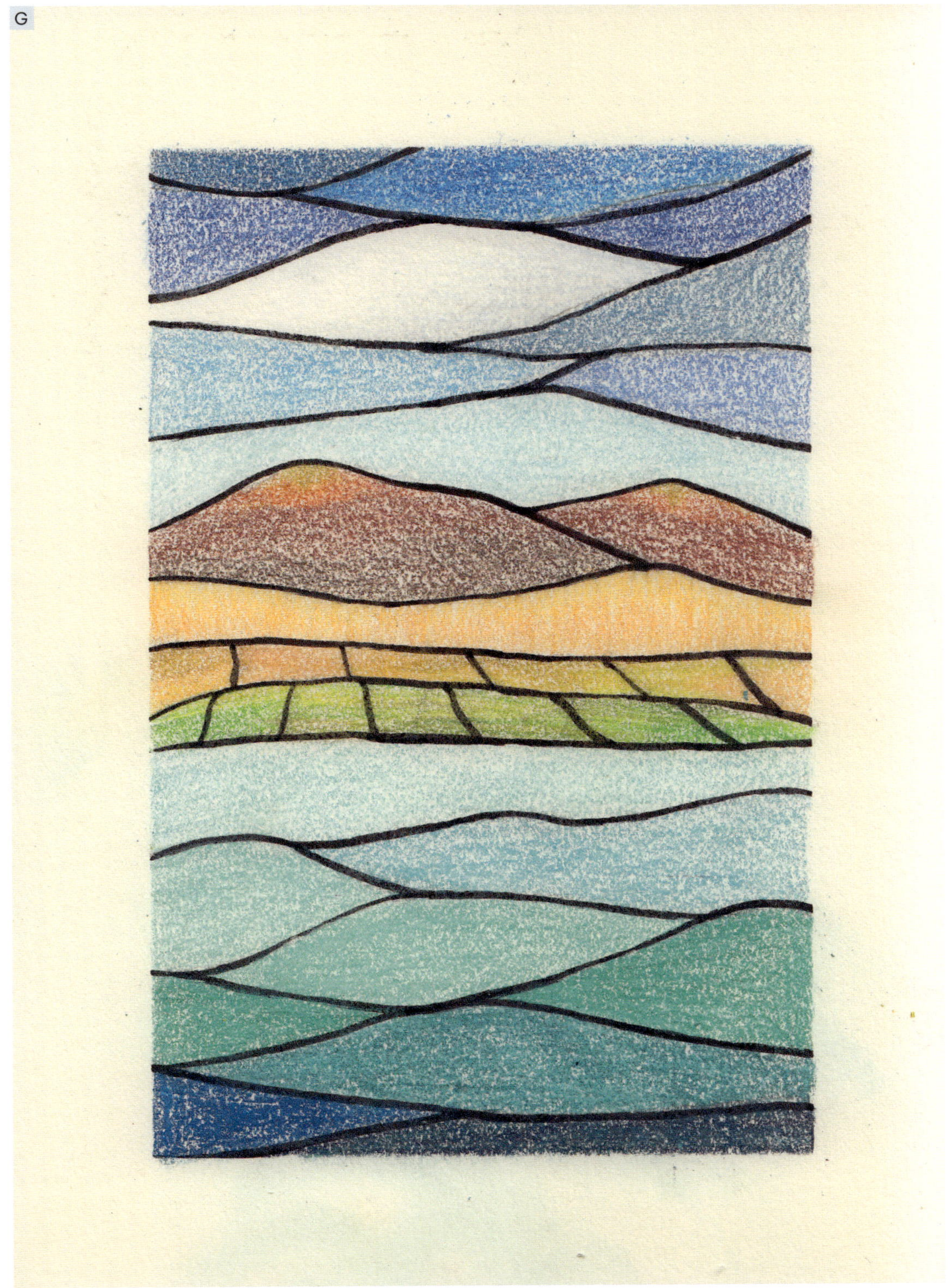
G

LESSON TWELVE

WEATHERED WISHES

When I was a young girl, my mom made these little pieces of art using brown paper bags. When finished, she would hang them outside on the tree branches so they could become seasoned by the weather. My very fuzzy memory is that we wrote wishes on these tiny drawings, with the idea that when the wind and rain weathered them away to nothing, our wishes would come true.

This is my version that I call Weathered Wishes. We will make three, using colored pencils on brown kraft paper, and hang them on string so they can be gently tied to the branch of your favorite tree.

TOOLS TO GATHER

- Graphite pencil
- Selection of colored pencils in a variety of hues, including black
- Ruler or straightedge
- 3 pieces of kraft paper, 5 × 7 inches (13 × 18 cm; like a brown paper bag)
- Medium- or brush-tip black marker or metallic gel pens (optional)
- Scissors
- Eraser
- Hole punch or something that can make a small hole in the paper
- 3 pieces of string or yarn, 24 inches (61 cm) each

COLORFUL FLAGS

This sample is created with the colors of the rainbow, but feel free to use any colors. With a graphite pencil and a ruler, mark off a center section on your paper, about 2½ inches (6 cm) wide. Draw a series of 7 misshapen rectangles with simple designs inside. Copy the sample or create your own! *See A.* Remember the technique of going over the fill area two or three times, in different directions, to achieve a smooth application. Use a colored pencil or metallic gel pen to connect the flags at the top. Trim away the outside edges of the paper by cutting along the pencil lines.

PEACOCK FEATHER

1- Begin by drawing lines with a pencil to create a 2½-inch (6 cm) section in the center of the paper. Using black colored pencil, draw a lightly curved line that gets wider at the bottom, as shown. Draw an upside-down heart at a slight angle, a bit above the thinner end of the line. *See B.*

2- Using a turquoise pencil, surround the heart with a thin line. Use a bright-green pencil to surround the entire heart shape, as shown. Using the black pencil, create a thin, curved line on the edge of the turquoise line, and then use a bright lemon-yellow pencil to surround the green color with a thin line. With a warmer yellow pencil, fill in a larger area, as shown, and then use a golden-brown pencil to create a thin line toward the outer edge of the yellow. Finally, use a rust- or sienna-colored pencil to create a final border, creating a small point at either end of the shape. *See C.*

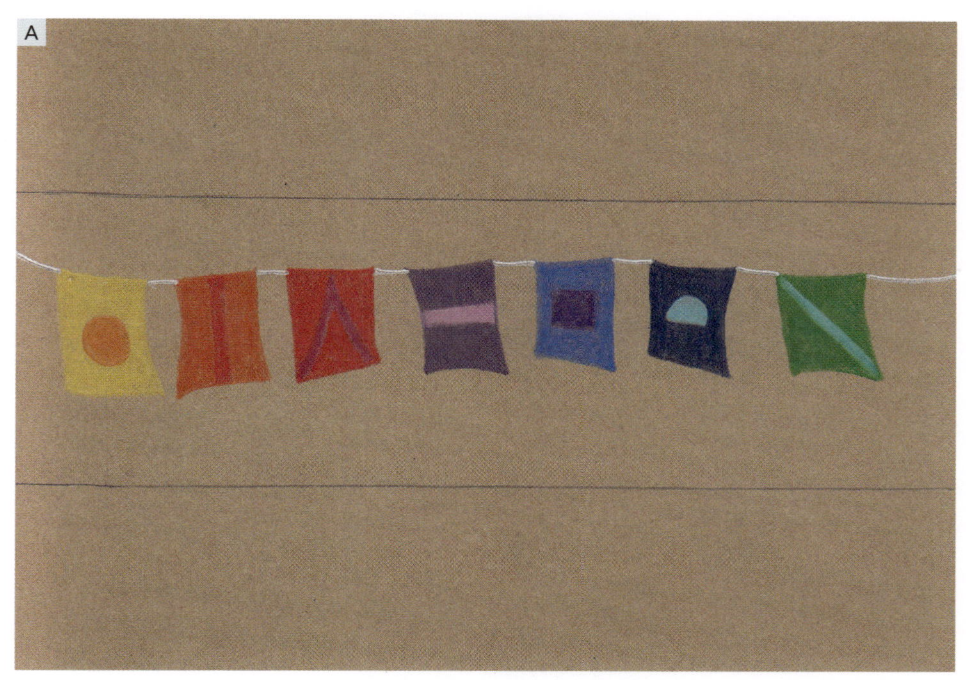
A

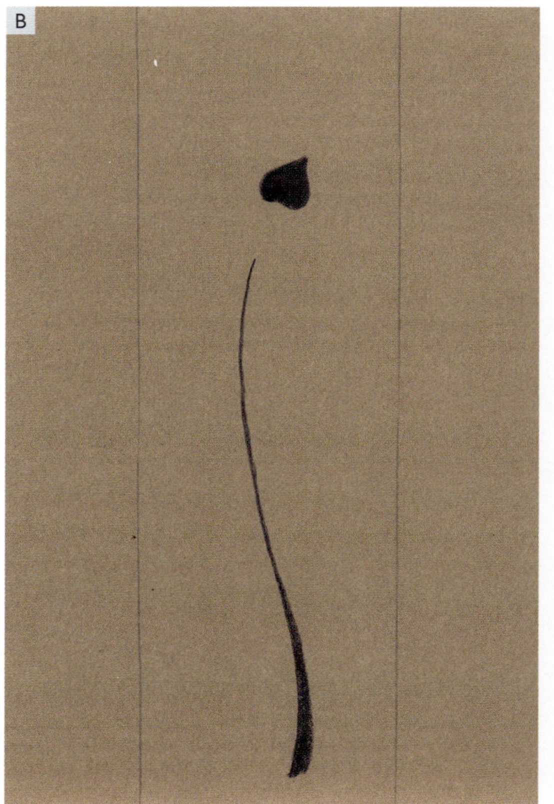
B

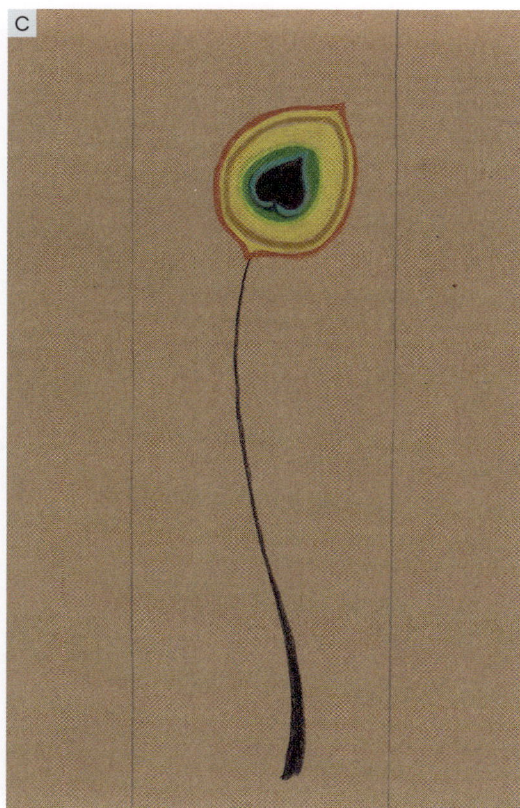
C

3 - Using a blue-green pencil, create thin lines that curve and radiate from the center black line, as shown. Notice how the line is drawn right over the pencil border. This allows for more fluidity. Also notice how the lines get shorter toward the bottom of the feather. *See D.*

4 - Using a variety of bright green pencils, draw more curved lines, filling in the spaces between the lines already present. Keep the fluidity going and use the sample image as your guide. *See E.* When finished, use scissors to carefully cut away the extra paper as for the Colorful Flags project.

WISHING BOWLS

1 - Prepare your paper as for the Colorful Flags project (see page 72). Using a pencil, draw 5 simple bowl shapes, as shown. Don't forget that you have an eraser, if you need it. These shapes do not have to be perfect. They are basically a flattened oval with a quarter-moon shape below. *See F.* You can do it!

2 - Choose 5 colors to work with, plus a medium-violet or gray pencil. Beginning with the top bowl, use one color to fill in the top oval shape. Use another color to fill in the bottom quarter-moon shape. Use that same color to fill in the top oval shape of the second bowl. Choose another color to fill in the bottom quarter moon of the second bowl. Use that same color to fill in the top of the third bowl and a new color to fill in the bottom. Continue in this same manner, ending with the first color you used in the top bowl. *See G.*

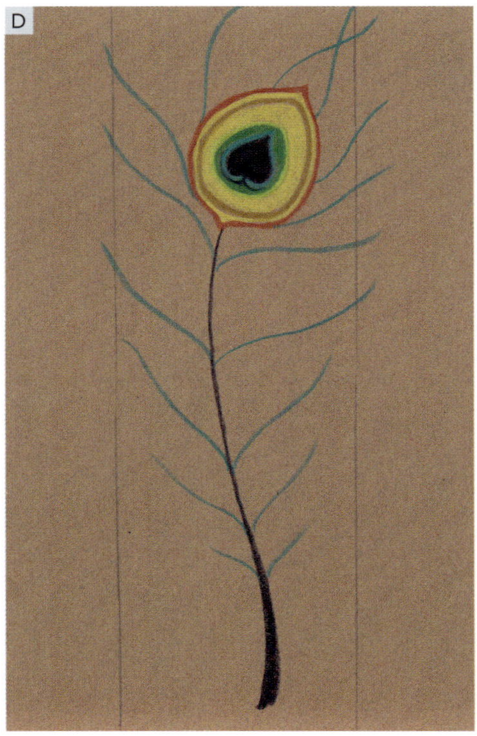
D

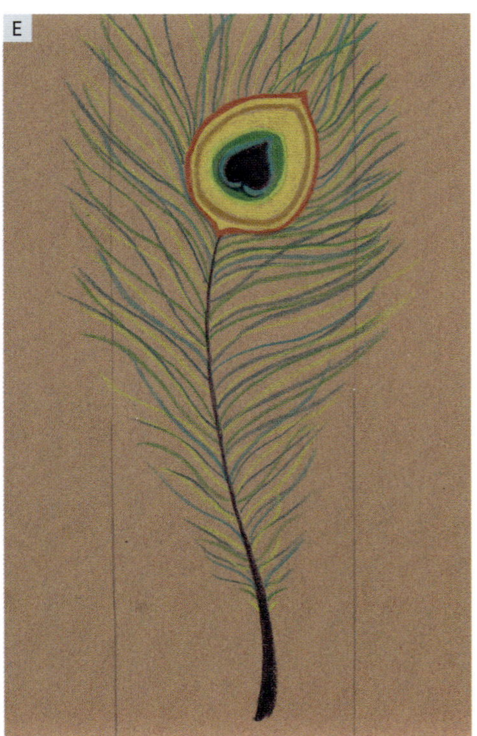
E

3 - Here's where the magic happens! Using the violet or gray pencil, with a gentle touch, very lightly shade in the right side of the top section of each bowl using feathery strokes, as shown. Do the same on the left side of the bottom section of each bowl, as shown. This will give your bowls the illusion of depth. Follow the sample image as your guide. *See H.* Trim away the edges of the paper along the pencil lines.

CREATE THE WISHES

With a hole punch, create a hole in the center top of each tag. Fold a length of string in half, threading the looped end through the hole and then pulling the ends through the loop to secure it to the tag. *See I.* The final step is to make a wish and write it on the back of the tags. Sometimes I write each letter of my wish in random places, so in the end, it is indecipherable to anyone but me. Hang the tags from your favorite tree and watch them as they weather in the sun, rain, and wind.

USE YOUR CREATIVITY

What if you created bookmarks instead of Weathered Wishes? For the Colorful Flags, use the patterns of international maritime signal flags to spell out someone's name and create a bookmark for them. How can you adapt some of the other lessons from this book to fit on this narrow strip of paper? So many ways to fill a rectangle!

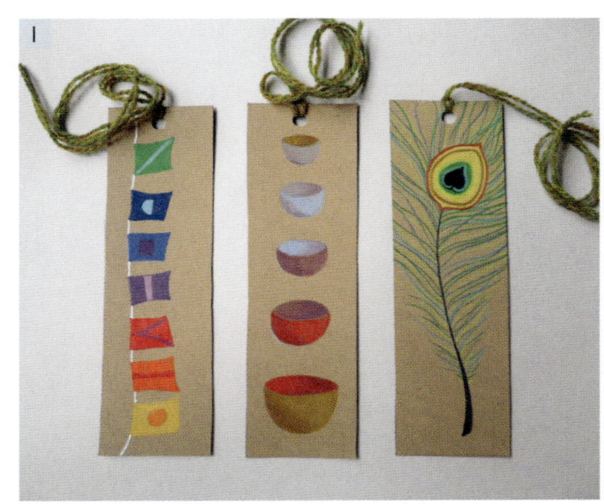
I

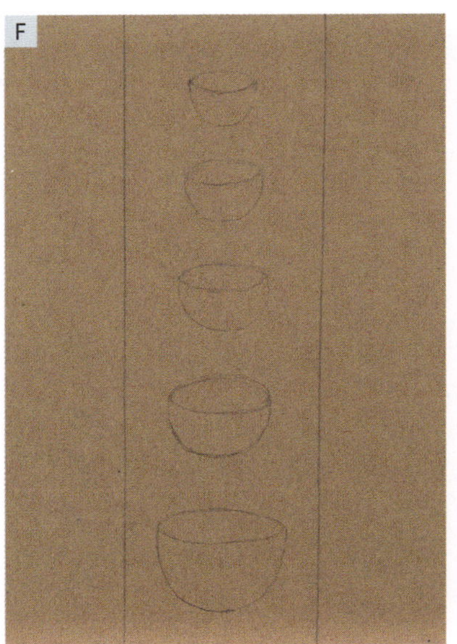
F

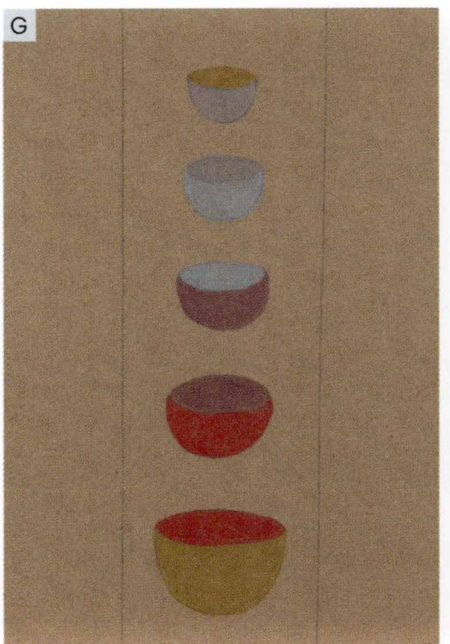
G

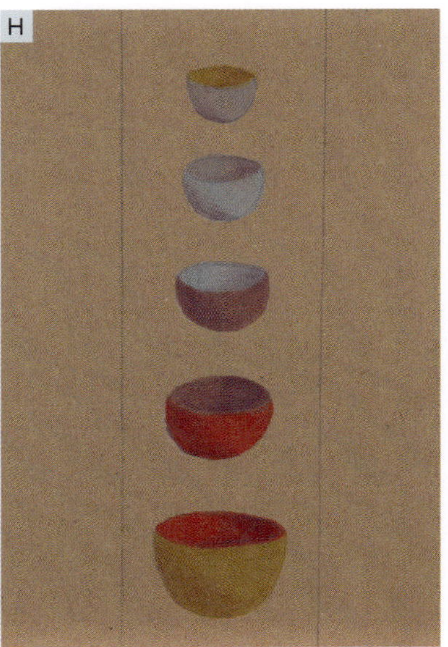
H

LESSON THIRTEEN

FANTASY FISH

When we use colored pencil as our drawing medium, there are so many bright colors available to create simple yet bold and graphic designs that sing on the page. Tropical colors are so much fun to use, and one of my favorite subjects to capture with those candy-colored hues is fantasy fish. Although they take on the basic shape of real fish, the color combinations are endlessly fantastical and create whimsical drawings perfect for framing to brighten any room.

Don't be intimidated by the result—these cheerful fish are simple to create, step by step. We begin with a graphite pencil sketch using basic shapes, refining them with an eraser, if we need to, and then add brilliant contrasting colors to make the simple design elements pop. This project works well with complementary colors, which are hues found across from one another on the color wheel, such as red/green, orange/blue, and violet/yellow. When these color pairs are used next to one another, they make each other even more brilliant! It's a simple magic trick—an illusion artists have used for centuries.

For this sample lesson, I chose shades of turquoise-blue and orange, with a bit of black for contrast. I suggest trying similar complementary colors for your first drawing and then using your imagination to come up with as many different combinations as you can.

TOOLS TO GATHER

- Graphite pencil
- Piece of drawing paper, 5 × 7 inches (13 × 18 cm)
- Eraser
- Colored pencils in a variety of turquoise, aqua, and green-blues, warm yellows, reds, oranges, and black
- Colorless blender pencil (optional)

STEPS

1- The best advice I can give you is take your time, keep it simple by following the sample, and use your eraser for the pencil line drawings. You'll draw 2 fish, as shown. *See A.*

• Using a graphite pencil and a light touch, draw an oval shape like you see on the bottom fish, and then draw a long, curved triangle shape like you see for its body. Don't worry if it's a little lopsided. Use your eraser if you want to make changes. Then, draw 2 teardrop shapes for the side fins and 2 more at the end of the tail, as seen in the sample.

• Let's look to the top fish for the final details. Draw a matching line above the curve where the oval-shaped head meets the body. Draw 2 lines in the center of each side fin and create a series of matching lines in each tail fin, as shown.

• Finally, draw the eyes and mouth on the head of the fish, as seen in the image.

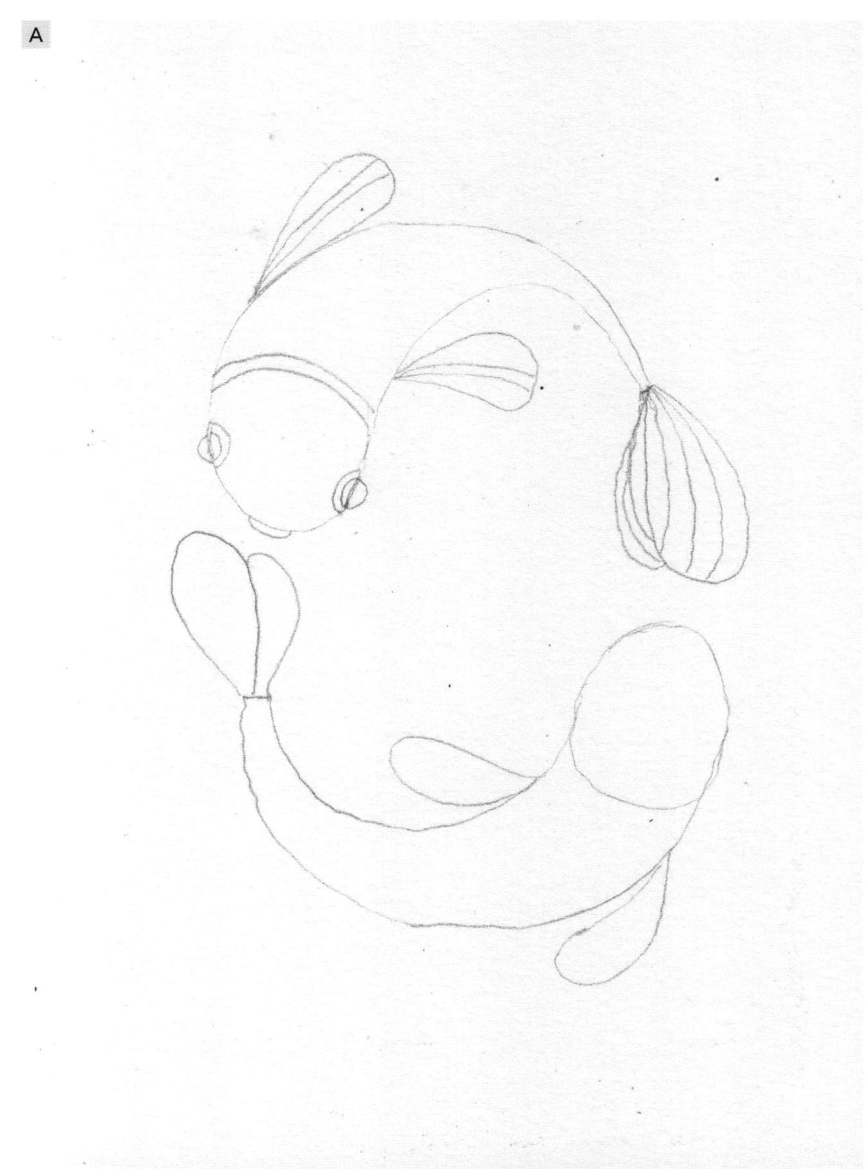

2 - Time to color! With a light orange pencil, color in the bands, as shown on the bottom fish. With a darker orange or red pencil, outline each shape you colored orange, as seen on the top fish. *See B.*

3 - Using different shades of yellow, orange, red, and black and one turquoise pencil, fill in the rest of the fin shapes, as shown. Fill in the outer half circle of the eyes. *See C.*

4 - Using a turquoise pencil, fill in the other half circle of the eyes. Then, with an orange pencil, fill in the outer section of each eye. Using a sharp black pencil, create tiny lines across the orange section of the eye, as shown. Finish by coloring in the mouth with black pencil. *See D.*

5 - With a medium turquoise pencil, draw half ovals in a pattern that builds off itself, starting larger at the top and getting narrower and smaller as it reaches the end of the tail. Use the sample as a guide as you draw this pattern on both fish. They do not have to be the same! *See E.* Relax and enjoy the meditative process of pattern drawing.

6 - With a lighter turquoise pencil, lightly fill in the bodies of both fish, including the heads. Use a darker turquoise pencil to fill in the space between the half oval pattern on the body with tiny quarter circles, as shown, for both fish. *See F.* At this point, you can call it finished; if you have a colorless blender pencil, complete step 7.

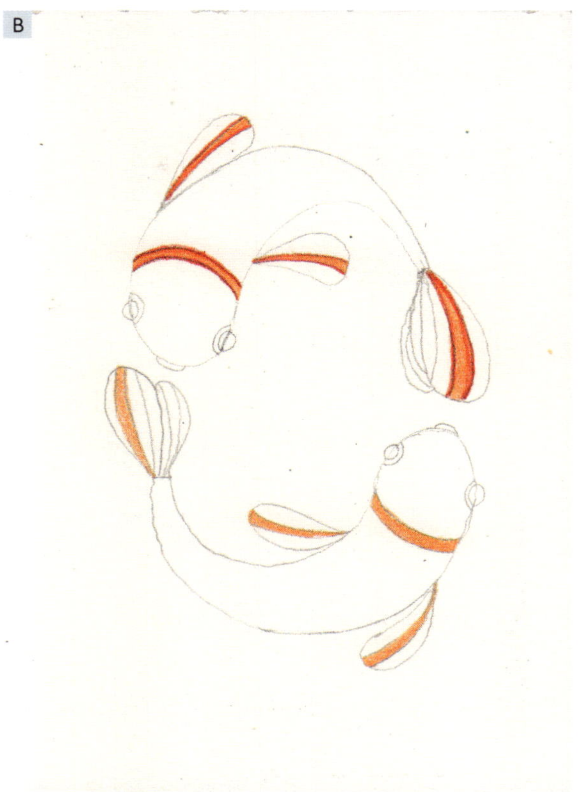

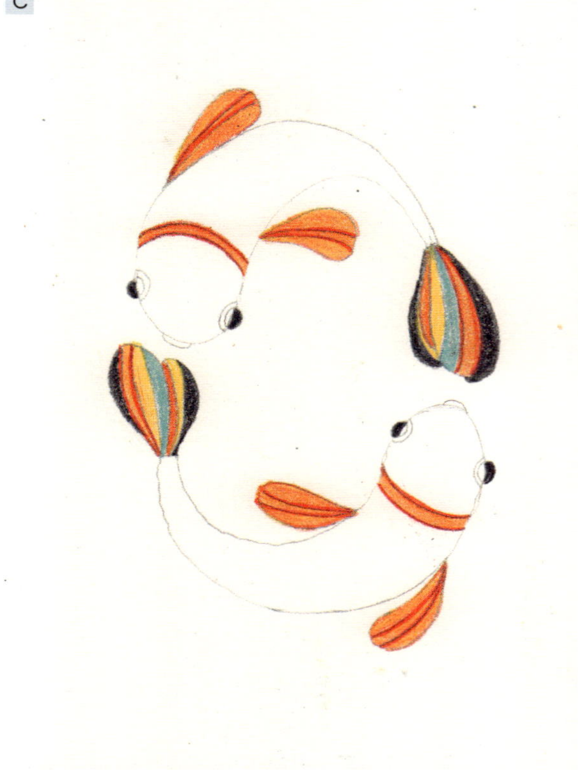

D

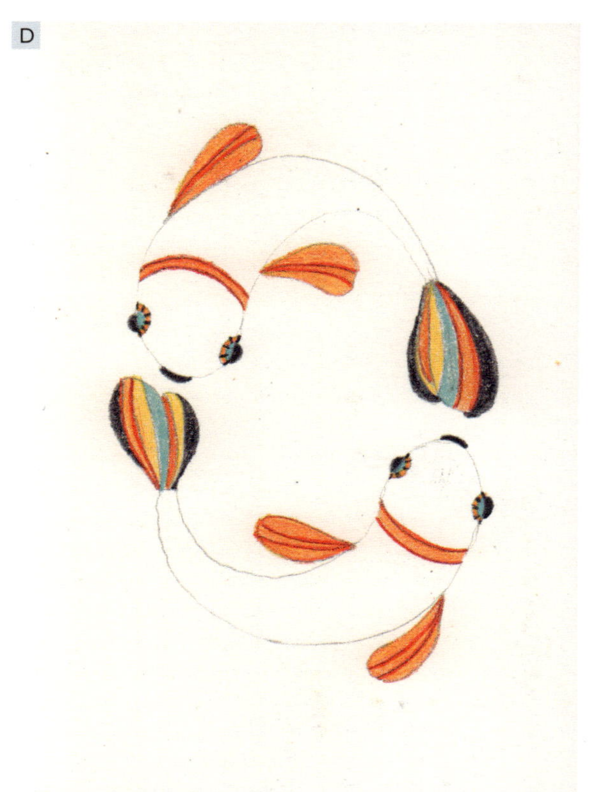

E

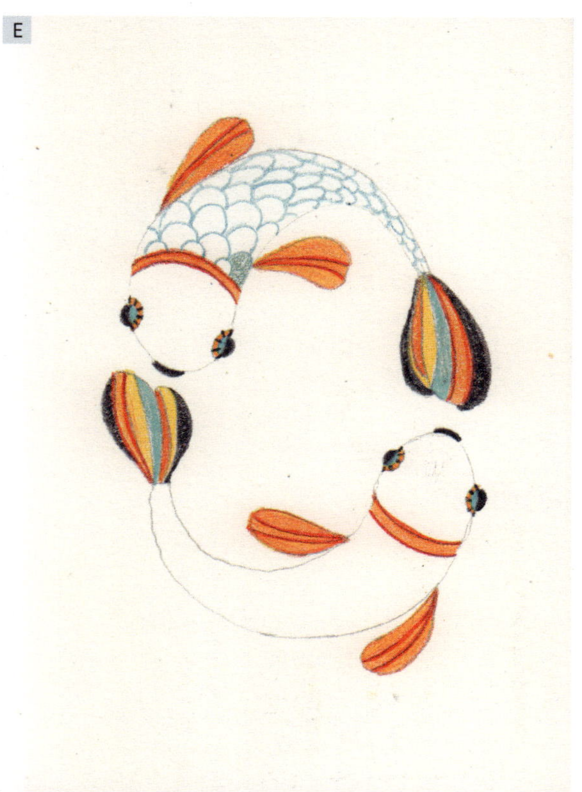

F

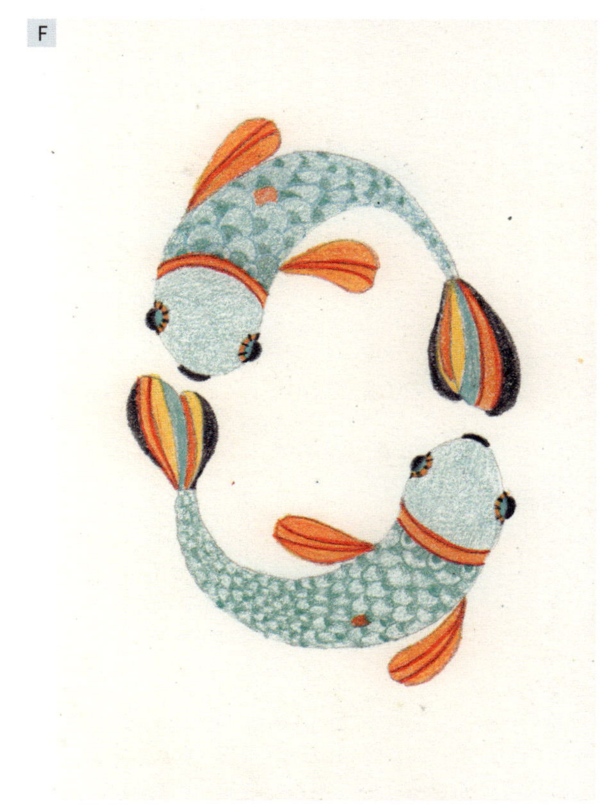

7 - Using the colorless blender pencil, gently go over the entire drawing, leaving the black areas for last. This step gives a richer, more jewel-like tone and smoothness to a colored-pencil drawing. *See G.*

USE YOUR CREATIVITY

What other color combinations could you try? Garnet reds and emerald greens? Dandelion yellows and regal violets? What about a rainbow fish? What other patterns could you use to fill in the fins, tails, and bodies?

G

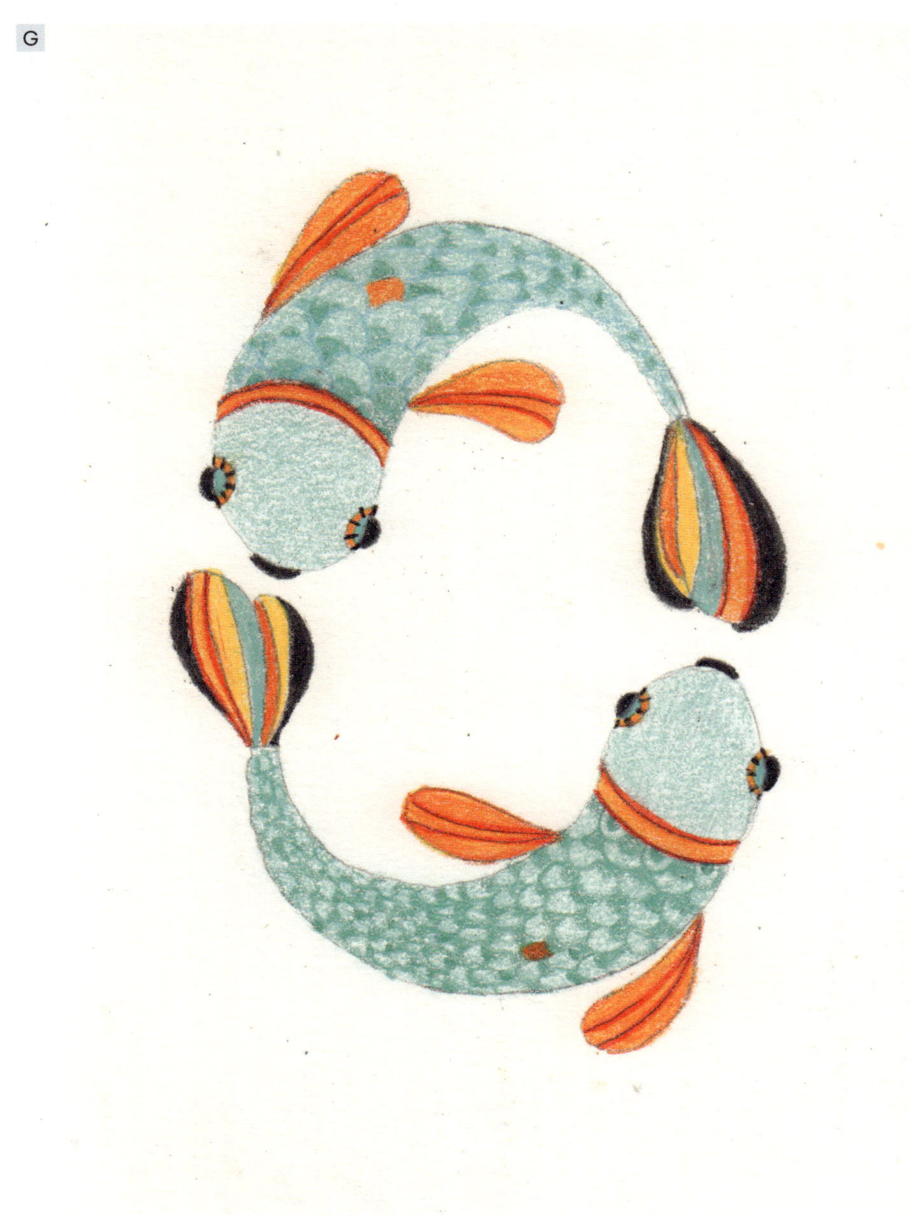

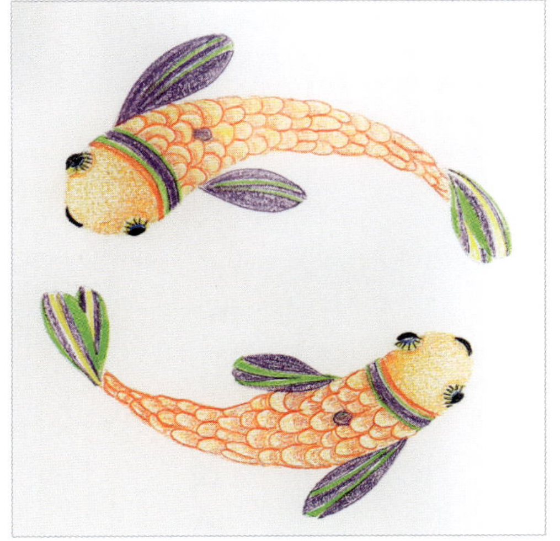

Jane Woker

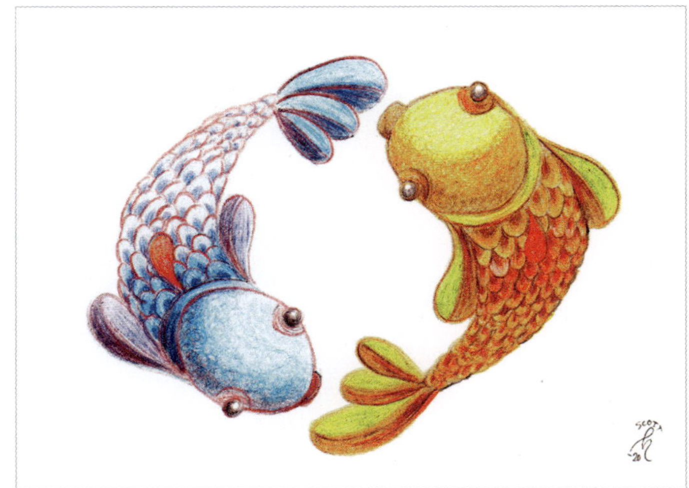

Hazel Scott

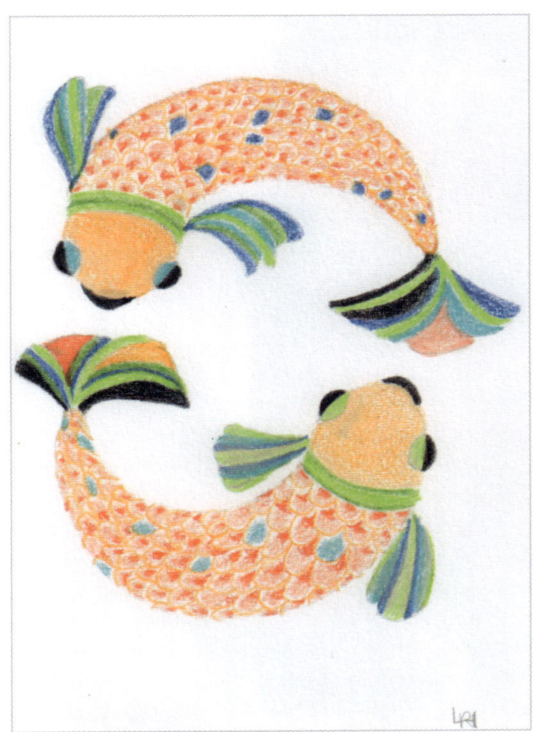

Lisa Hofmann

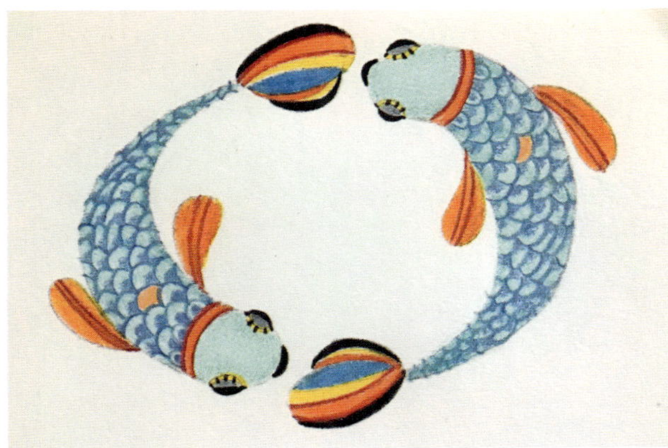

Lizabeth Craig

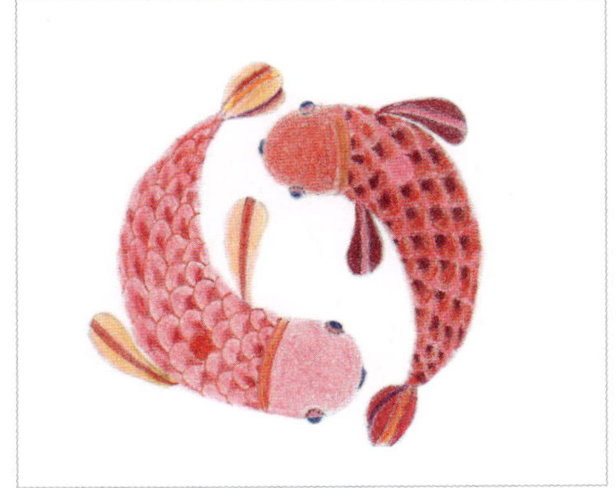

Wendy Ching

LESSON FOURTEEN

MAGICAL FOREST

This lesson brings together all we have learned so far. It might appear complicated, but if you take it step by step, you will be amazed at what a beautiful, magical scene you can create. Here, we'll use removable tape to create a random border, but you can forgo this step if you prefer to just draw a light border with pencil. I hope you choose the most cheerful colors from your set of colored pencils and enjoy creating this fantasy landscape full of patterns and lovely color transitions, layered with meditative mark making and beautiful imaginary trees.

I also hope you will try toned paper for this project. If you do not have toned paper, use a clean, unwrinkled piece of a brown paper bag. When we use a darker paper, we can make full use of the lightest values of our colored pencil sets. It's great fun!

TOOLS TO GATHER

- Graphite pencil
- Toned drawing paper, about 5 × 7 inches (13 × 18 cm; such as Stonehenge Kraft or a piece of brown paper bag)
- Eraser
- Washi tape (removable decorative paper tape) or masking tape
- Colored pencils in a variety of colors and values; pay special attention to selecting some lighter hues, especially white, pale yellows, blues, peaches, etc.

STEPS

1 - Using a graphite pencil, draw 3 tree shapes on your paper, as seen in the sample image. Use your eraser to make any adjustments. The third tree shape is just the trunk of a pine tree—a couple of parallel lines. Place a length of washi tape horizontally across the paper, sort of moving it around as you attach it to create a random border as a horizon line, as shown. *See A.*

2 - The sample image for this step shows the random application of lighter colors across the upper background (above the tape), avoiding coloring inside the trees. *See B.* On the left side, inside the tree branches, is random mark making with various tones of blue, including a small pattern of yellow ovals with bright-green centers. This is an example of how to include some random patterning. You can copy the sample image or create your own. Also note the vertical rainbow of markings to the left and right of the tree trunk, above and below the tape. Try this! It's great fun and adds a lovely element to the scene. You can finish it with white pencil markings, in the same vertical way, around the rainbow marks. Keep these background colors on the light side, as shown.

3 - Fill in the bottom section of the background below the tape in a random way, using vertical strokes, similar to step 3. *See C.*

4 - Remove the tape, revealing a clean border along the horizon. Use a selection of colors to randomly fill in this space, using horizontal strokes. Use mid-tones and light colors for this step, as shown. *See D.*

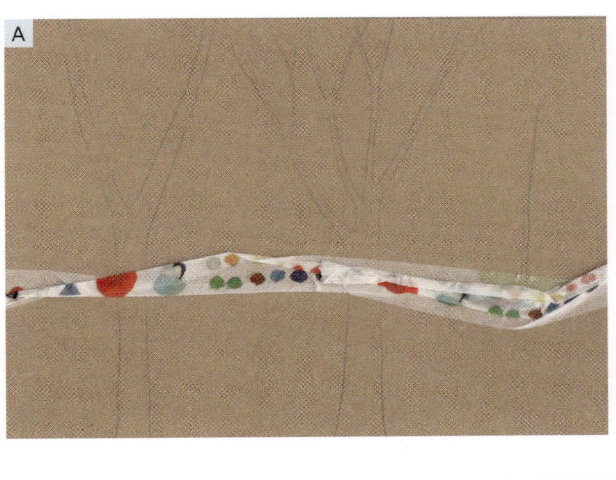

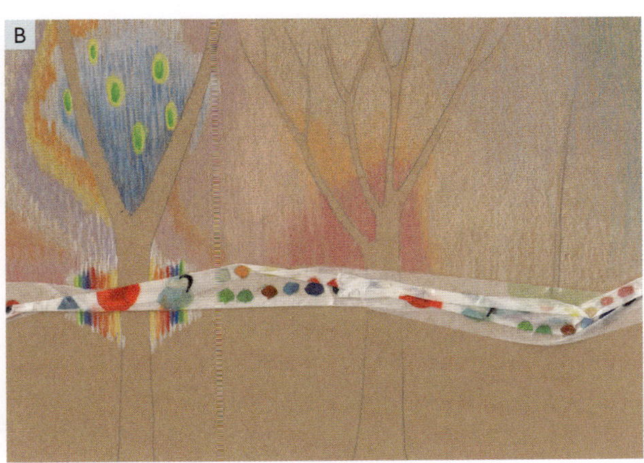

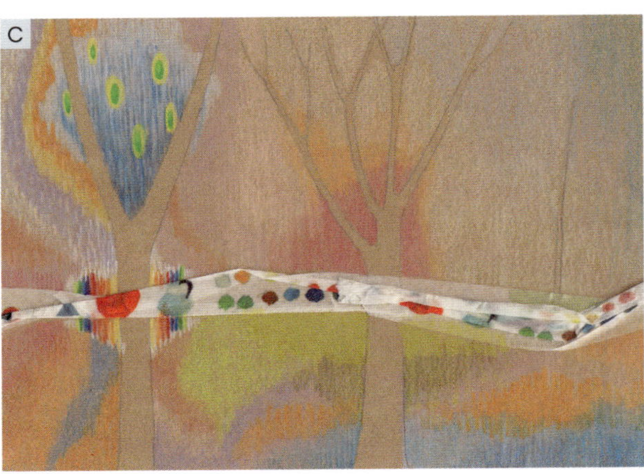

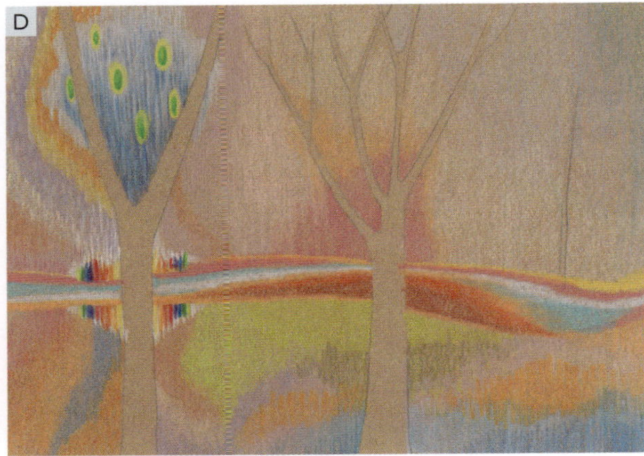

5 - This next layer is all about intuitive mark making. Study the sample image. *See E.* Notice how tiny tick marks in lighter hues are used to soften the borders between sections of color. Sometimes the marks are short and fine, other times a bit longer or wider. You can change this by using a duller pencil or a very sharp pencil, or with the pressure you exert while making the marks. You can also try different kinds of marks, such as tiny circles, squares, teardrop shapes, and the like. Whatever feels right, is right! Take your time and create a whimsical layer of tiny marks over the background to bring texture, color, and interest to your drawing.

6 - Let's add some tiny ferns to the ground under the trees, some leaves to the middle tree, and pine needles to the far-right tree. *See F.* For the ferns, use a bright-green pencil to draw the simple plant shape outlines, and then fill them in with a lighter yellow or green color, as shown. For the leaves on the middle tree, use a lighter green pencil to make lots of random oval-like marks all around the branches, as shown. Then, use a darker green color to make a few random darker leaves and a rose-colored pencil to add a few more, as shown. Use a white pencil to make a small mark next to each rose-colored mark. For the pine tree, use a mid-green or brown pencil to make slanted lines shaped like pine boughs, as shown. Use a lighter green pencil to add more strokes in the same direction. Finally, if you want some birds in the sky, use 2 shades of blue to create tiny bird shapes. I surrounded mine with tiny white marks to suggest movement.

7 - For the final step, we will fill in the tree trunks and branches. I used shades of violet and pale blue. Begin with a middle tone. Using vertical strokes, fill in the tree trunks from right to left, leaving the left side blank. Use a darker tone to add another layer toward the right side of the trunks and a lighter color to add marks toward the left side. For the tiny pine tree, use a middle tone with a touch of darker tone in it to color in the trunk, skipping where the branches are, as shown. On the left and center trees, use a darker pencil to enhance the areas where two branches meet, or where a branch meets the trunk. Study the sample image to see this in practice. *See G.*

USE YOUR CREATIVITY

I hope you feel proud of your lovely magical forest scene and confident in your ability to create some really fun things with colored pencils now. How would you approach this differently on white paper? What if you tried this technique to create an ocean or water scene? How about city skyscrapers? Keeping the shapes simple and making them come alive with vibrant colors and random marks can create a beautiful piece of art.

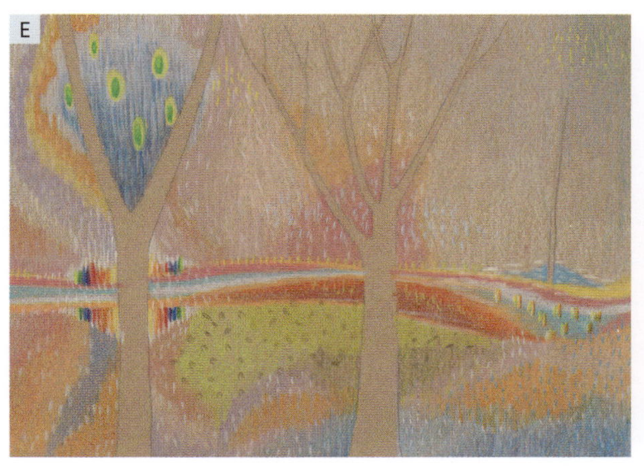
E

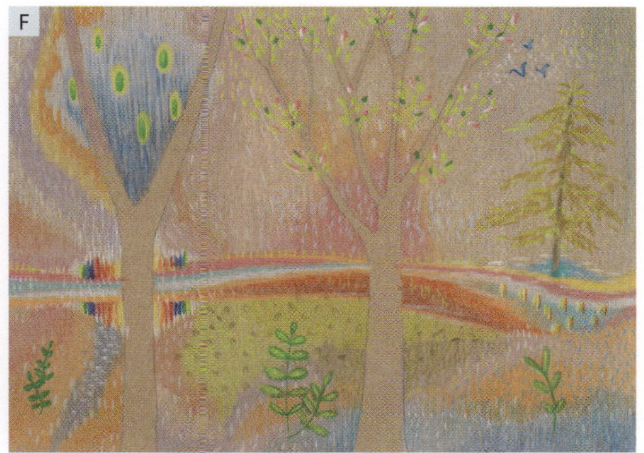
F

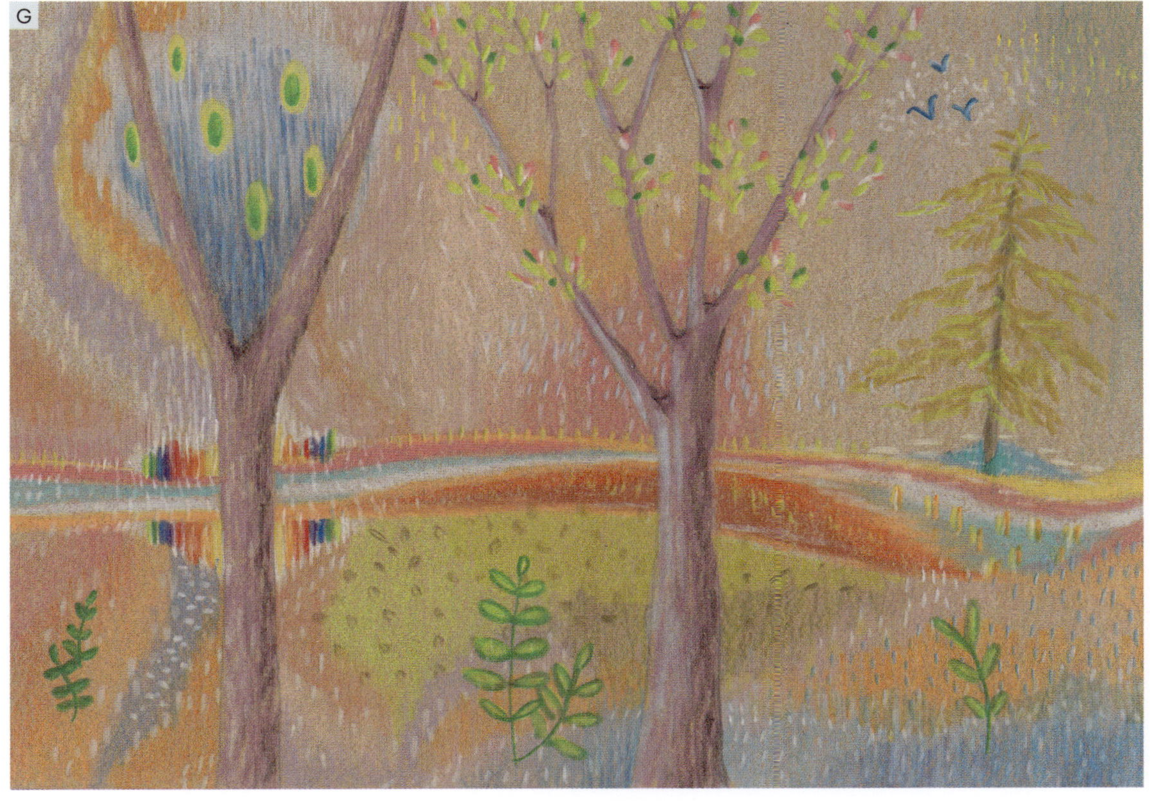
G

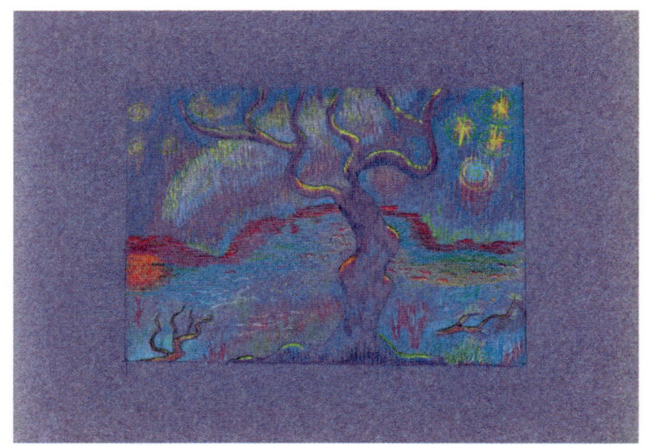

Helene Jorgensen

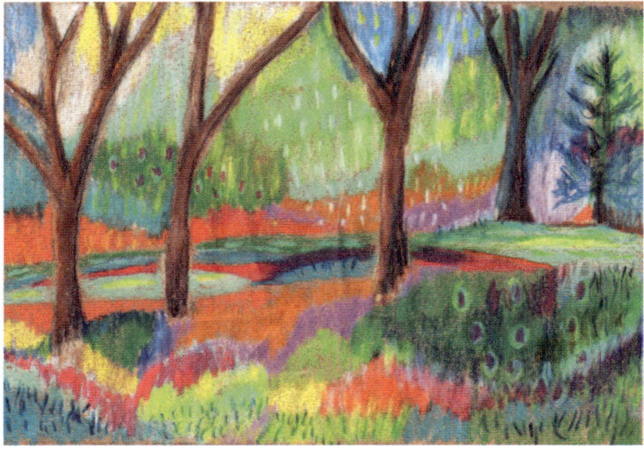

Lisa Hofmann

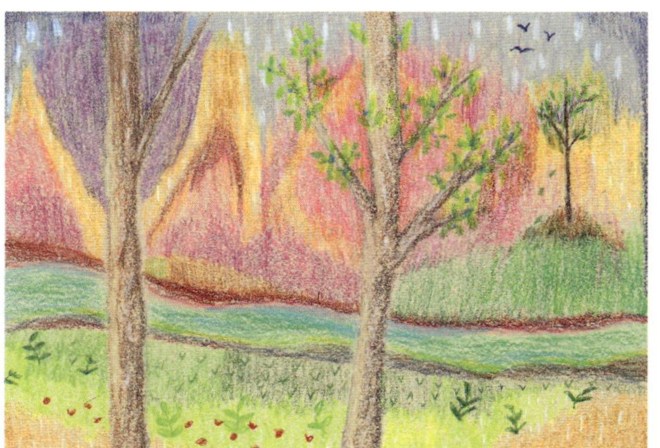

Wendy Ching

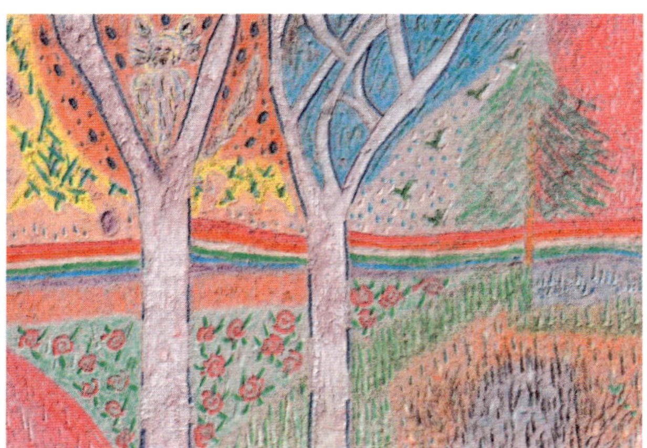

Debbie Brandecker

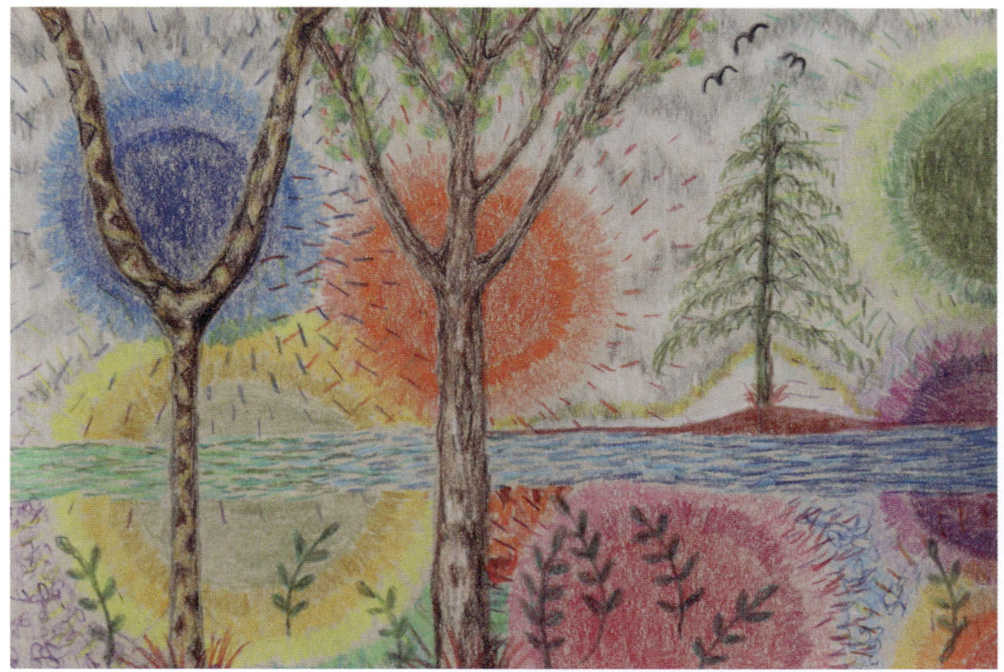

Liz Tobosa

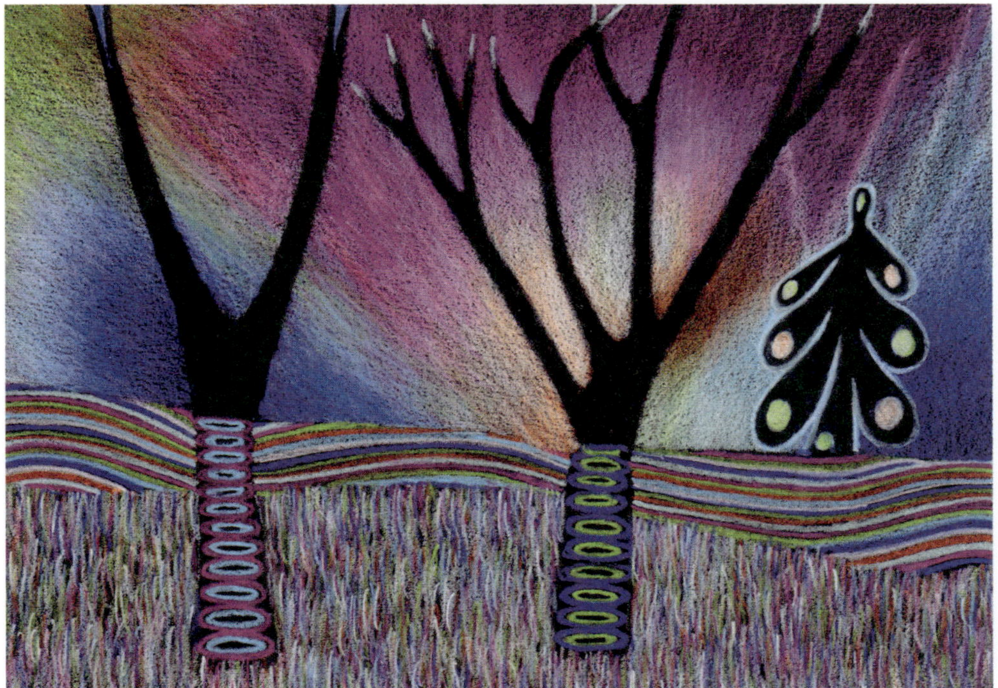

Jon Pedersen

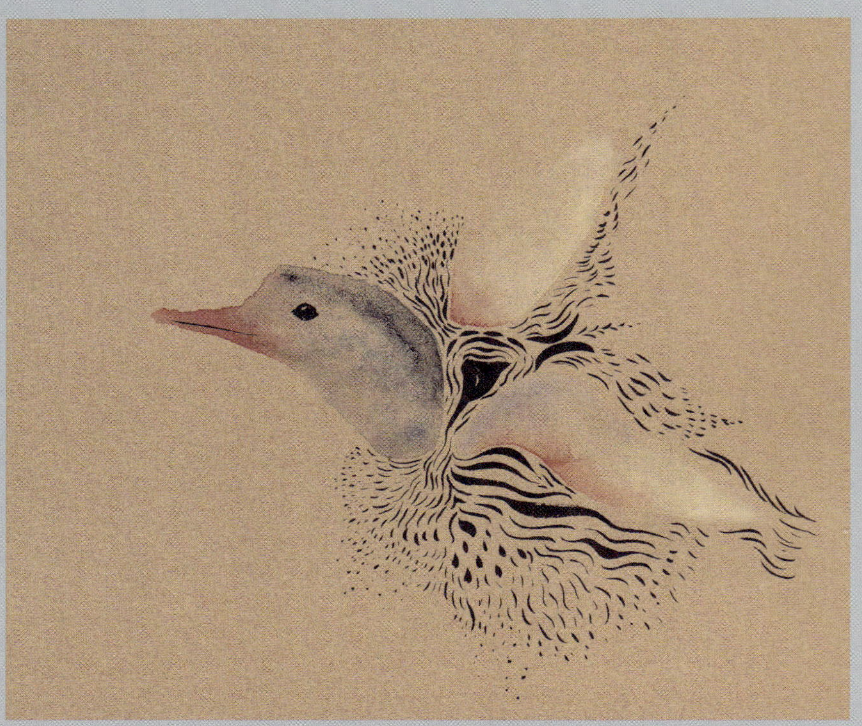

INK

Our next medium brings a whole new world to our drawing work—the ability to have the crisp brilliant line work of the pen plus the advantage of being able to use a wet brush to create beautiful washes of color. The types of ink pens we can use are so varied—from the bold graphic black line of a technical pen, to the fluid rainbow of colors available with markers and brush pens, to the metallic glimmer of gel pens. In this section, we explore them all.

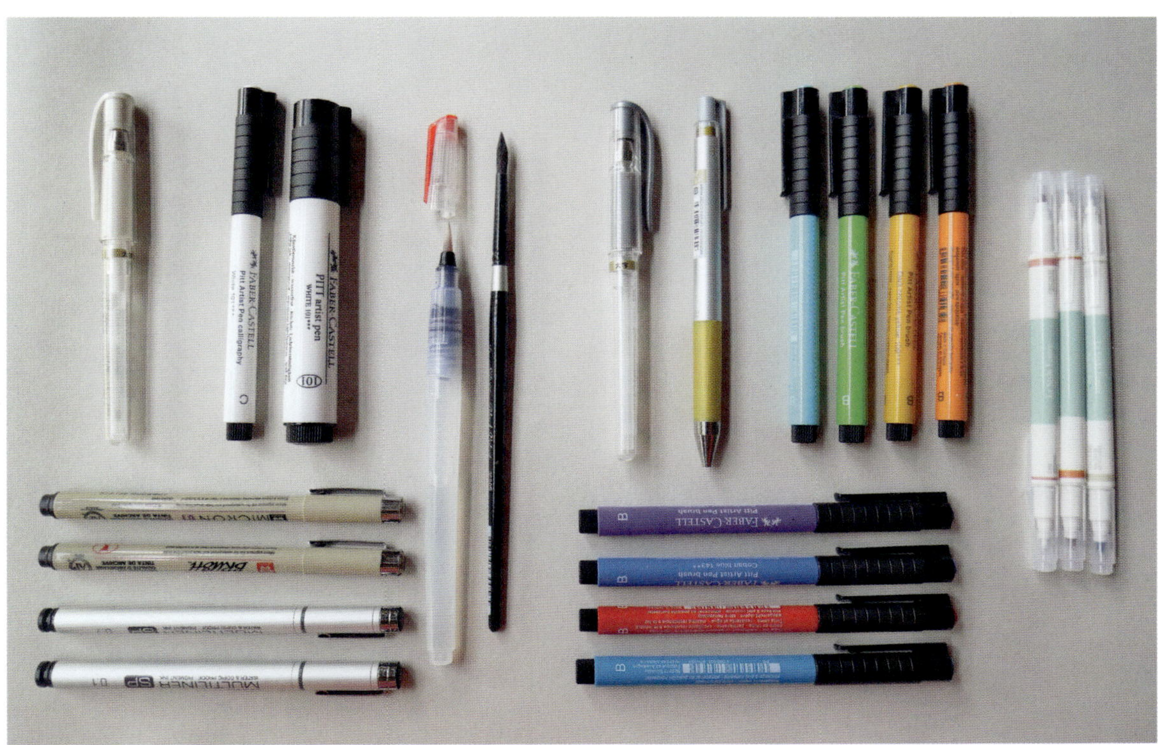

MATERIALS

You will find a list of my favorite ink pens of various kinds in the Resources section (see page 124), but any kind of pens you already have can be used—you don't have to spend a lot on professional artist-grade tools. A colorful set of children's markers is a great place to begin, and I use them often. The most important thing is having a wide range of colors, including black, gray, and browns. White gel pens are useful and fun, as are gel pens in various metallic hues, such as gold, silver, and copper. You will also find that pens come with different types of tips—from the very thin line of micron pens to the chisel tips of calligraphy pens to flexible brush tips and everything in between. I suggest trying them all.

For paper, you can use the same 5 × 7-inch (13 × 18 cm) pieces of drawing paper you used for graphite and colored pencil work. Be creative with your paper choices. Nothing we are doing will be so wet that you would need a watercolor paper. You will also need a round watercolor brush in a size 6 or 8. Portable water brush pens are also great to try. The only other supply you will need is a pencil. My favorite supplies are listed in the Resources section (see page 124), so give that a look before you make any purchases. Once you have gathered your supplies, let's get started with the magical medium of ink.

LESSON FIFTEEN

SCRATCH AND HATCH

The foundation of all pen-and-ink work is the line, but oh the variety of ways we can make lines! In this lesson, we will explore traditional ways of making lines as well as more intuitive ways. Once you add these different techniques to your drawing toolbox and give them a bit of practice, you will be able to call on them for any subject you wish to draw. It's all about value, texture, and our familiar friend, direction of form.

Let's keep it simple with our materials and use a black pen on white paper. The effects of these different types of lines, or as I like to call them, "scratches and hatches," are best demonstrated and learned without the use of color. Choose any black pen you like, but make sure it has a fine point, so, in other words, it does not make a wet, bold line. It can be a ballpoint, felt tip, gel, or micron pen. Now, let's get scratching and hatching.

TOOLS TO GATHER

- Drawing paper, 5 × 7 inches (13 × 18 cm)
- Graphite pencil
- Ruler or straightedge
- Fine-point black pen (I used a Pigma micron)

STEPS

1- On a piece of paper, use a pencil and a ruler to create a grid of 8 even rectangles. Leave a ½-inch (1 cm) margin all around to give you the size shown. In the upper-left rectangle, use your pen to draw horizontal lines, as shown. Start with the lines a bit farther apart, draw them closer together until you reach the center, and then begin to draw them father apart. Do you notice how the image appears lighter when the lines are father apart and darker where the lines are closer together? Drawing parallel lines like this in one direction is called *hatching*. It's a great way to show simple values of light and dark as well as depth. Things closer to the horizon line will appear closer together; they will appear farther apart as you move away from the horizon line. *See A.*

2- In the next rectangle, use your pen to draw diagonal lines going in one direction, then in the other direction, across the top half of the space, as shown. When we cross lines over one another in the opposite direction, it's called *cross-hatching*. Notice that where the lines are closer together it appears darker, and when lines are broken it appears lighter. In the bottom section, make different areas of cross-hatching with lines going in 4 different directions: diagonally in 2 directions and sometimes horizontally and also vertically. The more directions used, the darker the area appears. Cross-hatching is a highly effective technique for creating different areas of value between dark and light. *See B.*

3 - Moving to the next space, use broken lines to create the image shown. Continue to draw broken lines, following the curves of the first lines. Then, begin creating curved lines in new directions, as you desire, to create overlapping, curved cross-hatching of solid and broken lines, as shown. You can hatch and crosshatch with any shape of line. Notice how the areas that overlap appear darker and the areas with lines that are farther apart appear lighter. *See C.*

4 - In the left side of the next space, use the point of your pen to make tiny dots that are far apart at the bottom and gradually closer together and more plentiful moving toward the top. This technique of using tiny dots is called *stippling*, and it is a wonderful way to show value and shading. Even though all the dots are the same size, creating lots of dots close together creates the illusion of darkness. On the right side of this space, do the same exercise, but make some of the dots gradually larger as you move toward the top. This is another way to use stippling—with dots of various sizes. *See D.*

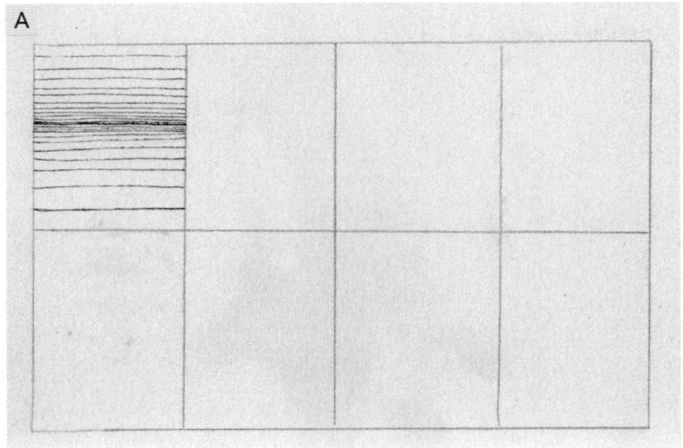

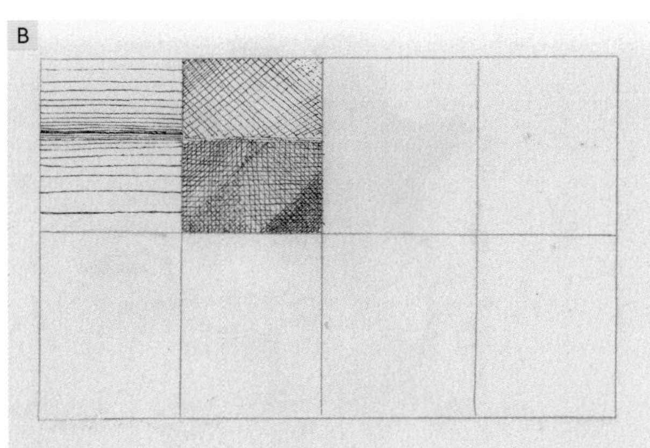

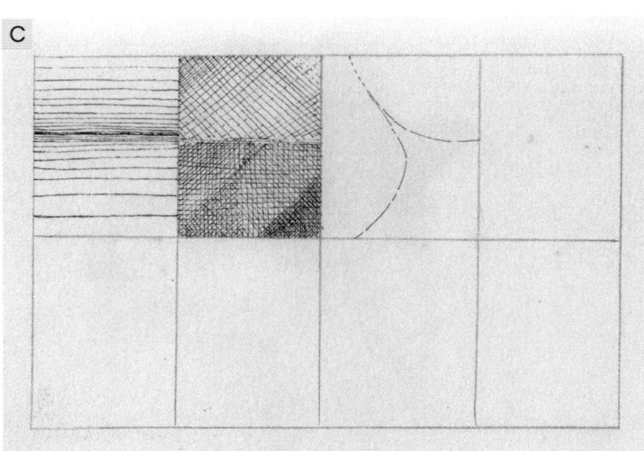

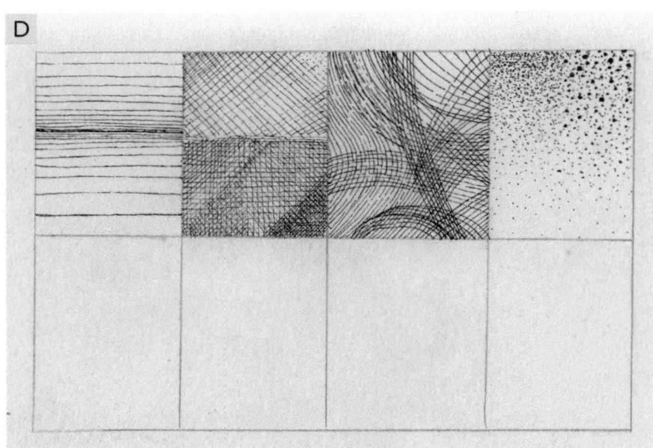

5 - In the next space, use your pen to create rows of tiny hatch marks that slightly overlap one another. Try them straight, father apart, closer together, curved in different directions, horizontal, long, short, and wavy. These types of tiny hatch marks are effective for creating fur, hair, feathers, waves, and other textures in subjects you might choose to draw. *See E.*

6 - Now it's time to *scribble*! Scribbling creates amazing textures that can be used for simple shading and textures. It feels free and easy. Try scribbling with the lines farther apart at the top, then gradually becoming closer together toward the bottom for great effects. *See F.*

7 - I call this texture *tick marks*, and I use it a lot. Using tick marks is not only a great way to hatch large areas with even values, but they also make a wonderful decorative pattern. Try them vertically, horizontally, closer together, farther apart, in a curved shape, and even in varied lengths. *See G.*

8 - This final pattern uses diagonal lines with little bends, along with small areas where the lines create tiny random shapes. Use this to create patterns and designs. Fill in the open shapes with cross-hatching, scribbles, and stippling. *See H.*

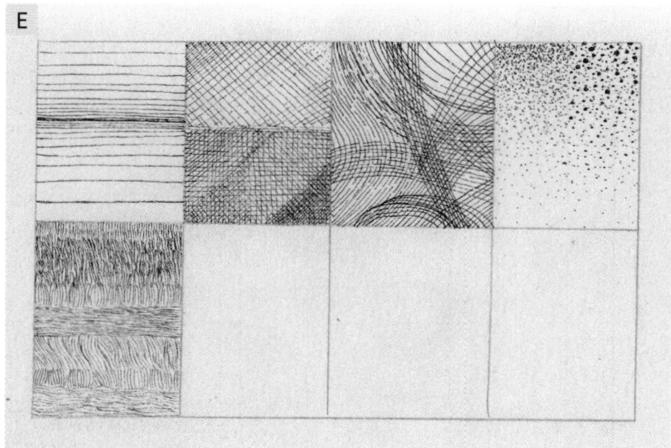
E

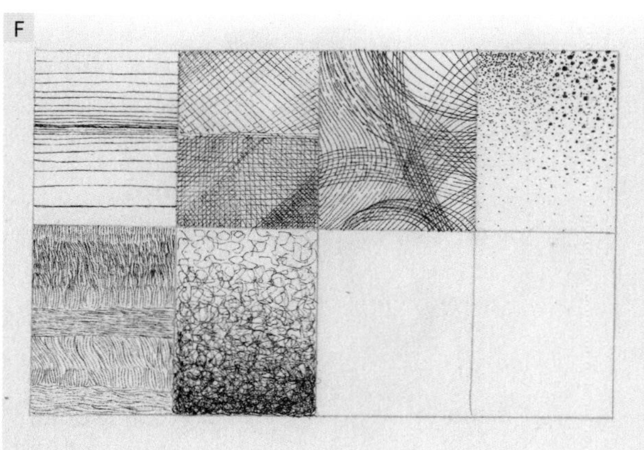
F

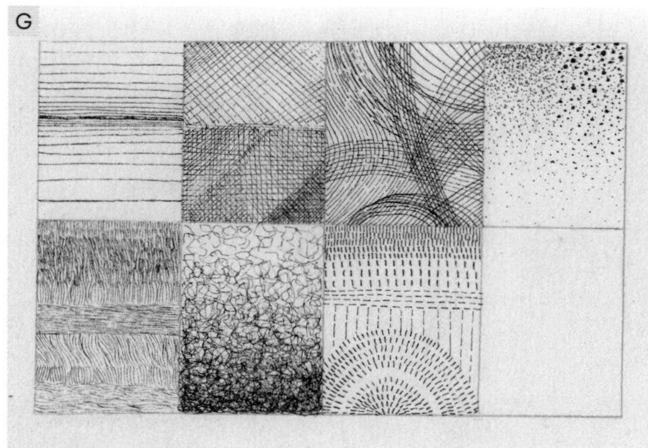
G

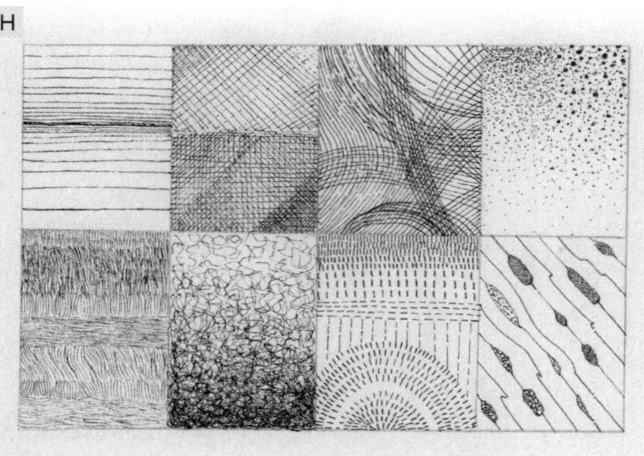
H

USE YOUR CREATIVITY

All these ways of making marks can be combined and altered to suit any subject you wish to draw and embellish with patterns. What if you started a freeform drawing combining many of these textures? What if you used a brush-tip pen? Sometimes, when we make random marks, as in the drawing below, it begins to appear as something we recognize.

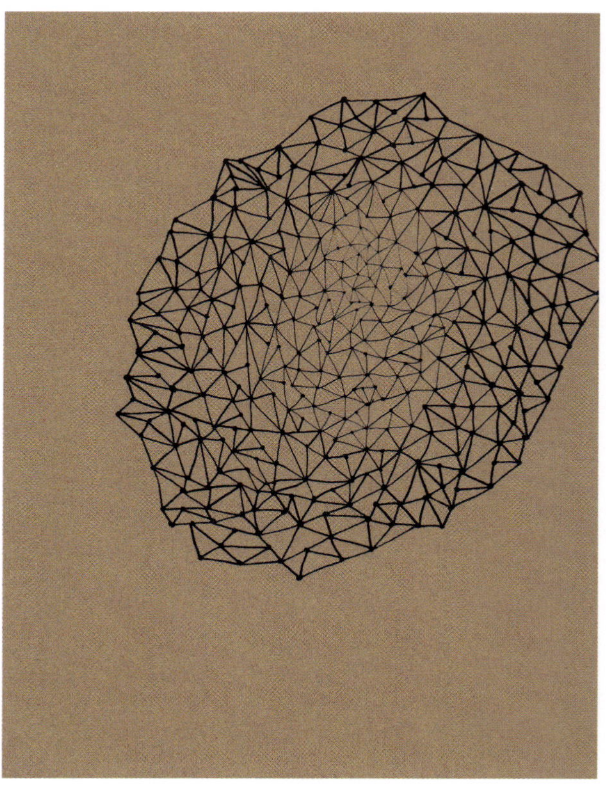

This drawing using pens of different line widths became a geometric pattern. Try it!

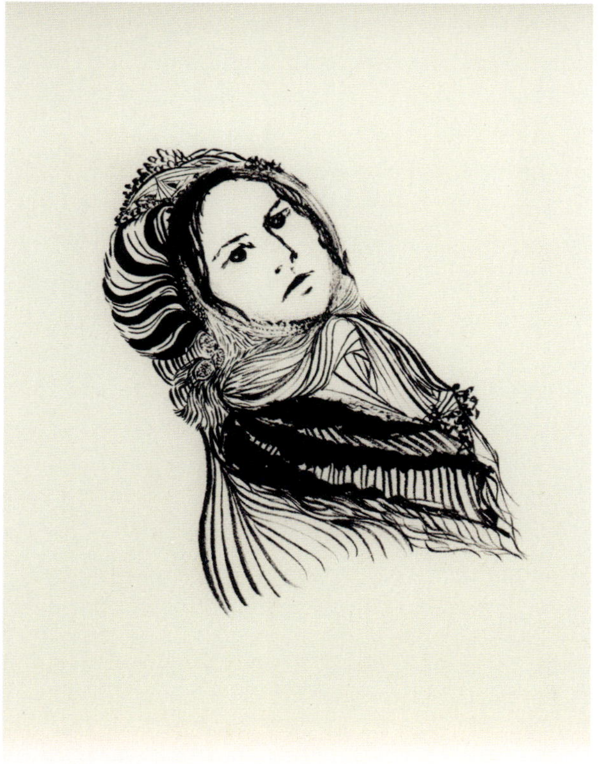

This random mark making with a brush-tip pen started to look like a person, so I embellished it with a simple face.

LESSON SIXTEEN

EXPRESSIVE LINE AND WASH

One of the interesting things about using ink in a pen or marker is that, although you are always working with the line in various forms of mark making as we saw in Lesson 15 (page 90), because it is a water medium, you can also use a brush to wet it and create a wash. Even when using a waterproof ink, if you wet it before it dries, it will dissolve into a wash of color. This simple fact allows us to create beautiful effects in our drawings with pen—from crisp lines to dreamy swatches of transparent color.

In this lesson, we will use the line to create expressive marks and then use a brush dipped in water to create softer edges and areas of beautiful color. Make note that if you use some pens with waterproof inks and allow them to dry, then use water-soluble inks in the same area, the waterproof inks will stay put but the water-soluble inks will dissolve into a wash. I use mostly water-soluble ink pens, such as Crayola markers, in the sample images, but for a few areas, I use waterproof pens such as Faber-Castell Pitt Artist pens to create some diversity in the finished drawing. I suggest experimenting with both. Try to recreate the image, as shown in each step, and begin again with your unique marks and colors. The student drawings are examples of a few more possibilities you can achieve when you take this lesson a bit further on your own.

TOOLS TO GATHER

- Good selection of markers and pens in colors you love (I mention the colors used in the sample images, if you want to try to match them.)
- Drawing paper, 5 × 7 inches (13 × 18 cm)
- Round watercolor paintbrush in size 6 or 8
- Glass of clean water
- Paper towel or cloth to wipe your paintbrush

STEPS

1 - Choose 5 different colors to begin. I use a bright blue, violet, magenta, orange, and golden yellow. Draw 5 interlocking circles in the center of the paper. Dip your paintbrush into clean water and use the tip of the brush to apply a thin layer of water in each of the circles, as shown. Notice how the brilliant inks dissolve and move, mixing and mingling with each another. *See A.*

2 - Choose 3 values—light, medium, and dark—of another color. I chose warm grays. Using the tick mark technique (see page 92), surround the circles with 3 rows of tiny tick marks, beginning with the darkest color, then the medium color, then the lightest, as shown. *See B.*

3 - Using the same 5 colors you used to draw the circles, use the stippling technique (see page 91) to make tiny dots along the outer edge of the tick marks, starting with one color and then switching to each of the other colors, as shown. Use the tip of a wet brush to dissolve the inks so they create a fluid line containing all the colors used, as shown. *See C.*

A

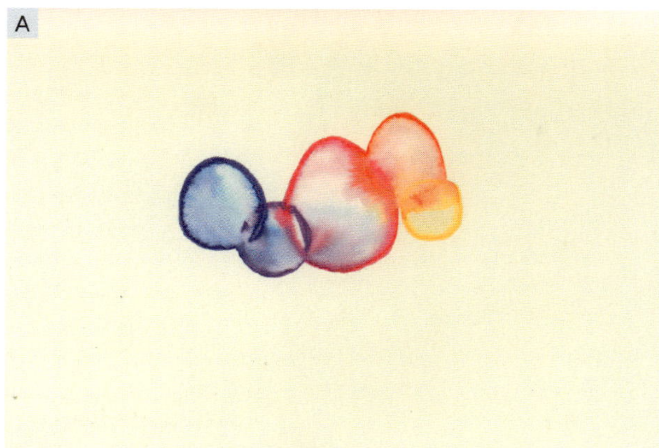

B

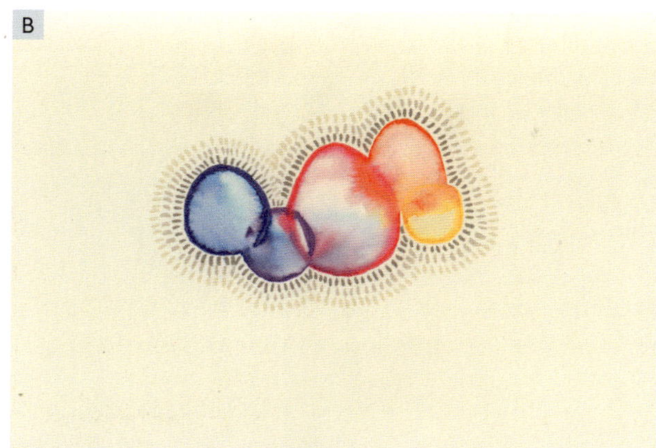

C

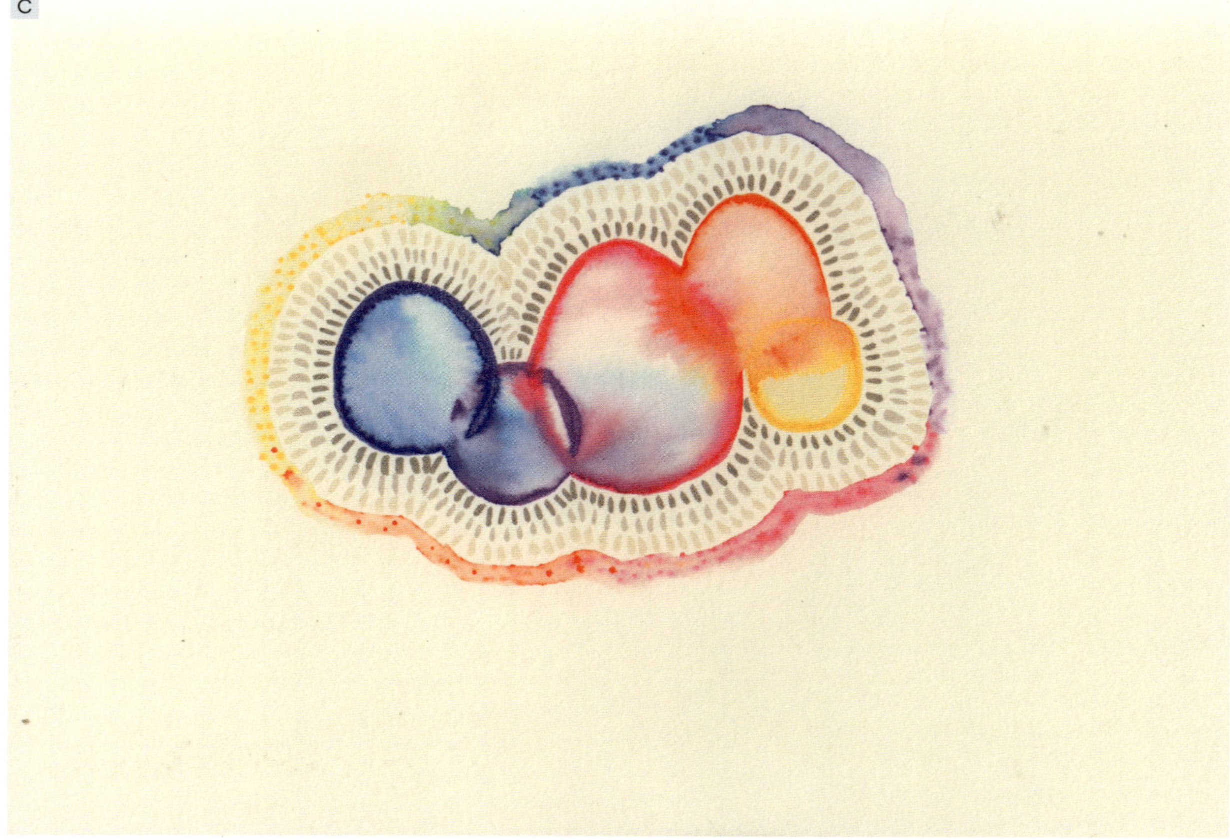

4 - For the first part of this step, choose 2 shades of pink and a golden yellow. Lay one of the pink markers so the length of the tip is flush with the paper, and then roll it on its side to create a random wider line in a half-circle shape along a small part of the rainbow line, as shown. Use the other pink to create a similar line inside the first line. Use the golden yellow marker to color in a small circle in the center, touching the rainbow line from step 3. Dip your paintbrush into water and use it to wet the area inside the first wider line all the way to the rainbow line, as shown. Create 3 of these shapes, as seen in the sample image. Use a light blue marker to create a thin line of stippling around each shape. Finish by using a light green marker to apply another thin area of stippling, as shown. *See D.*

5 - Using the same light green marker, draw tiny leaf shapes between the stippled areas, as shown. Use one of the pink markers to draw tiny ovals scattered to the outside of the leaf shapes. Use an orange marker to create another oval shape around the pink shape. Finally, use a wet paintbrush to fill in each leaf shape and the pink oval shapes, leaving the space between the pink and orange ovals dry. Study the sample image to see how it should appear when you are finished. *See E.*

D

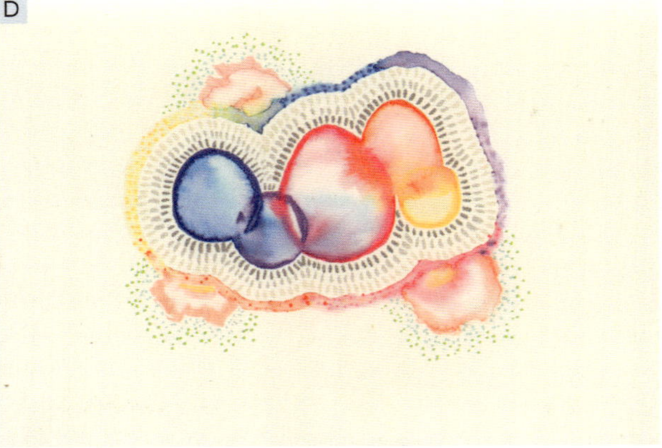

E

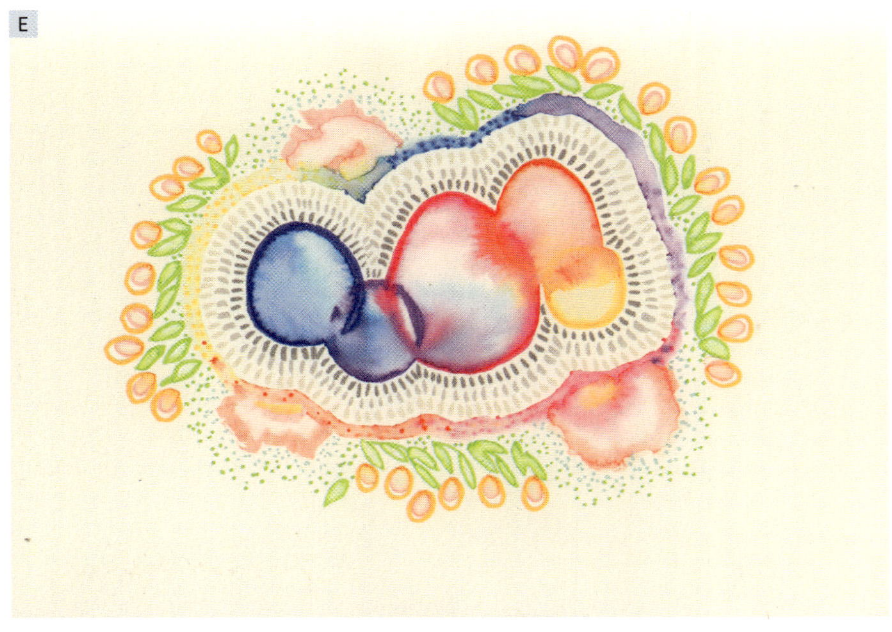

USE YOUR CREATIVITY

This is a wonderful way to create a cheerful greeting card or gift. You could also spell a word, writing the letters inside each of the larger circles with dark-gray ink. What about the word *bloom*? Or the name of the recipient? You can always adjust the number of circles to reflect the number of letters in the word or name you choose!

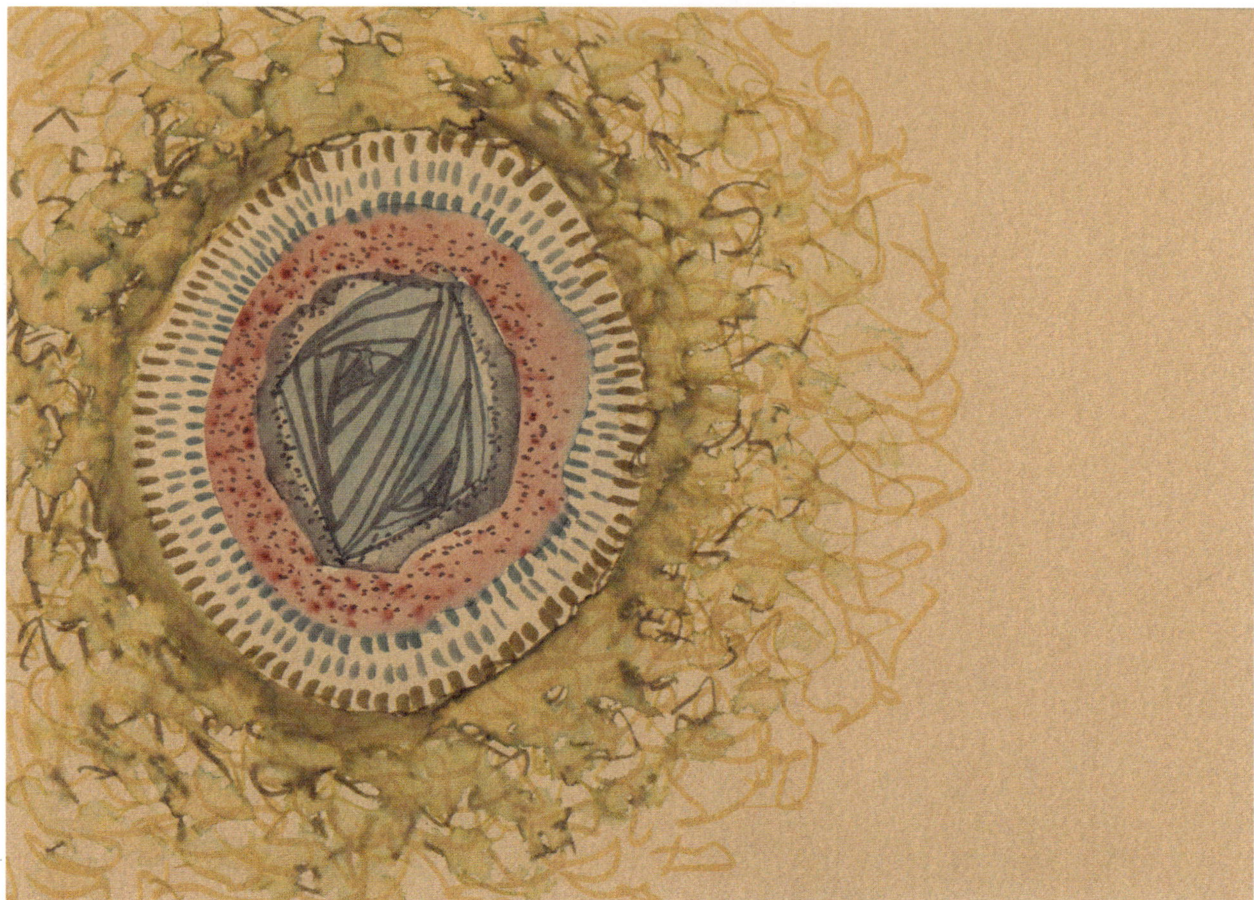

Here is an example of the same techniques used in a different way on a piece of Kraft paper. Turn the page to see some beautiful works by my students that show even more possibilities.

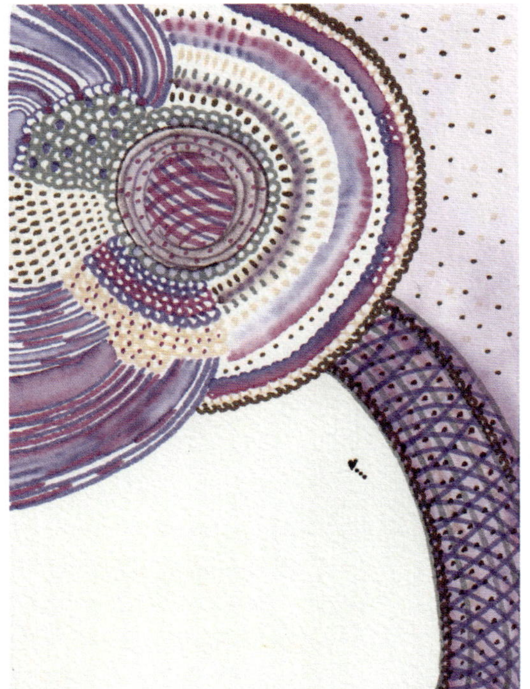

Debbie Brandecker

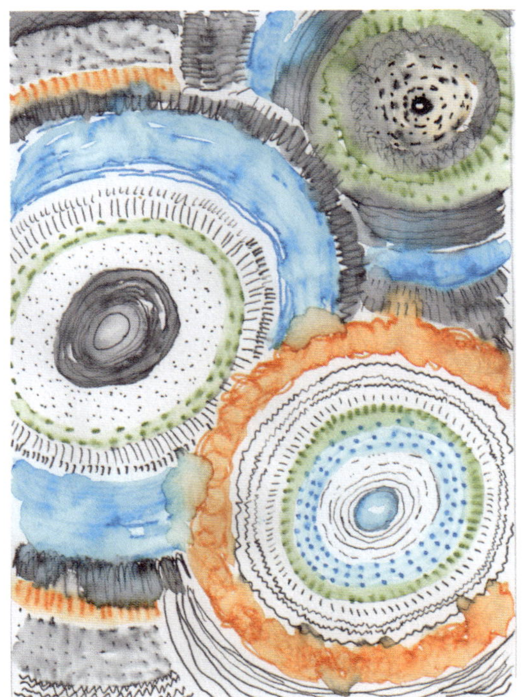

Lisa Hofmann

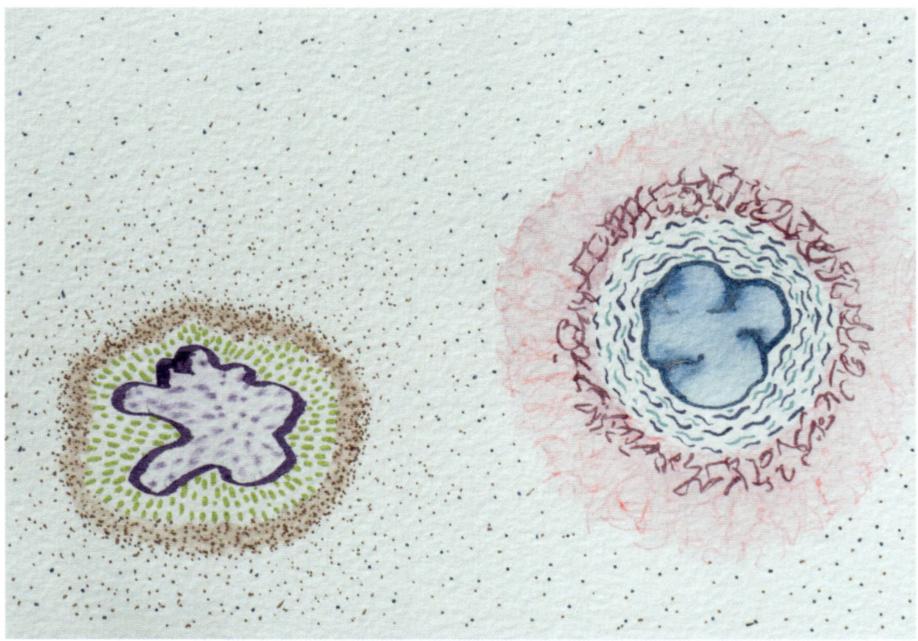

Nathalie Bélanger

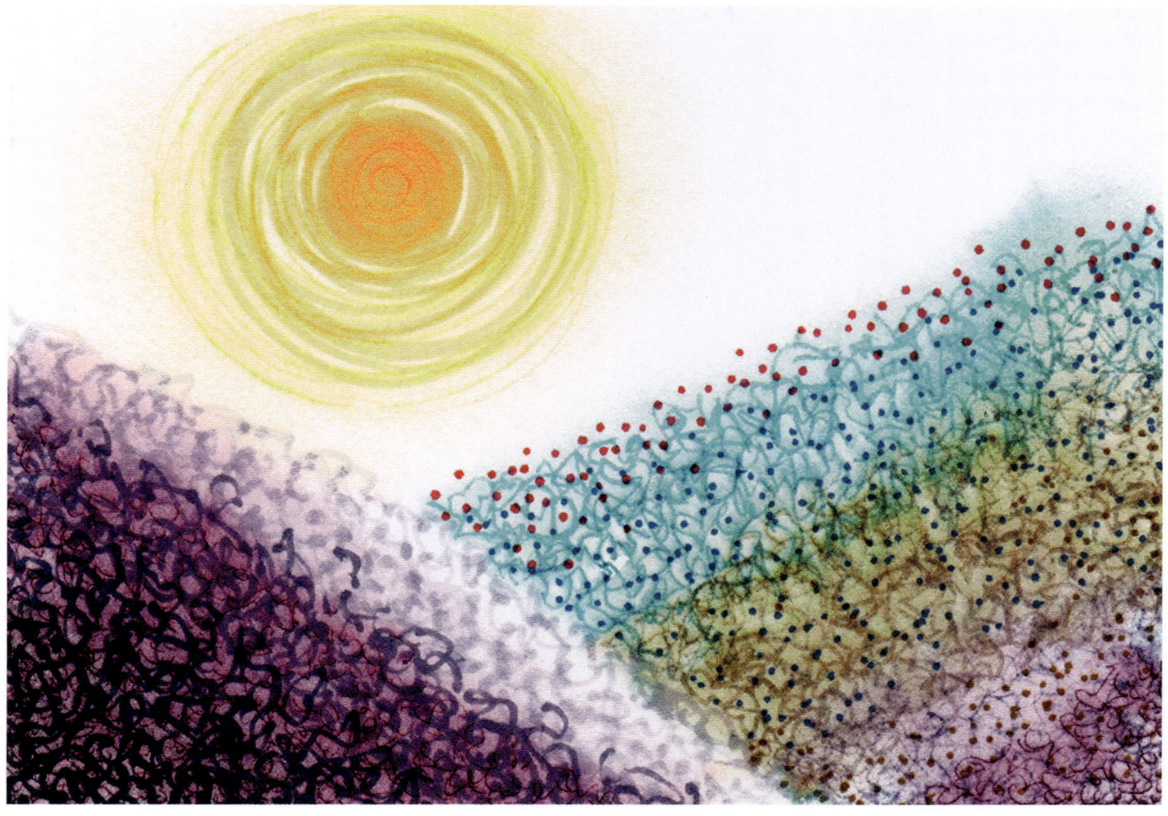

Hazel Scott

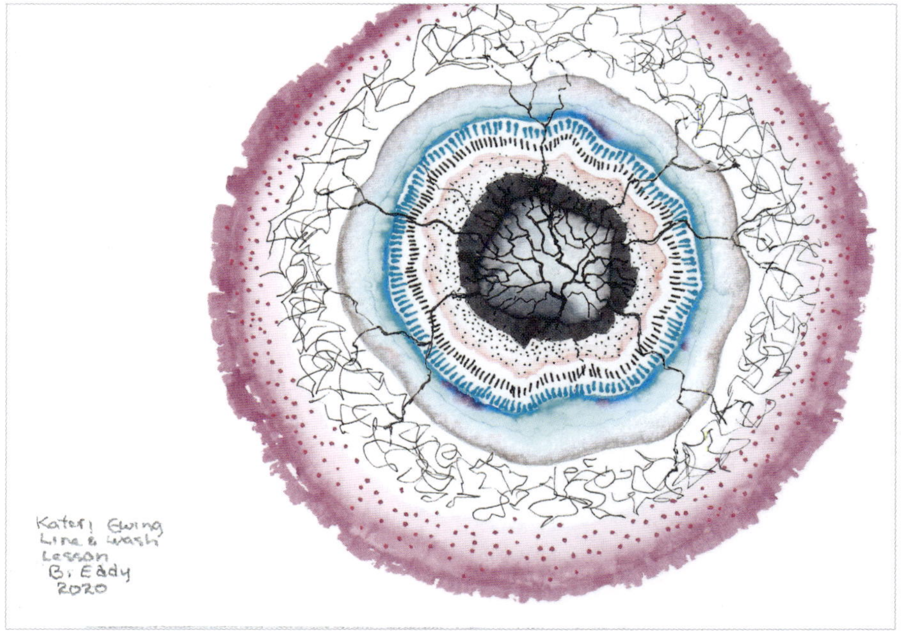

Beverly Eddy

LESSON SEVENTEEN

CIRCLE FLOWER POWER

One of my favorite flowers is the dandelion. Every spring when it presents those cheerful golden faces en masse in my yard, I cannot help but smile. I love its determination, its ability to be so proliferate—its tendency to spread joy far and wide. I also love the seed heads, those pearly, luminous white domes of fluff. This lesson is inspired by those sunny, yet humble weeds (at least to lawn perfectionists) and is a bridge between our expressive mark making and our beginning to create more representational drawings.

I have chosen a more subtle palette of colors, but feel free to go as vibrant as you wish. We will use bits and pieces from previous lessons to create a page full of blossoms that would make a wonderful get-well card or a postcard to cheer someone. If you have metallic gel pens or a white gel pen, try them in this lesson. There is also a sample image showing how you can make the images a little more flowerlike. This exercise is kind of magical and great fun.

TOOLS TO GATHER

- Selection of markers and pens in 8 colors that you love (These should **not** be waterproof. I use Crayola markers.)
- Drawing paper, 5 × 7 inches (13 × 18 cm)
- Round watercolor paintbrush in size 6 or 8
- Glass of clean water
- Paper towel or cloth to wipe your paintbrush
- Metallic gel pens
- White gel pen

STEPS

1 - With a marker, draw an imperfect circle in the center of the page. Using each of the 8 colors, some more than once, draw a total of 15 circles, as shown. Dip your paintbrush into clean water and fill in each circle with water, making sure to take the brush all the way to the edge of the circle to activate the ink. *See A.* Let dry completely before moving on.

2 - Draw a smaller imperfect circle inside each of the existing circles, using a different color marker from your selection of 8. Use a wet paintbrush to fill in each smaller circle with water, as in step 1. *See B.* Let dry completely before moving to step 3.

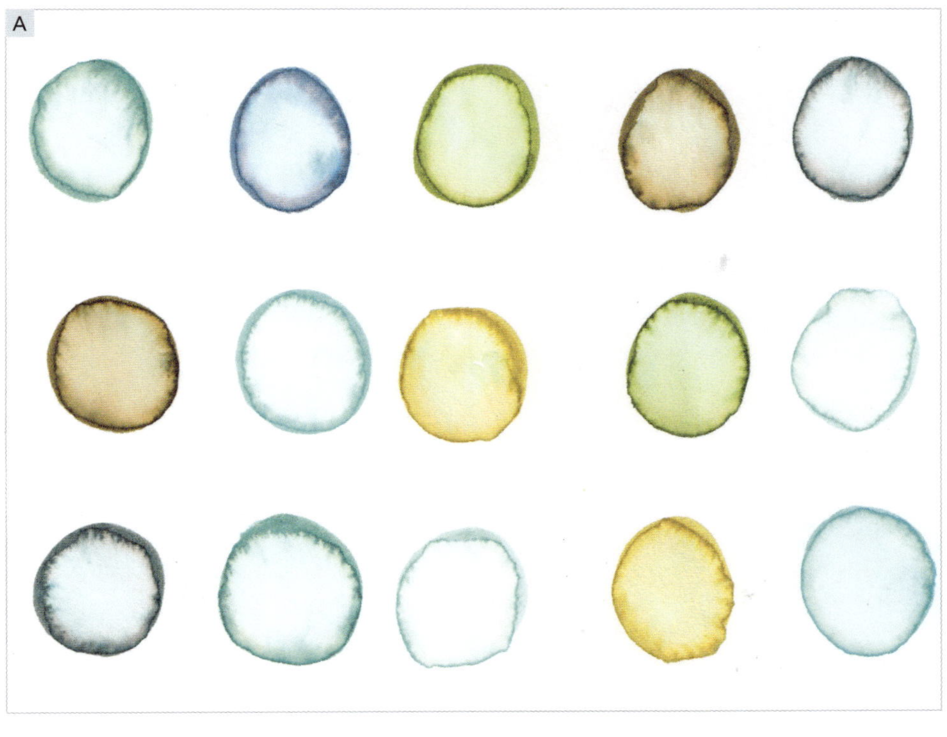
A

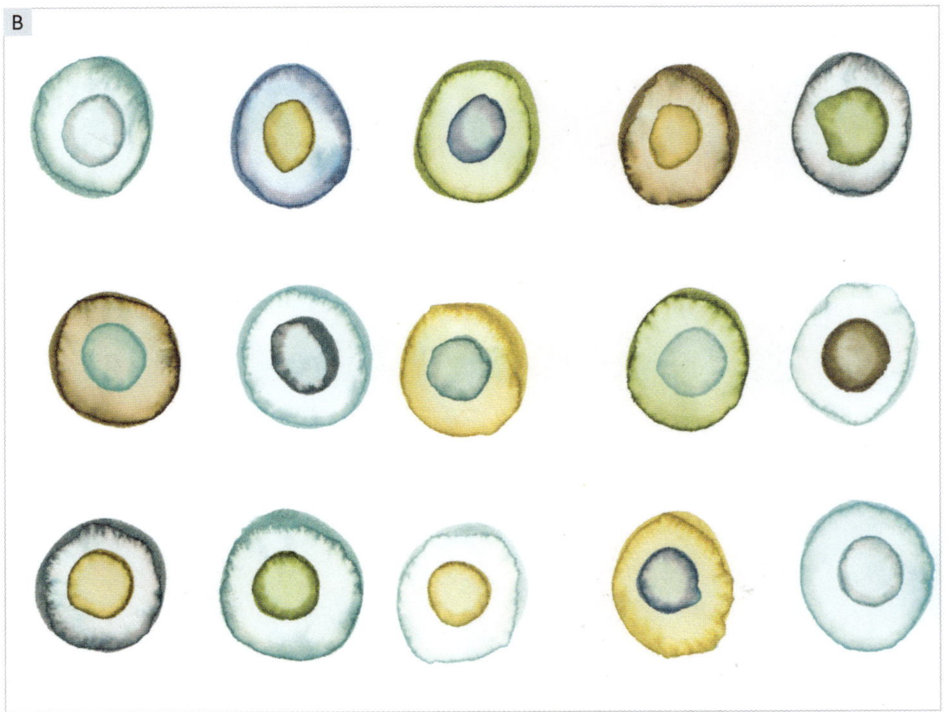
B

3 - With a metallic gel pen (I used a fine-point gold pen), draw 2 loose, very imperfect circles around each circle. Now, create some marks to decorate each blossom. Here are some ideas, as seen in the sample image *(see C)*:

- With metallic gel pen, draw scribble marks around the inner circle.
- With metallic gel pen in another color, make stipple marks to create tiny dots around the edge of the inner circle.
- Using a marker in a contrasting color, create tick marks around the inside circle.
- Using a marker in a contrasting color, create uneven hatch marks radiating from the inner circle.
- Using a marker in a contrasting color, create a series of tiny half circles around the center circle.

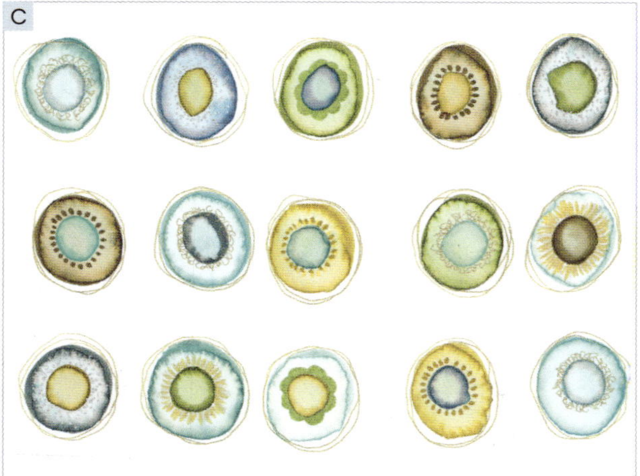

4 - Use metallic and white gel pens to add even more details *(see D)*, such as:

- Stippling inside the smaller circles
- White dots inside the circles, in the half-circle shapes, around the edges of things
- Larger metallic gel pens dots at the very center of the circles

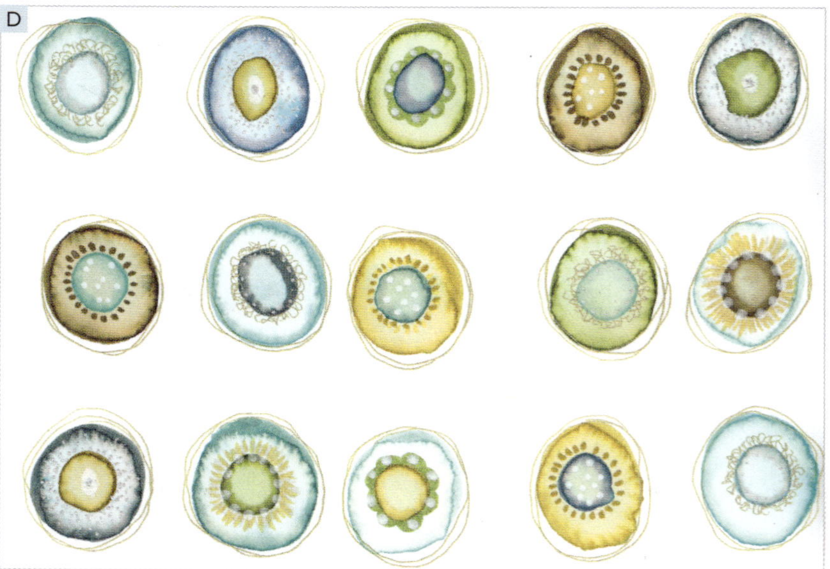

USE YOUR CREATIVITY

The image below gives an example of how to create a little garden row of flowers using the same techniques but adding long green stems with tiny leaves. *See E.* What if you drew them closer together, as if in a bouquet, and then cut a vase shape out of patterned paper to glue on top? What if you drew individual petal shapes from the edges of the circles to create daisy and sunflowerlike flowers, using the same expressive types of marks? I would love to see the gardens you create. Tag me on Instagram: @kateriewing.

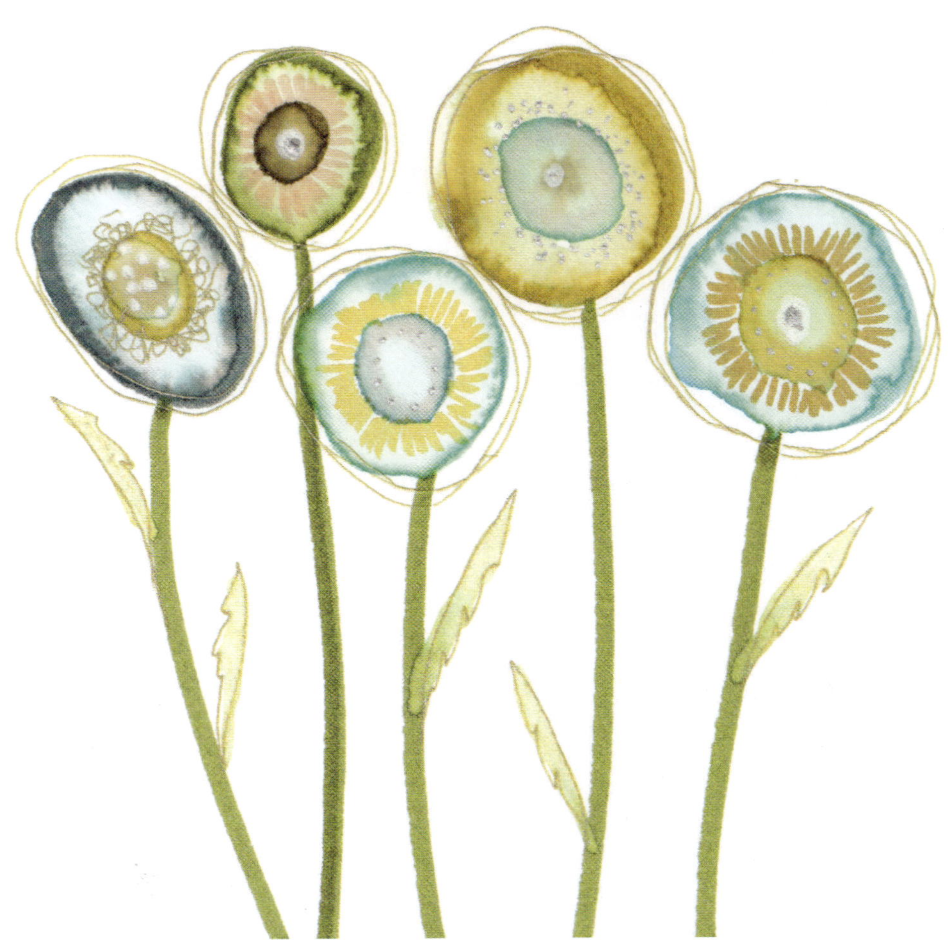

LESSON EIGHTEEN

FEATHERFALL

One of my favorite stories from childhood is the fairy tale *Mother Holle* collected by the Brothers Grimm in 1812. There is an image of old Mother Holle shaking her feather pillows high in the sky, and as those feathers fall to earth, they become snowflakes. In this lesson, we will use softly curving hatch marks to create a page full of ink feathers, so they appear to be falling from the sky. Then, with a sprinkle and splash of clean water, they will melt and transform before our eyes.

Feathers are a wonderful subject to draw with colored pencils or ink—try both. You can either use a selection of hues inspired directly from nature or use your imagination to create a rainbow of feathers straight from a fairy tale. Remember, use your feather touch with any medium you choose. Also, this lesson starts out feeling loose and easy, and it is, but the results can be so beautiful. Keep it loose and free—don't try too hard. Let's draw some feathers.

TOOLS TO GATHER

- Selection of water-soluble markers and pens in colors that represent feathers to you, or simply colors you love (I use a mix of Pitt Artist pens and Crayola markers in similar shades of blue, aqua, and gray with a touch of rust to make it pop. If you have waterproof pens, use them a bit with the others to get some fun results.)
- Drawing paper, 5 × 7 inches (13 × 18 cm)
- Round watercolor paintbrush in size 6 or 8
- Glass of clean water
- Paper towel or cloth to wipe your paintbrush
- Metallic gel pens
- White gel pen
- Graphite pencil

STEPS

1 - Choose 2 colors. At the upper left of your paper, use one color to draw a slightly curved line, and then create feather strokes starting from the center line (quill of the feather) and moving outward. Leave some areas blank to fill in with the second color. Remember, keep it free and easy using a light touch. It will look more featherlike than if you use a heavy, perfect line. *See A.*

2 - Continue to draw tiny feathers in this way, selecting 2 new colors for each feather. Keep the feathers random in size, direction, shape, etc. Use the sample image as your guide. *See B.* If you have waterproof markers, mix them in. It will create fun results!

3 - Dip your paintbrush into clean water. Holding it over your drawing, shake it or tap it with your other hand to create water droplets on the drawing. *See C.* Let dry completely without touching the droplets.

4 - When completely dry, use your metallic gel pens to draw finer feathery lines on the tip of each feather, as shown. *See D.* These should be very random and dreamy—not realistic.

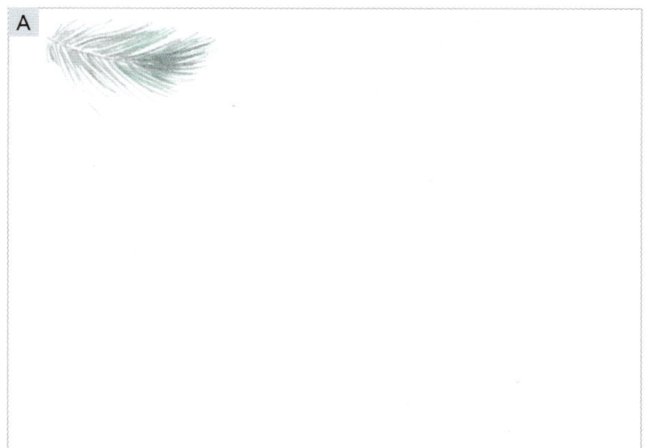
A

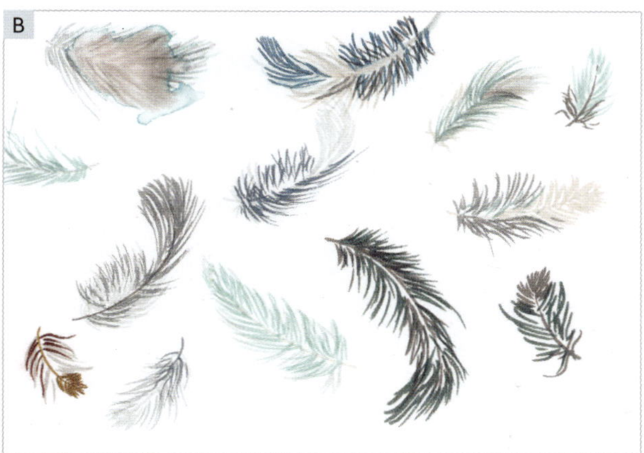
B

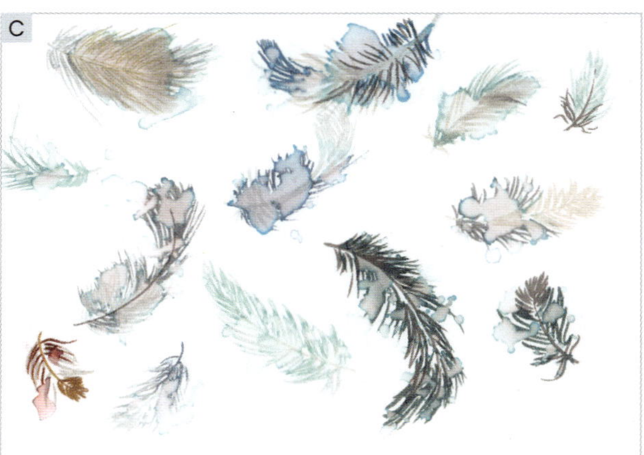
C

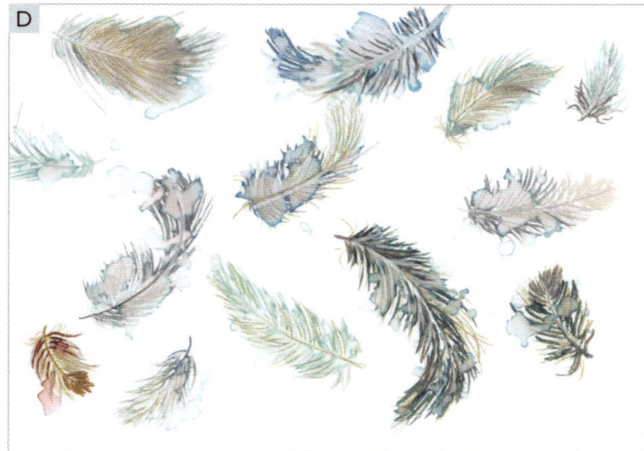
D

ANOTHER APPROACH

1 - Using a pencil and following the sample images, draw 2 lines to represent the center lines of 2 feathers. Use the pencil to create the tiny feathery lines, paying a bit more attention to keeping them more realistic and thinking of them as forming a heart shape when finished. *See E.*

2 - Choose 2 colors for each feather and create the feathery strokes right on top of the pencil lines. Take more time, really getting a nice integration of the colors and more realistic-looking feathery lines. *See F.*

3 - Using a wet paintbrush, sprinkle clean water over the feather drawings. *See G.* Let the water dry completely.

4 - Once the drawing is dry, use a fine-tipped metallic gel pen to create more feathery lines in the same way as the first layer. Notice the random, but delicate curve to the lines and how they are wispy at the ends, not harsh or ending abruptly. *See H.*

USE YOUR CREATIVITY

What would happen if you made a circle or wreath of feathers in the colors of the rainbow, or in the colors of the birds from your neighborhood? What if you mixed colored pencil with ink? What if you used black ink with a silver gel pen for a very elegant, monochromatic look?

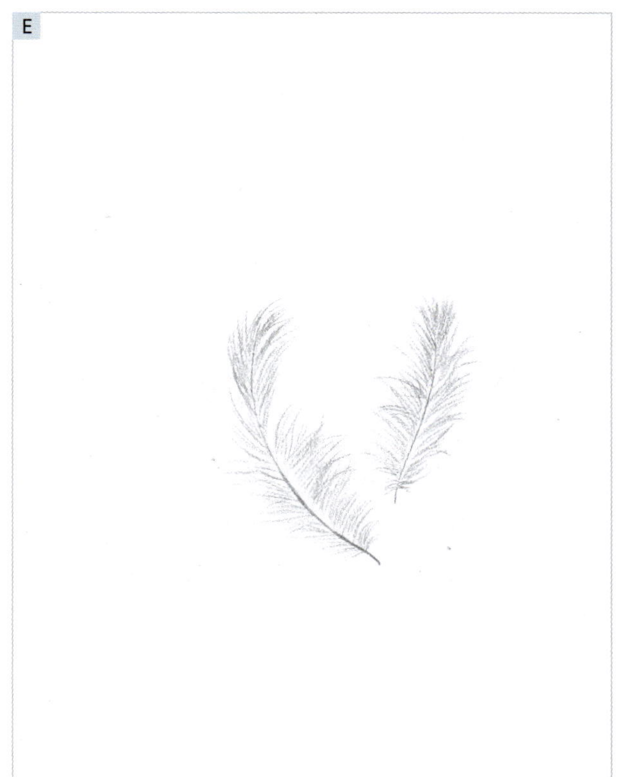
E

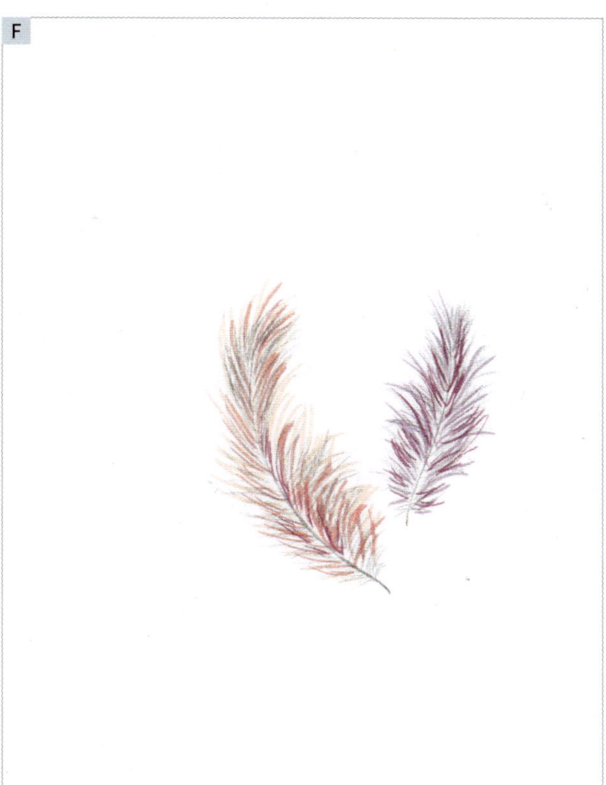
F

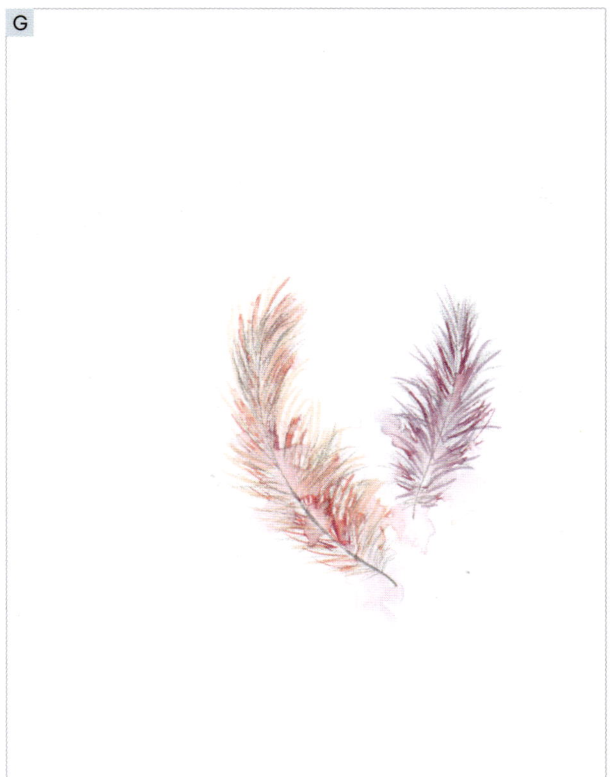
G

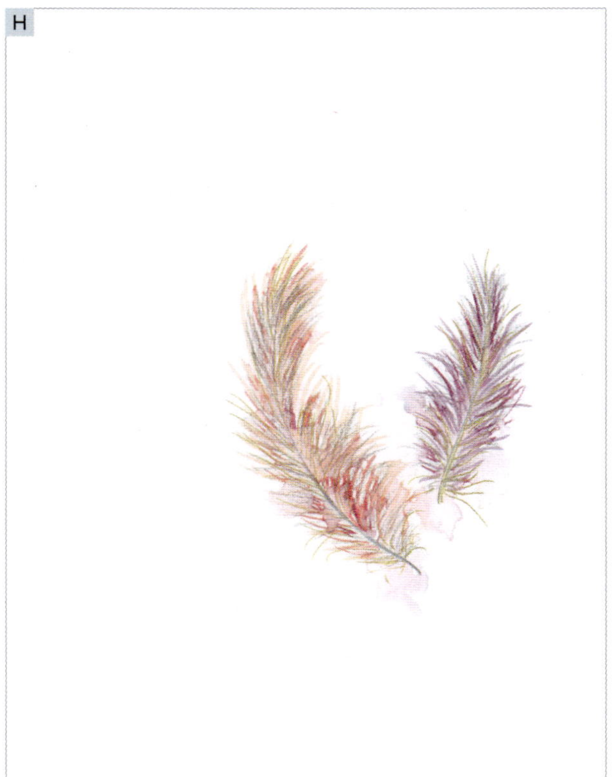
H

LESSON NINETEEN

A SIMPLE LANDSCAPE

Of all the subjects my students wish to learn to draw, the most popular by far is the landscape. We are all filled with a certain sense of place, and being able to make even a simple drawing of a view we love is a worthy goal as a beginning artist. The obvious dilemma in teaching this to an entire class is that we each have different ideas of how that landscape should look. The best solution? I teach the landscape I know and love best—a summer field with distant trees. Once you see how simple mark making can create the different parts of the landscape, you can adapt the shapes and colors to fit your own. Biggest tips: keep it simple at first and practice!

TOOLS TO GATHER

- Fine-point permanent marker in gray, black, or brown (If you have Pitt Artist pens or other permanent ink fineliners or brush pens in golds, greens, or browns, they will be great to use, too.)
- Drawing paper, 5 × 7 inches (13 × 18 cm)
- Selection of water-soluble markers and pens in greens, golds, rusts, and browns (Try to match the colors you see in the sample, but don't worry if yours are a bit different. I used Crayola markers.)
- Round watercolor paintbrush in size 6 or 8
- Glass of clean water
- Paper towel or cloth to wipe your paintbrush

STEPS

1 - To begin, use a light golden–yellow permanent marker or a brown, gray, or black permanent fineliner pen (PFP from here on) to create a random grassy textured line, as shown. *See A.*

2 - Choose 2 green permanent markers—a light green and one a bit darker—or PFPs, and use them to create a random section of marks that resemble the treetops. The best way to learn this is to study my example and practice it a bit. Randomness is not always easy, but once you get it, it's simple. Let the tip of your pen skip around. And dance. Don't try to be perfect! Follow my sample, do your best, and it will work beautifully! *See B.*

3 - Using the same pens, fill in the space between steps 1 and 2 with similar random mark making. Use hatching, cross-hatching, scribbling, stippling—whatever feels good. Follow my sample for guidance. *See C.* We are using permanent ink pens for now to build a foundation for the water-soluble markers later.

4 - Select some golden yellow– and rust-colored permanent markers, or use a PFP, to create random marks in a horizontal format to resemble grassy areas, as shown. Use the darker green permanent marker to create 2 small shrubs with scribble marks, as shown. *See D.*

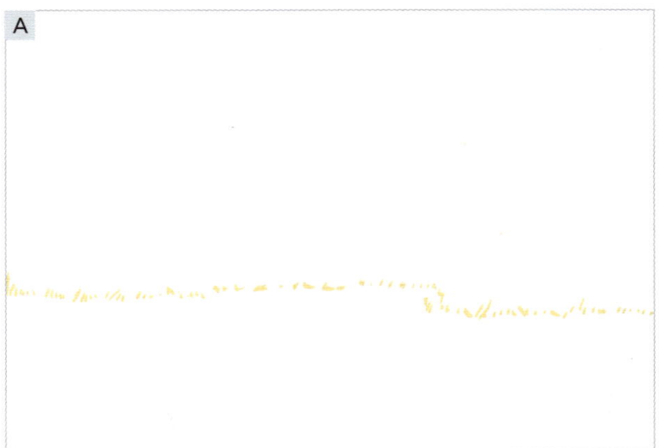
A

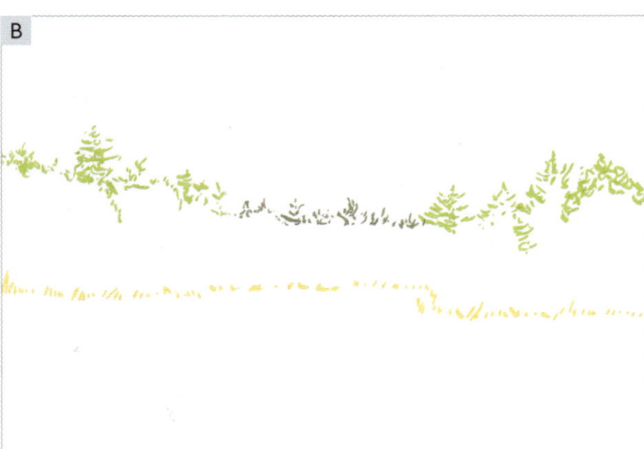
B

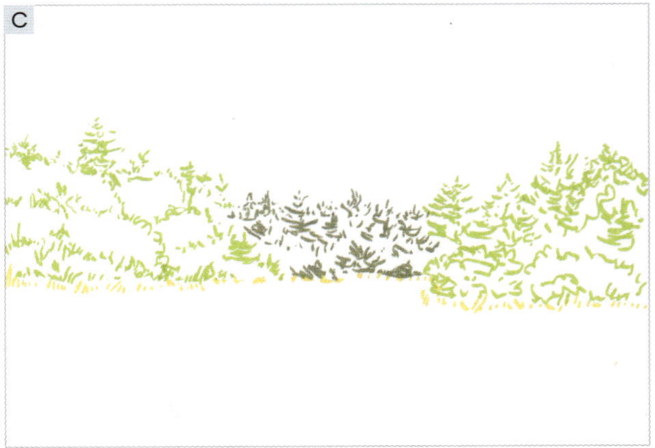
C

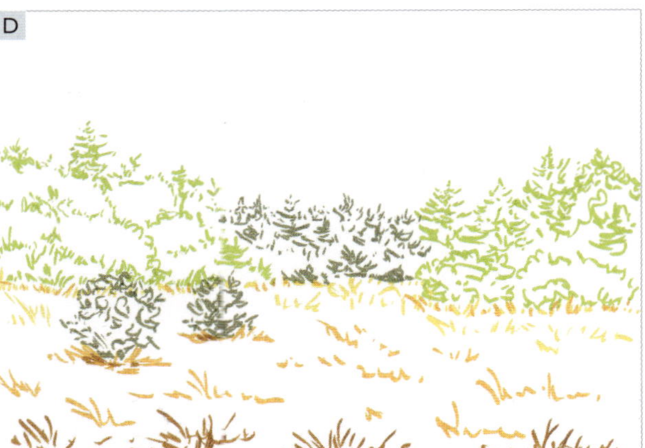
D

5 - It's time to use the water-soluble markers. Choose a variety of greens for the trees and golden yellow, rusts, and browns for the field. Use the stippling and tick-mark techniques to fill in the trees, shrubs, and grassy mounds with a variety of these colors, as shown. You do not need to copy my marks exactly. This exercise is about freedom with no expectations . . . be free and easy with your marks! *See E.*

6 - Now, it's time for magic. Dip your paintbrush into clean water and use the tip of the brush to wash over the trees and shrubs (all green areas). Do not saturate the paper; simply let the tip of the brush dance over the paper to activate the ink so it creates a lovely wash. Notice how the permanent marker lines stay put, giving the trees some structure. *See F.* Let dry completely before moving on.

7 - Repeat step 6 for the field area—everything golden, rust, and brown. *See G.* Let dry completely.

8 - For a final step, no matter which pens you used, use a PFP to create tiny hatch and tick marks where the trees meet the field and on the two shrubs, as shown. *See H.* This just gives a bit more dimension.

USE YOUR CREATIVITY

You have drawn your first landscape! How can you personalize it to fit your favorite landscape? Can you find more natural-looking colors? Are the tree shapes different? Is there green grass instead of a golden field? Is there an expanse of water, or even beach sand? How would you draw beach sand? Maybe tiny stipple marks, or tiny circles? So many possibilities. I hope you will share your results with me on Instagram: @katериewing.

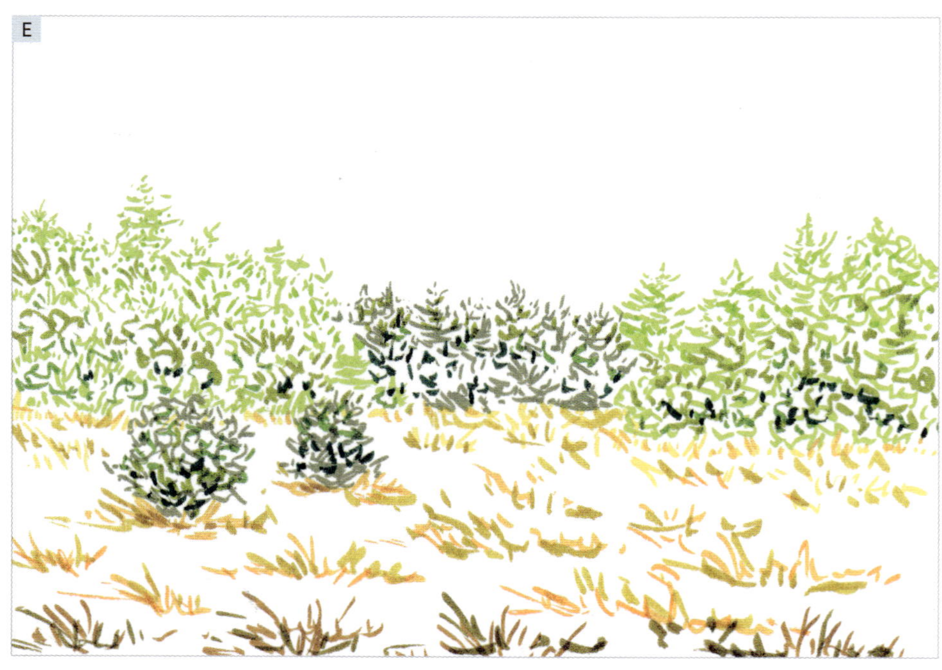

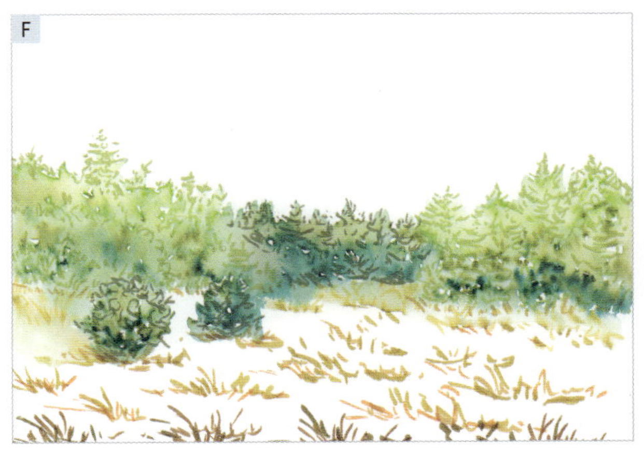
F

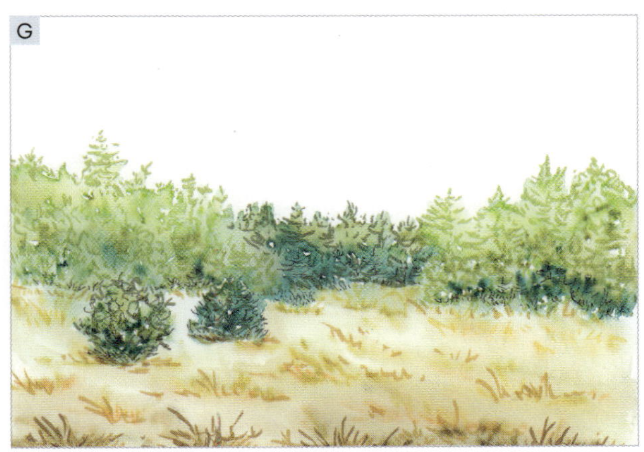
G

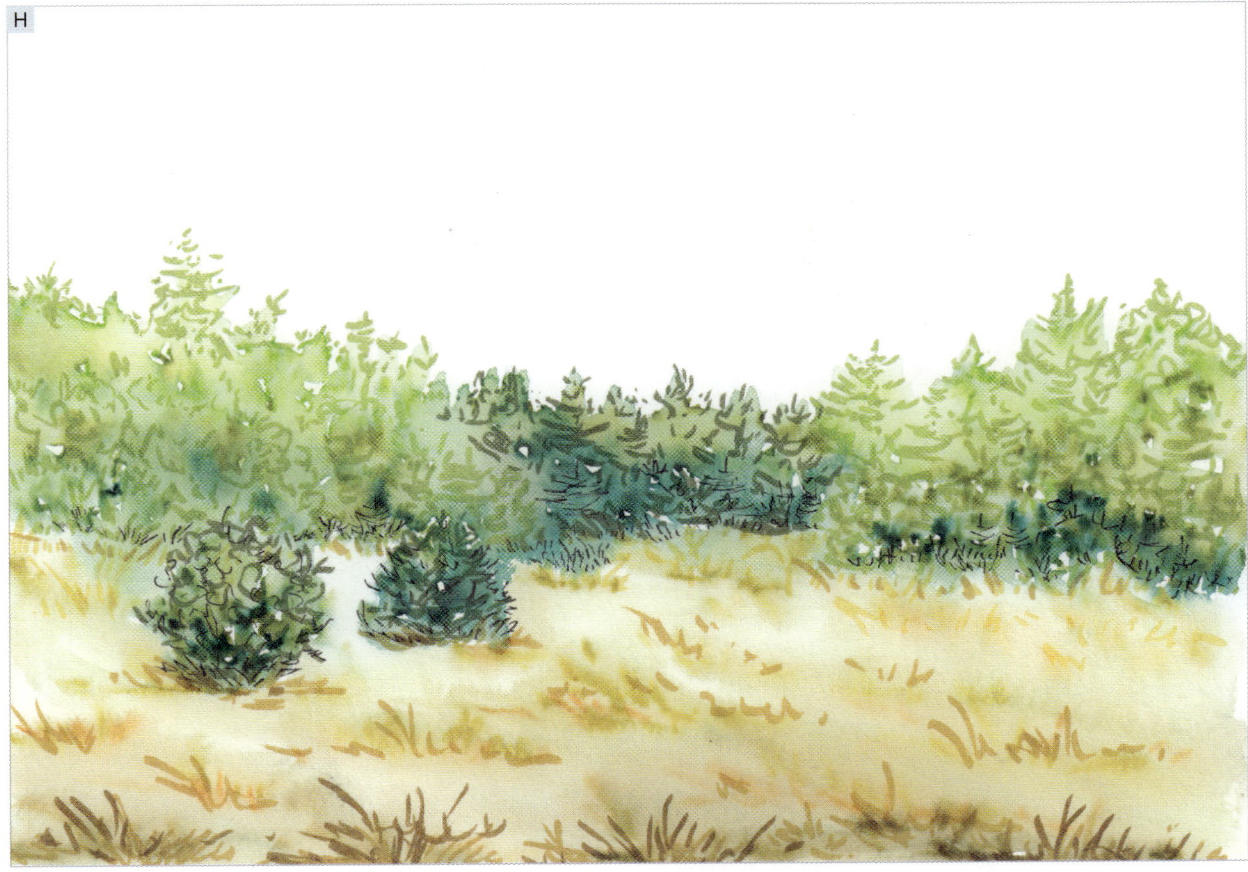
H

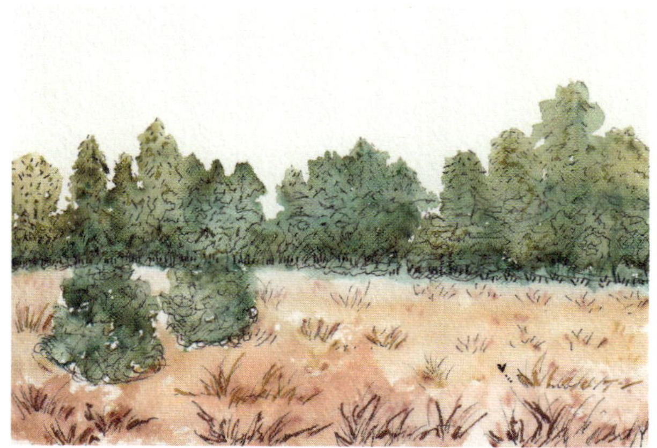

Debbie Brandecker

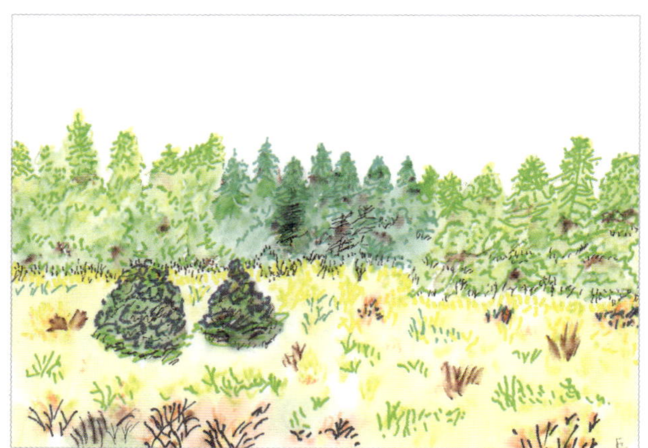

Fran Lowell

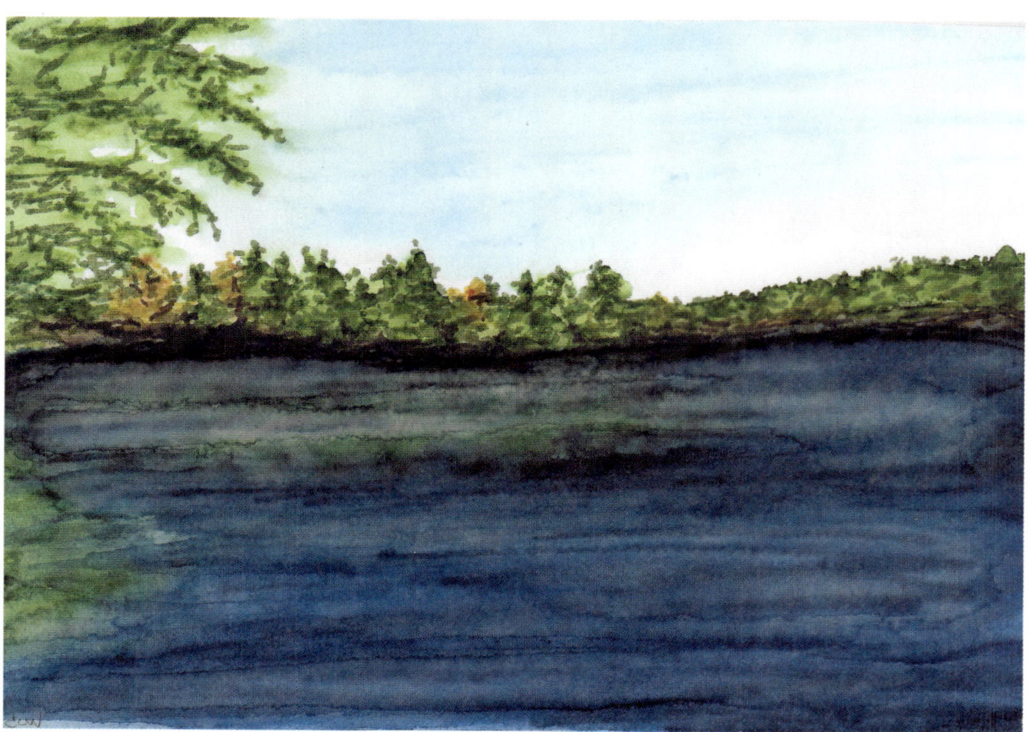

Carol Williamson

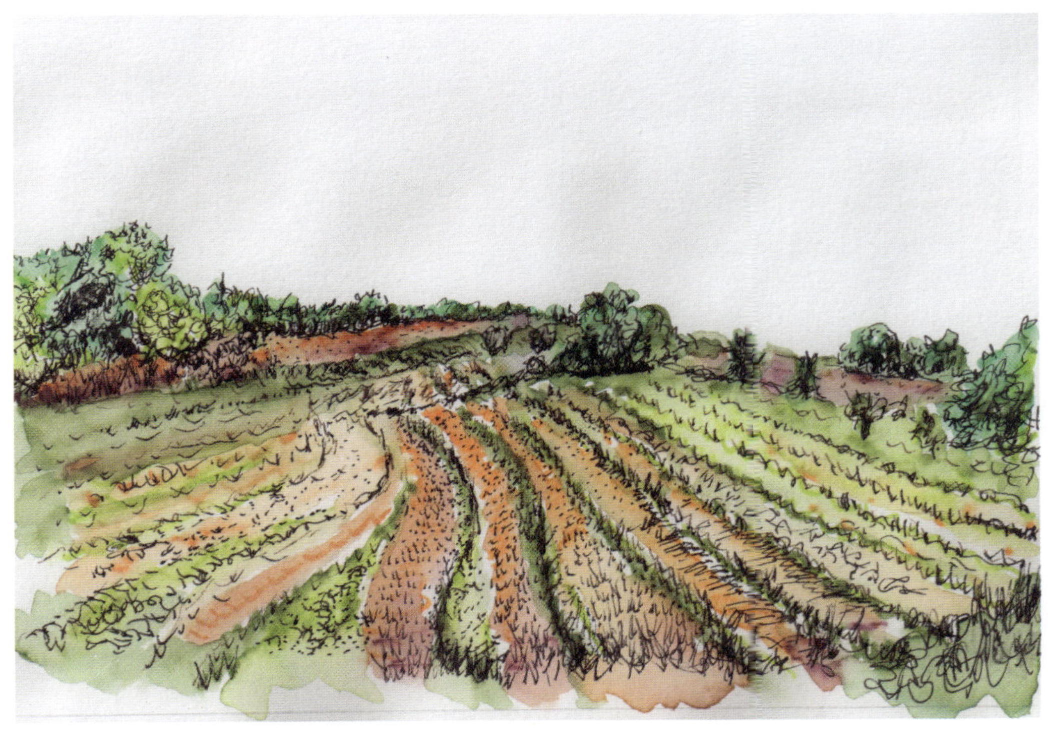

Lisa Hofmann

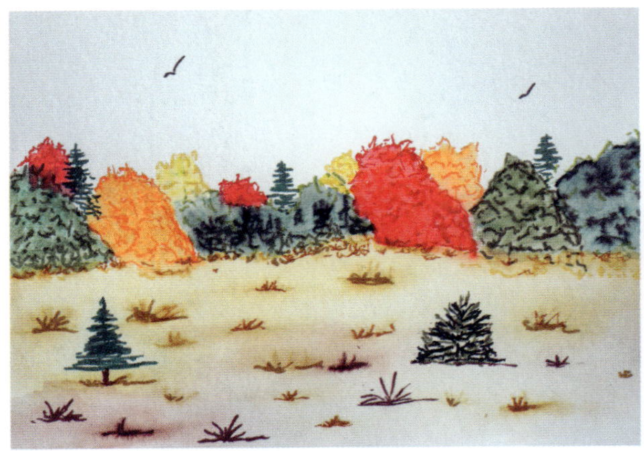

Nathalie Bélanger

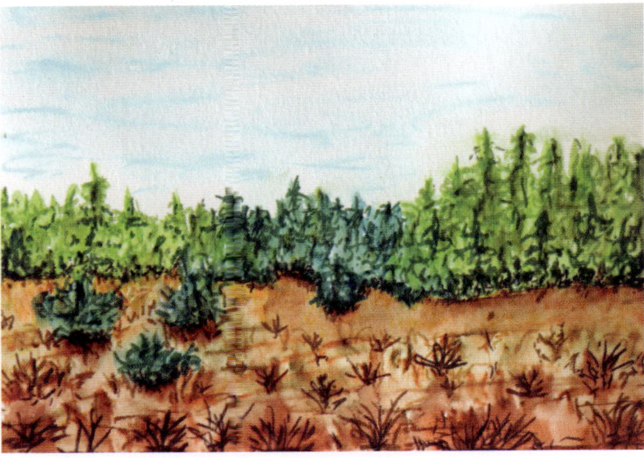

Liz Tobosa

LESSON TWENTY

RIVER STONES

When I am anxious, I draw or paint circles. It's just this thing I do—and for some unknown reason it always calms me down. Perhaps it has something to do with ensō, the Zen meditation practice of painting circles, but I believe it's all about the repetition of all those tiny marks that requires every bit of my focus. I have many pages in my sketchbooks of patterns made from tiny circles, and sometimes they are quite beautiful and worthy of framing. This lesson came from that practice, and I would go so far as to call it a mindfulness practice of its own.

The key to this lesson is the variation of line weight, which simply means using different-size pen tips. If you buy fineliner or micron pens, you will notice they come in various tip sizes. I recommend having 4 different tip sizes—and a brush pen is nice to have, too. If you only have one micron pen, such as a .005, you can draw double or triple circles, making the lines wider yourself, but this is really time-consuming. If you like the way this project looks, get a set of micron or fineliner pens in various nib sizes. They are useful for many types of drawing and are good to have available. It's also important that the ink you use is watercolor, so you can color over it and it won't bleed or smudge.

I call this project River Stones because I used some of the muted shades of the kinds of rocks I see in river beds and it absolutely reminded me of stones. However, this project is great for any creative color combinations. Use your imagination to create all sorts of shapes and effects.

TOOLS TO GATHER

- Graphite pencil
- Drawing paper, 5 × 7 inches (13 × 18 cm)
- Selection of permanent black fineliner or micron pens in various nib weights (I used a brush pen and .07, .03, .01, and .005 pens.)
- Markers in assorted colors

STEPS

1 - Using a pencil, draw a curved line from the top of your paper to the bottom, as shown. *See A.*

2 - Using the .07 pen (or the thickest line weight), draw a series of randomly shaped and sized circles and ovals all along the pencil line, leaving a tiny bit of space between them, as shown. *See B.* For this entire project, some shapes are bigger, some are smaller, some go left, right, or sideways, some are skinny, and some are fat—random is key.

3 - Continue with the same pen, adding more circles, but now make sure they all touch one another, as shown. *See C.* Do this on both sides of the line from step 1. Use the sample for guidance.

4 - With the brush pen or the same .07 pen, fill in all the spaces left between the circles, as shown. *See D.* Take your time with this and aim for nice clean circles.

5 - Changing to a smaller nib size, .03, repeat step 3, keeping to your goal of randomness and clean circles. Take your time, relax, and focus. This is a particularly good thing for calming the mind. *See E.*

6 - Change to an even smaller nib size, .01, and repeat step 3 again. *See F.*

7 - Finally, change to the smallest nib size, .005, and repeat step 3 one more time. *See G.*

8 - Now for the color! There are no rules . . . choose some colors and fill in each circle individually. Use one color at a time and skip around to create any patterns you like, or be completely random, like the sample. *See H.* Leave some white, or fill in every one. It's up to you!

USE YOUR CREATIVITY

What if you made the line in step 1 a circle, or any other shape? What if you drew tiny squares or triangles instead of ovals and circles? What if you used colored pencils to fill in the shapes? What if you used metallic gel pens to fill in a few? Experiment. Oh, and what if you filled a piece of paper that was 3 feet × 5 feet (90 cm × 150 cm)? That might be modern art. Experiment. Relax. Enjoy.

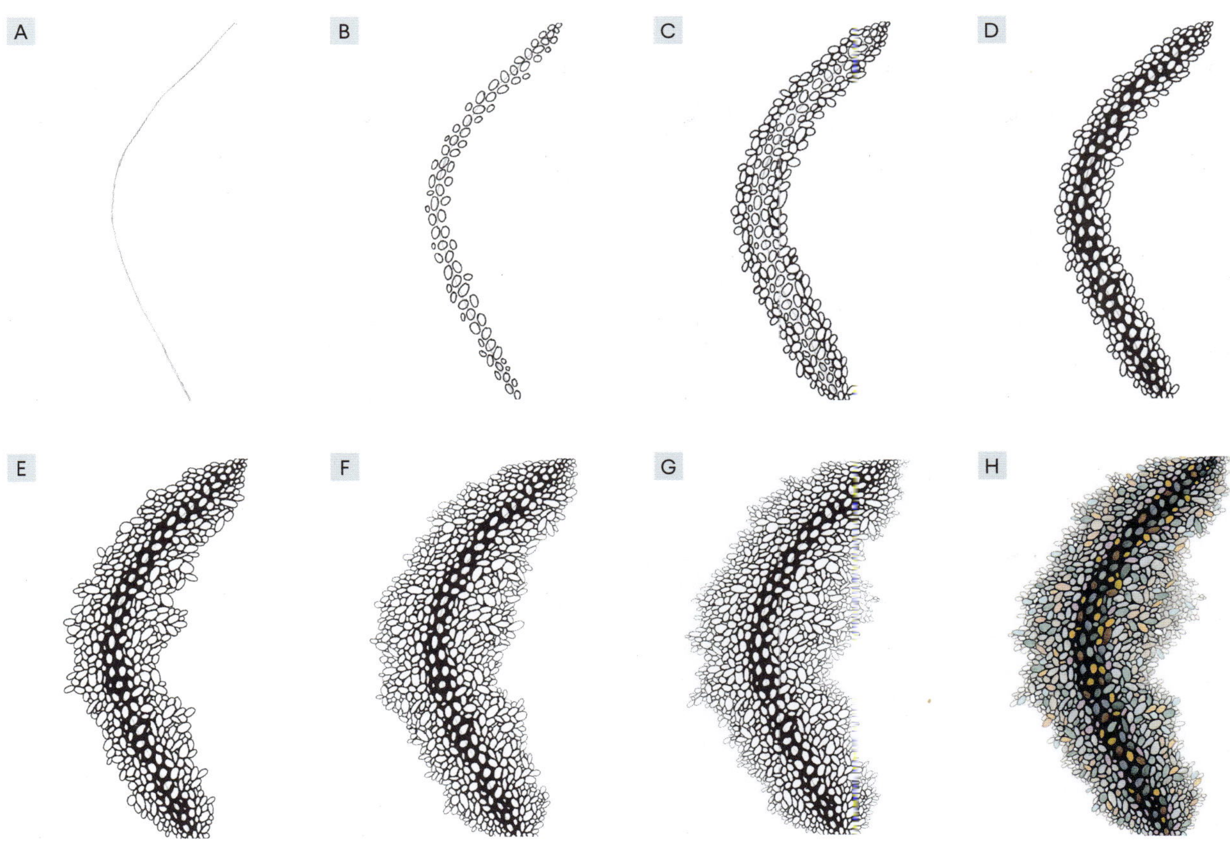

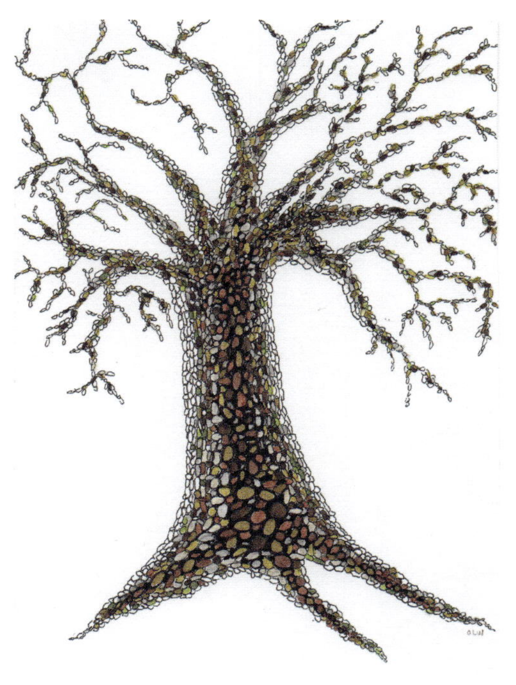

Carol Williamson

Liz Tobosa

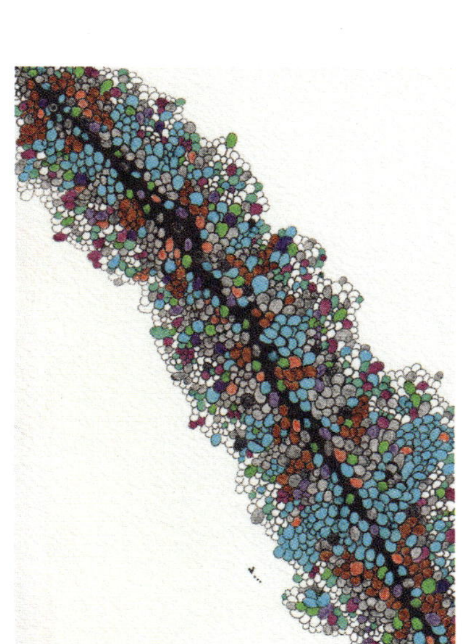

Debbie Brandecker

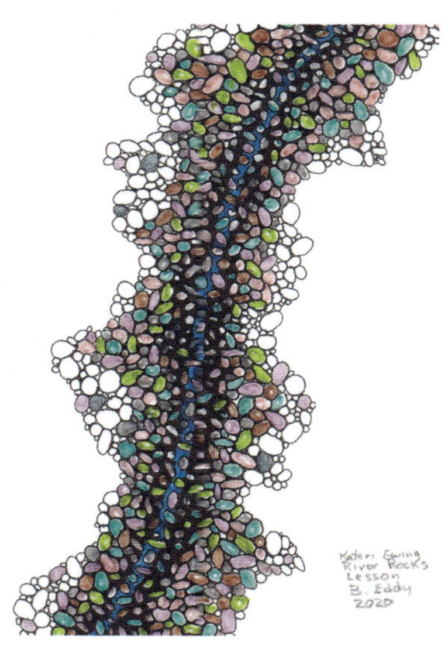

Beverly Eddy

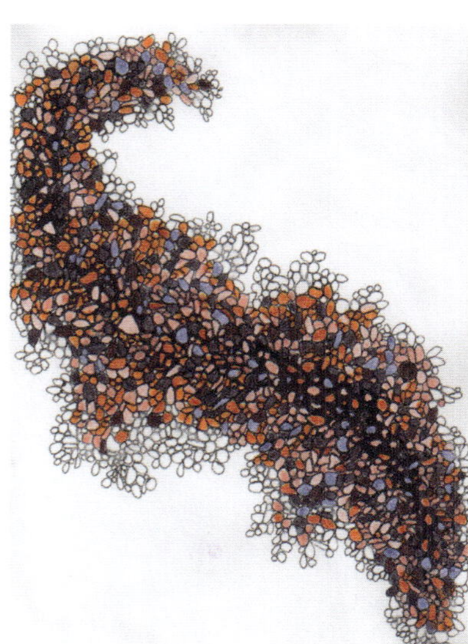

Lisa Hofmann

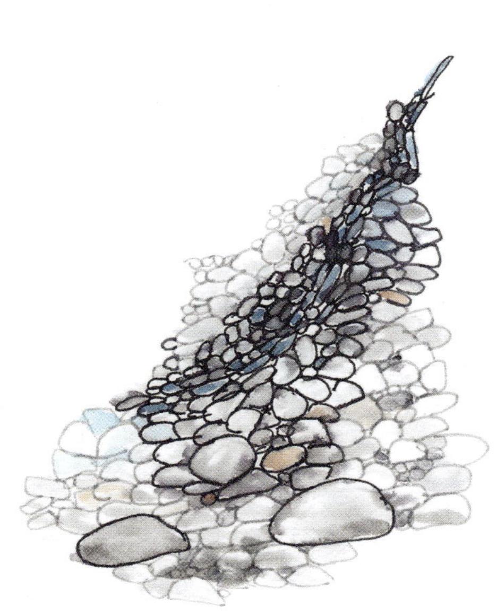

Helene Jorgensen

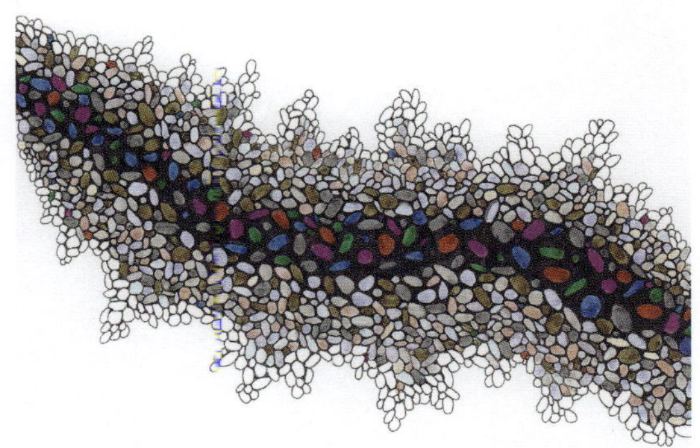

Wendy Ching

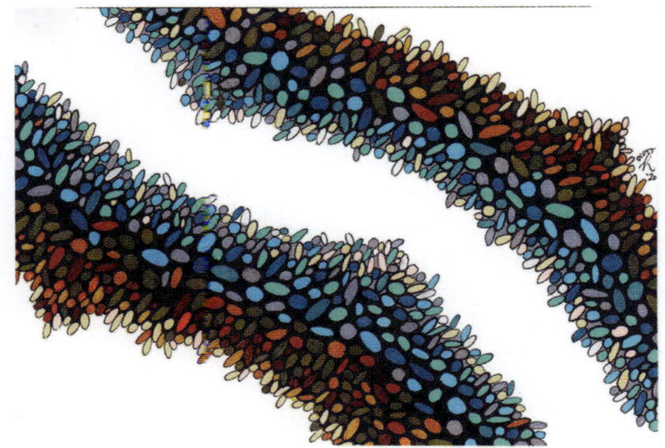

Hazel Scott

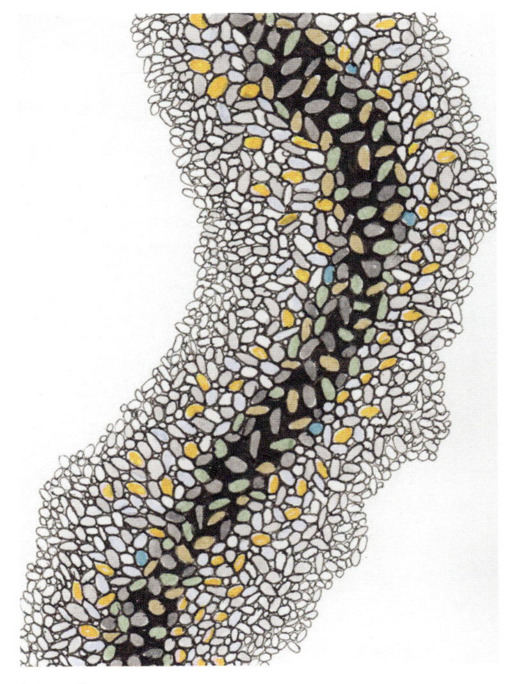

Mary Dowson

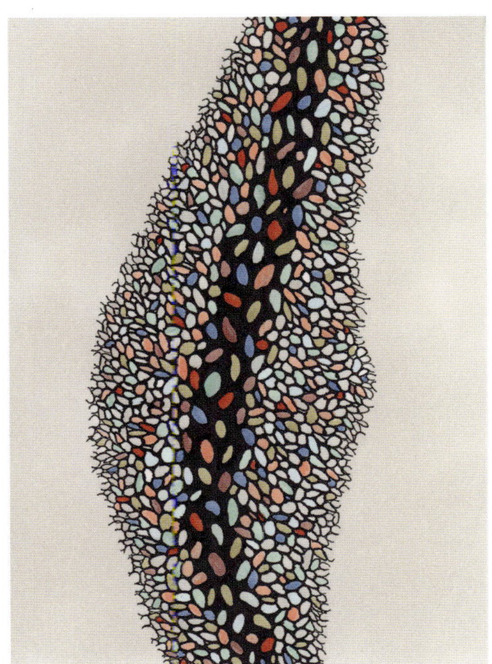

Jon Pedersen

LESSON TWENTY-ONE

A TINY BIRD

We have arrived at our final lesson in this book. You have learned so much and, hopefully, your confidence has grown and you now see that drawing isn't just for professional artists—it's truly for everyone.

For this lesson, we are going to draw my personal favorite subject, a bird on a branch. What I want you to know most is this: *you can do this*. Step by step, shape by shape, we will draw a bird. Yours will look different from mine and, if I drew it again tomorrow, mine would look different, too. This is desirable. We each can create something in our unique way. So, relax and remember your greatest ally when drawing with a pencil—your eraser! And your second greatest ally is beginning again, if you must.

This is an imaginary bird, which means we can use any colors we desire to give it our unique touch. For your first try, feel free to use similar colors, but after that . . . experiment! I used only Crayola markers for this drawing and, of course, a pencil and a permanent black fineliner pen. If you have a brush pen, get that ready, too! Let's draw a bird.

TOOLS TO GATHER

- Graphite pencil, HB or no. 2
- Drawing paper, 5 × 7 inches (13 × 18 cm)
- Eraser
- Permanent black micron or fineliner pen
- Markers in assorted colors, including browns and greens
- Round watercolor paintbrush in size 6 or 8
- Glass of clean water
- Paper towel or cloth to wipe your paintbrush

STEPS

1 - Let's get the trickiest part out of the way first. With an HB or no. 2 pencil (and your eraser nearby), draw a series of shapes, as shown, allowing them to overlap. Be messy, erase, whatever you need. Keep your lines light (feather touch!) so they are easy to erase. I made mine darker so you could see them. Start with the small oval (the head), and then add the larger oval (the body), curved triangle (a wing), and rectangle (the tail). Try to keep proportions and angles similar to the sample, but remember this is your drawing, not mine, and it will be different by nature. *See A.*

2 - Now, we refine. Using your eraser when needed, follow along by comparing the drawing in this step with the drawing in step 1. With your pencil, change the shape of the lines connecting the head to the body, as shown. Then, starting a little bit out from the

head, draw a straight line that eventually curves down toward the body—this creates the area for the beak and eye. Make the beak as shown, like a tiny triangle with a line through it, and create the eye by drawing a tiny circle on the line, as shown. Erase any extra lines. *See B.*

Then, work on the wing. Draw in the lines, as shown. Erase the outer edge and any extra lines in the original curved triangle. Do the same for the tail. Now, look at the bottom side of the body. Notice how the lines have changed. Make that correction on your bird and erase the old lines. Finally, draw two legs and feet, as shown. Remember, your eraser is always there. We are learning to refine our line drawing from the initial basic shapes we put down. We can begin *any* drawing with simple shapes and refine it using new lines and an eraser.

3 - Using the same pencil, draw a simple branch with tiny leaves, as shown. Follow the lines in the sample or create your own branch shapes. The only caveat is, make sure the branch fits under the bird's two feet. *See C.*

4 - The hardest parts are over! Use your black permanent pen to trace over the pencil lines of the bird and each leaf. Do not leave any parts untraced. If you have a brush pen, use it to create a thicker, rougher tracing of the branch. If not, use the fineliner pen. Let it dry for at least 20 minutes. Use an eraser to remove any pencil lines you see. You should have a clean ink drawing now. *See D.*

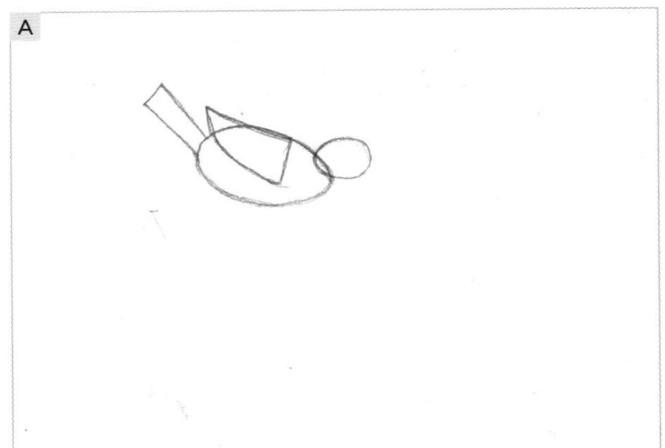

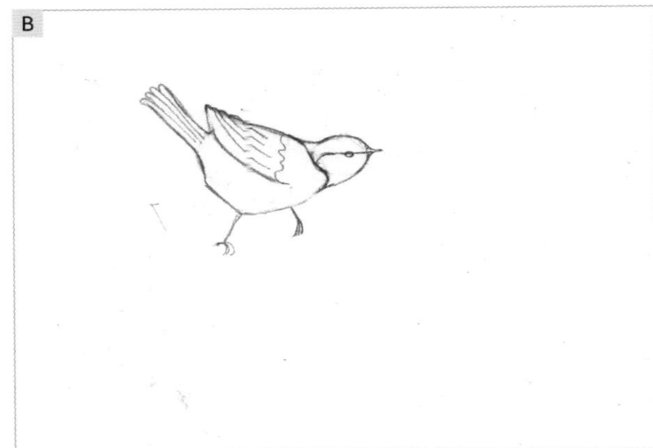

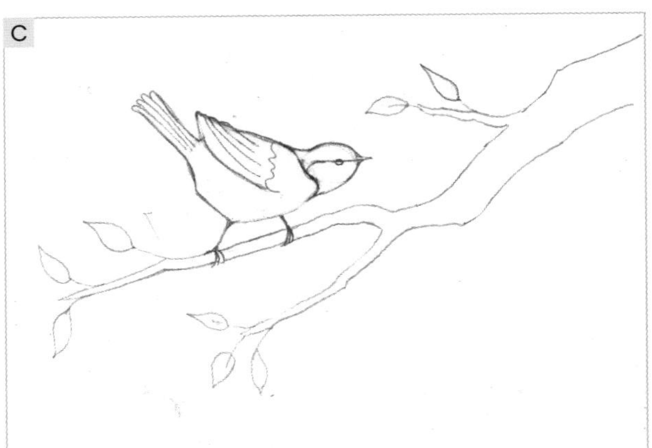

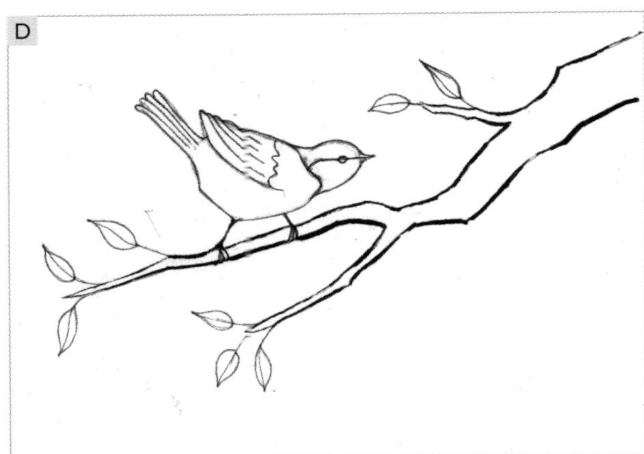

5 - Below is a close-up of the technique for the branch. Using markers in 3 shades of brown—light, medium, and dark—create lines of color from light to dark inside the branch, as shown. Light colors go on top, darker colors on the bottom. Then, use a light green marker to draw a line under the top of each leaf, a medium green to draw a line under the center line of each leaf, and a darker green to put a small line where each leaf meets the stem. *See E.*

6 - Dip your paintbrush into clean water and paint over each leaf and the entire branch, allowing the ink to soften and create a lovely wash. Choose your colors for the bird, making sure you have a dark version and a lighter version of each color. I chose rusts for the bird's head, blue for his wing and tail, and a buff color for his body. Follow the markings, as shown, using your color choices. Notice the lighter blue is used separately from the darker blue; the same is true of the rust colors. The buff color is all the same, but you could certainly use a bit of a darker color right along the bottom of the body. *See F.*

7 - Dip your paintbrush into clean water and carefully paint over the bird, creating lovely washes. I did each color section separately, letting them dry a bit before moving on, so that they didn't completely mix and mingle. *See G.*

USE YOUR CREATIVITY

What if you drew tiny flowers at the base of each leaf for a springtime branch? Or, how about using the colors of autumn leaves instead of green? What if there were two birds, or three, all facing different directions? Use the basic shapes to create the bird with different angles to see how you can create different pictures and positions. Look at pictures of real birds and see how you might break them down into simple shapes. Birds are endlessly satisfying subjects. I hope you try many and that you will share one with me on Instagram by tagging @kateriewing.

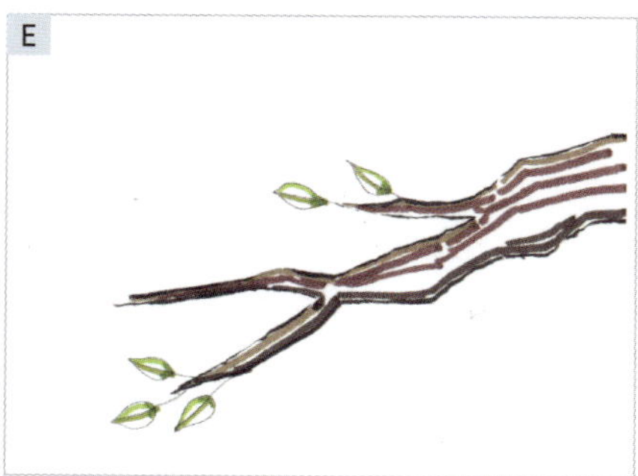
E

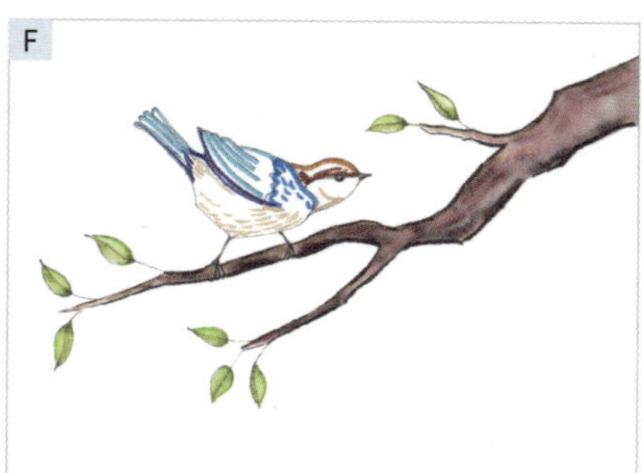
F

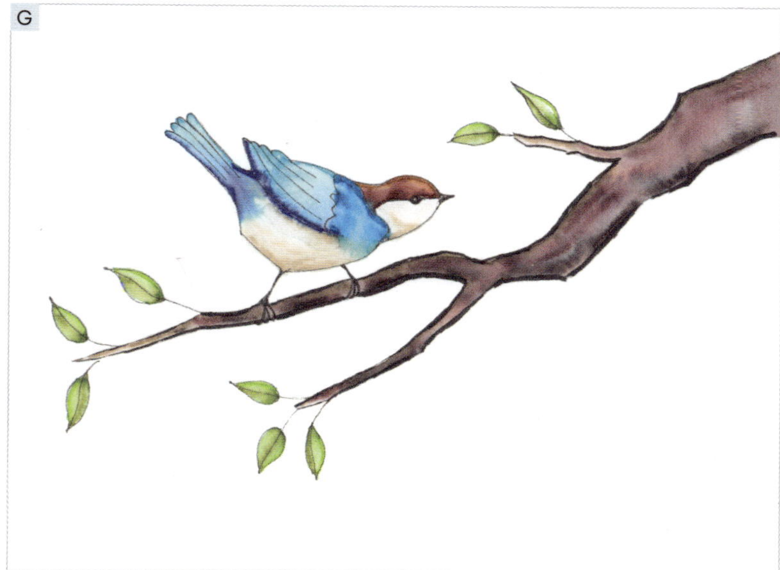
G

/ STUDENT GALLERY

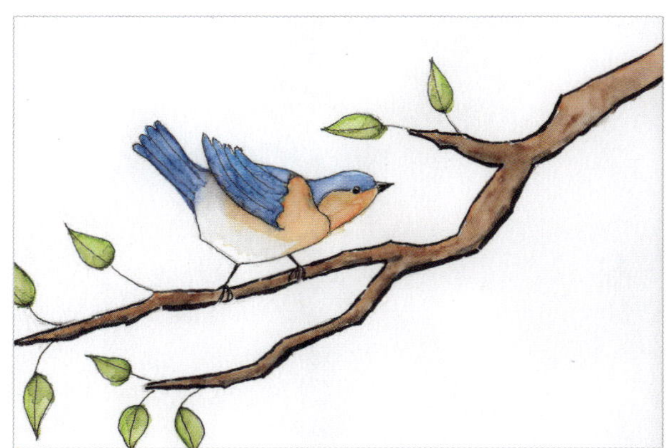

Carol Williamson

Nathalie Bélanger

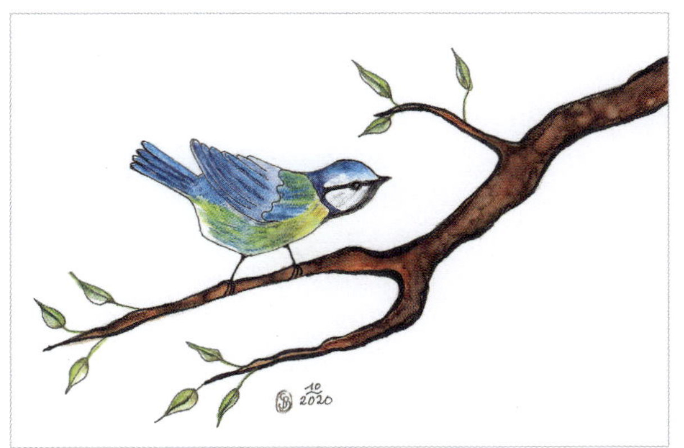

Sallie Binder

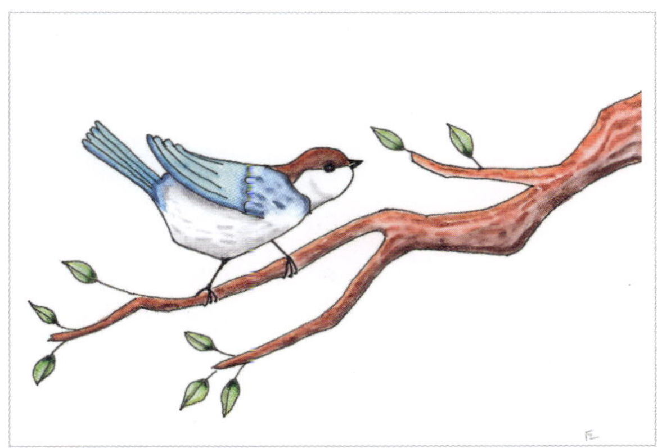

Fran Lowell

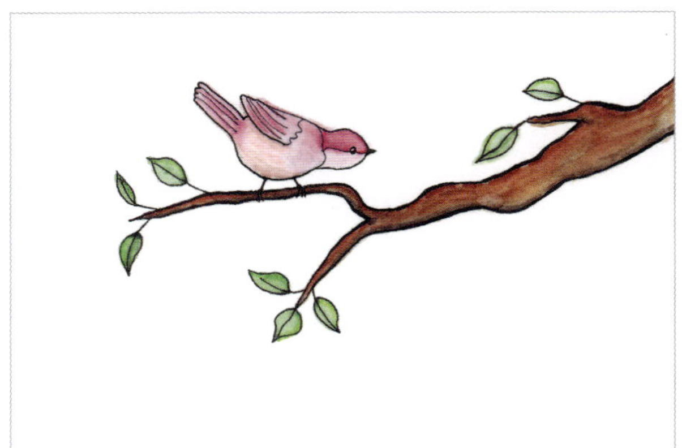

Wendy Ching

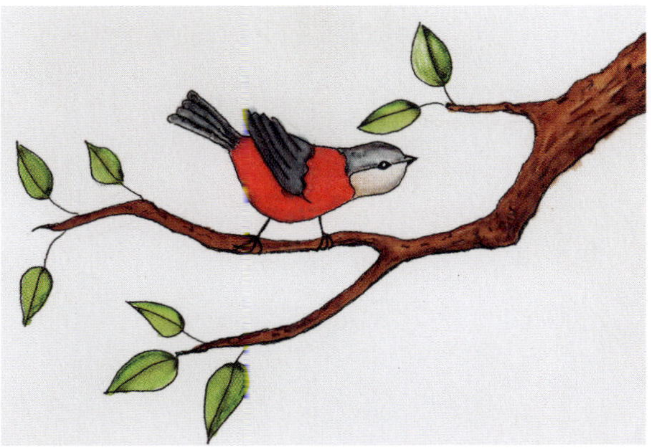

Liz Tobosa

FINAL THOUGHTS

We have journeyed through 21 lessons together, exploring different ways to make your mark with graphite, colored pencil, and ink. How does it feel? Do you have a favorite medium? Where will you take it from here?

Scattered throughout these lessons, I have shared some of my students' beautiful work. Their drawings represent the work of everyday people, trying these lessons for the first time, and demonstrate how they made them their own. I hope they help you see the possibilities for creating small works of art with the simplest tools and techniques. One of the most fascinating things I have learned as a teacher is how much diversity I see when many people use the same tools and lessons. Even if you do the same lesson over and over, you will never create the same drawing twice.

My hope is that you will continue to gather your simple tools and carry on with your unique mark making, stretching yourself to try new things and even new mediums, like watercolor. I can't wait to see what you create! You can find me on Instagram: kateriewing; on Facebook: Kateri Ewing ~ Watercolors; and on my YouTube Channel (lots of free lessons!) by searching for Kateri Ewing. You can also study with me online in my warm, supportive Patreon community of worldwide explorers, where we learn and create together every day: Patreon.com/kateriewing.

Thank you so much for choosing to bring a daily creative practice into your life. When we bring beauty into the world, we make it a better place, mark by mark, color by color.

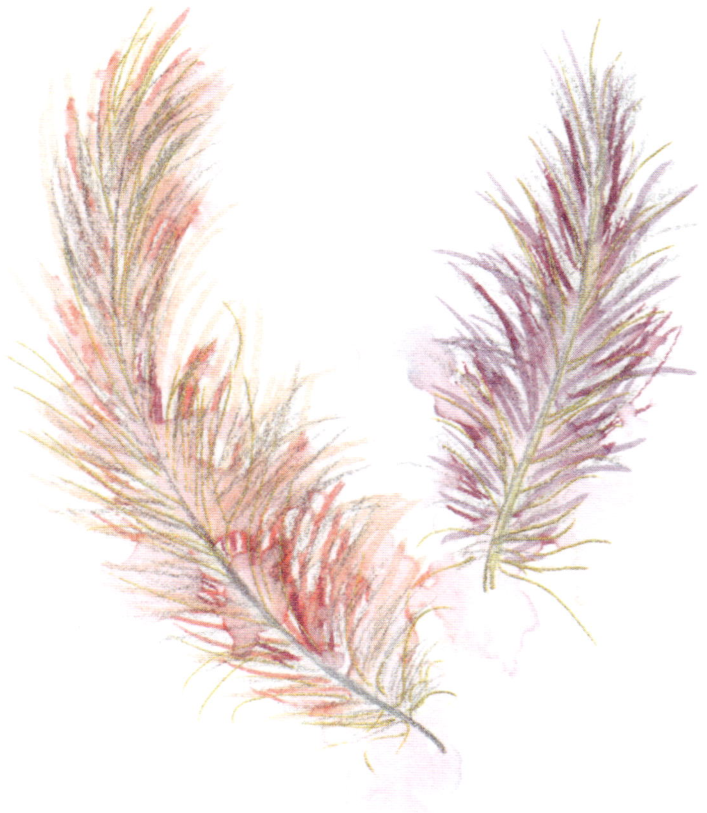

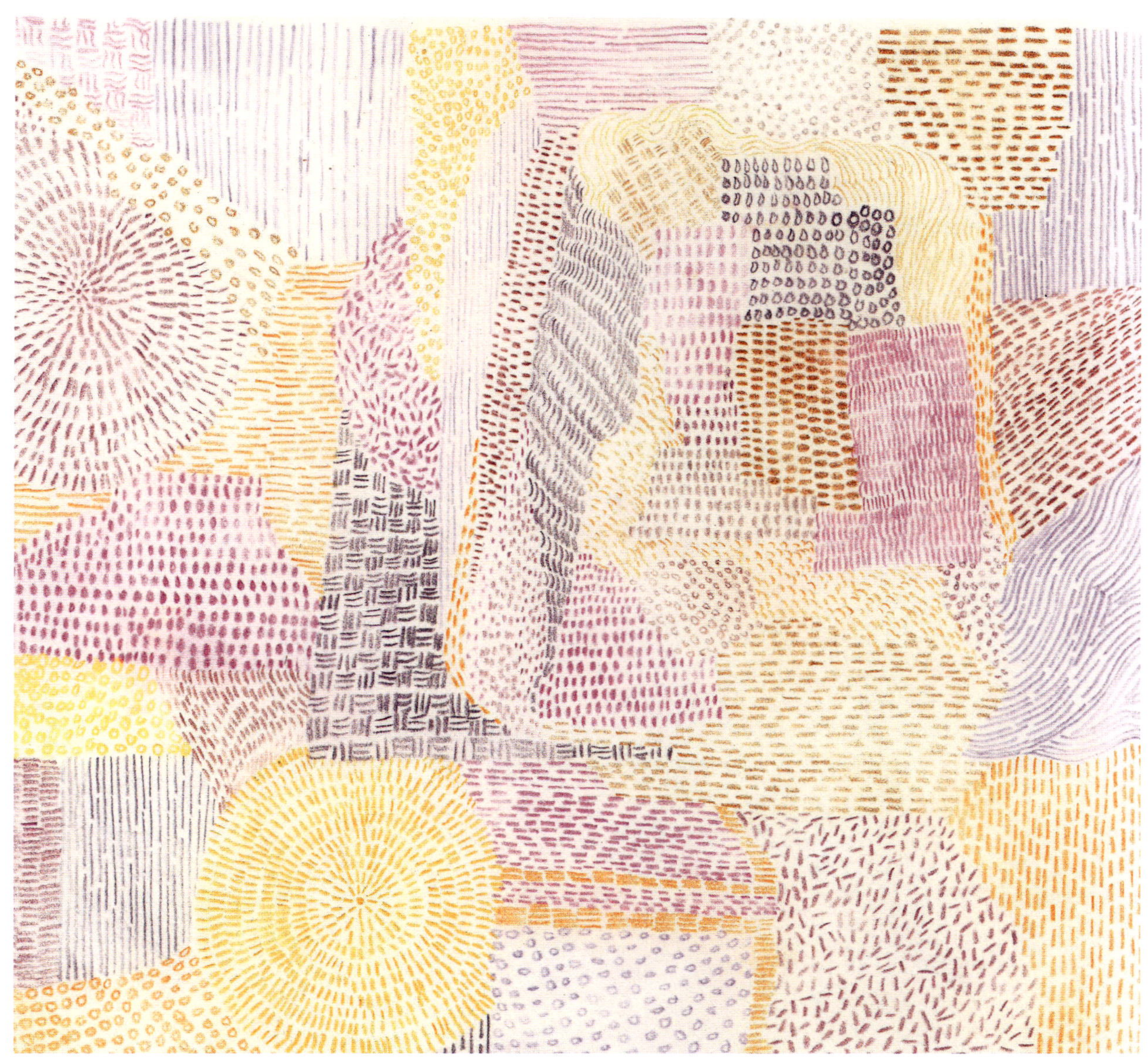

RESOURCES

PAPER

I recommend paper cut or torn to 5 × 7 inches (13 × 18 cm) in size to keep the painting area manageable. You can buy pads this size or buy larger sheets and cut them to size.

Student Grade (more affordable)
Canson XL Series Bristol pad
Strathmore 400 drawing paper

Artist Grade
Strathmore 500 mixed media paper
Stonehenge drawing paper (comes in many colors, including kraft, and in 5 × 7-inch, or 13 × 18 cm, pads)

PENCILS

If you only want one pencil, buy an HB, also known as a no. 2 pencil. My favorite drugstore brand is Dixon Ticonderoga. Artist Andrew Wyeth used only no. 2 pencils he brought at a hardware store. Different types of pencils are fun, useful, and can make our job easier, but they are not necessary.

Graphite Pencils
Caran d'Ache Grafwood
Faber-Castell 9000
Staedler Mars Lumograph

Colored Pencils, Student Grade
Arteza
Crayola
Faber-Castell Premium

Colored Pencils, Professional Grade
Caran d'Ache Luminance
Derwent
Faber-Castell Polychromos

INK

Fineliner Pens
Copic Multiliners
Sakura Pigma micron
Sharpie

Water-soluble Markers
Arteza brush tip
Crayola Super Tips

Waterproof Markers (India Ink)
Faber-Castell Pitt Artist pens

Metallic gel pens
Pilot G2
Uni-ball Signo
Uni-ball Signo broad-point gel pen (white gel pen)

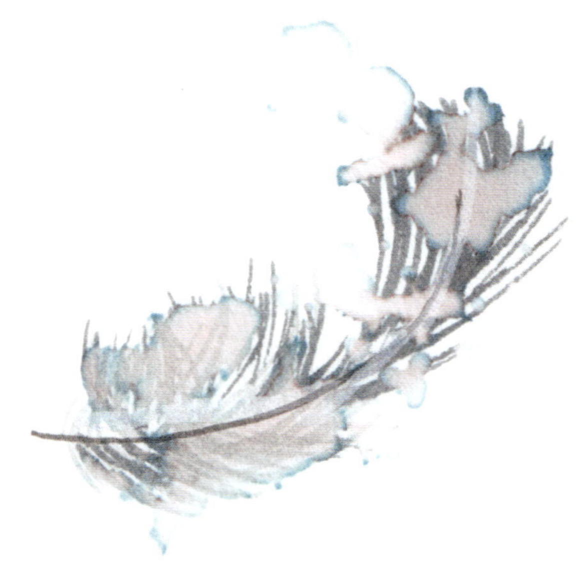

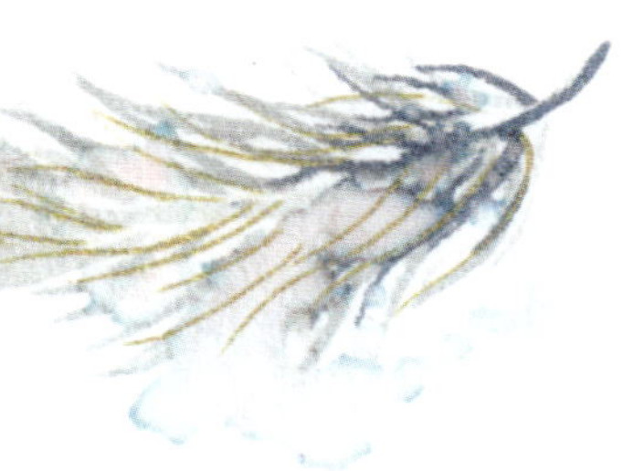

ACKNOWLEDGMENTS

There are so many people to thank—even some I've never met, but who have helped me find my way to where I sit right now. Here are a few I wish I could gather around an enormous table for a warm celebration of gratitude.

My mom, Kateri; my dad, Donald; my stepmom, Diane; my brother Michael—for being my family, the people who are always there for me, through thick and thin, and who have encouraged me to follow my path. I love you all far more than I can express.

My children, Kristoffer and Anna, for being my constant True North, my reason for pushing through the hardest times, my forever cheering section. You are my greatest treasures and most beloved. I am so proud of you. My son-in-law, Kevin, and my daughter-in-law, Katya, and my two grandchildren, Dima and Anneke, for all the love you bring into my life. I am so lucky.

My sweetheart, Rick—my best friend in the whole world, my fellow artist who understands the path and walks beside me. It is an immense gift to share my life with someone who appreciates the work I do every day and who every day celebrates my efforts, achievements, and helps me remember that my failures are what help me grow, with such steadfast love and compassion. I am truly, really truly, the most grateful and lucky woman. I never knew this kind of love until I knew you. I could not do the work, the way I need to do the work, without you by my side.

My stepdaughter, Mariah, for also being my cheerleader, and for your love and acceptance of me in your life. I'm so grateful for you.

To my friends near and far: Barb T., Barb Q., Beth H., Cassandra B., Cristina M., Dori S., Janet S., Kathy D., Kelli F., Lisa C., Lisa M., Lynne H., Mary G., Michelle H., Nancy J., Sara C., Wendy K., Zorana. Thanks for the conversations, messages, encouragement, inspiration, and friendship. You each bring something special to my life.

My friend, Grace Meibohm, owner of Meibohm Fine Arts, and her staff, David, Mark, and Nancy, who have become like family to me. Thank you for seeing in me what I could not see for myself. Thank you for every opportunity, for your nurturing kindness, for believing in me. How can I ever say thank you enough?

My editors and art directors: Joy Aquilino, Heather Godin, and Renae Haines, for your vision of this book, for believing I had it in me, for your guidance and patience and kindness all along the way. Thank you!

My students, the ones who encourage me to share my love for drawing and my deep belief in the power of the creative practice. It is my honor to share it all with you. Thank you for giving me the gift of seeing things through your eyes, as I continue to practice the gift of seeing through my own. We are, all of us, eternal beginners . . . the most wonderful thing to be.

And to my greatest teachers, John Ruskin and Andrew Wyeth, whose life's work and words have been a never-ending fount of inspiration and wisdom.

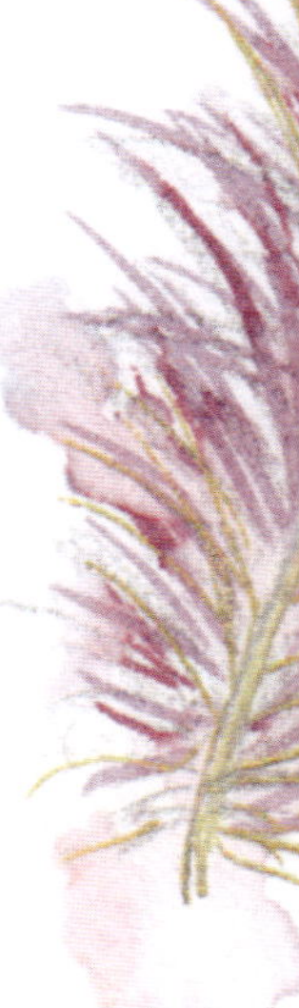

ABOUT THE AUTHOR

The author of *Look Closer, Draw Better, Watercolor Is for Everyone*, and *Drawing Is for Everyone*, **Kateri Ewing** is an artist in residence and teacher at the Roycroft Campus in East Aurora, New York. For her artistic and writing endeavors, she was honored with the 2012 Mary and Gil Stott Award at Roycroft. Her artwork has also won numerous awards in both local and national exhibitions. She uses her Patreon virtual classroom to interact daily with her worldwide students. She lives in Western New York. Learn more at kateriewing.com.

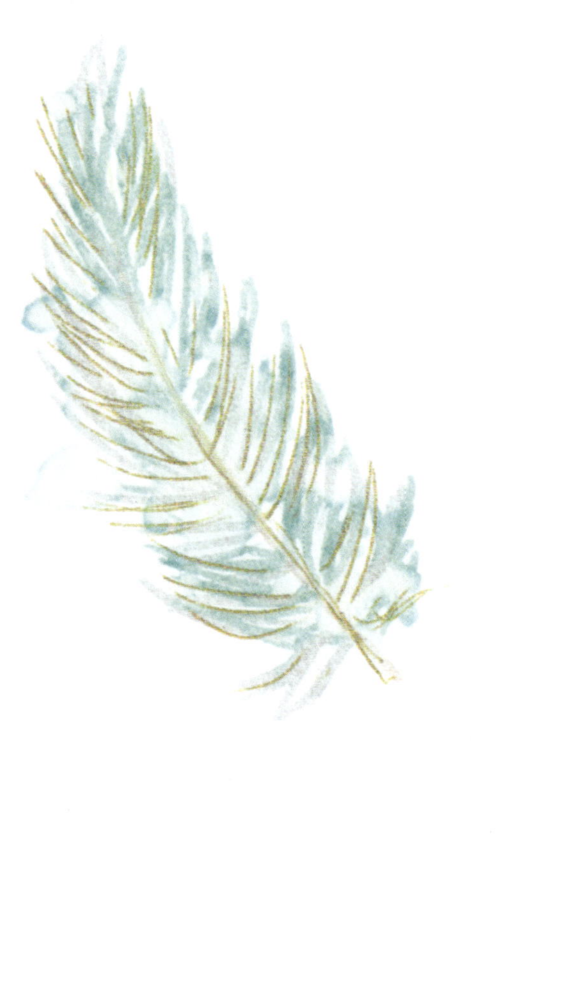

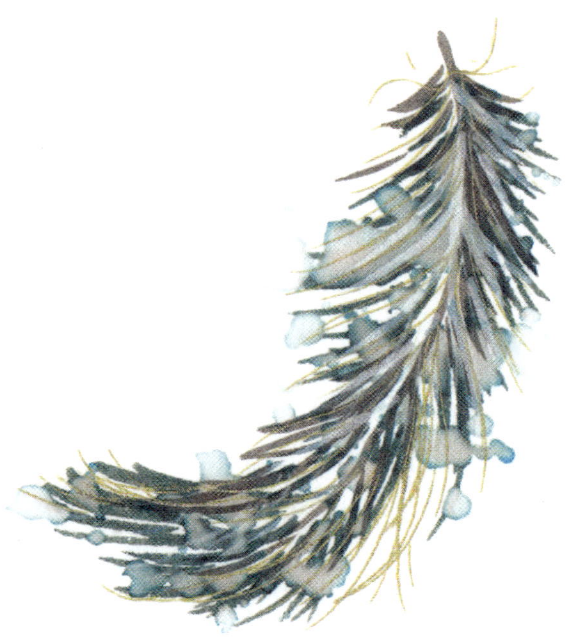

INDEX

ALSO AVAILABLE FROM QUARRY BOOKS

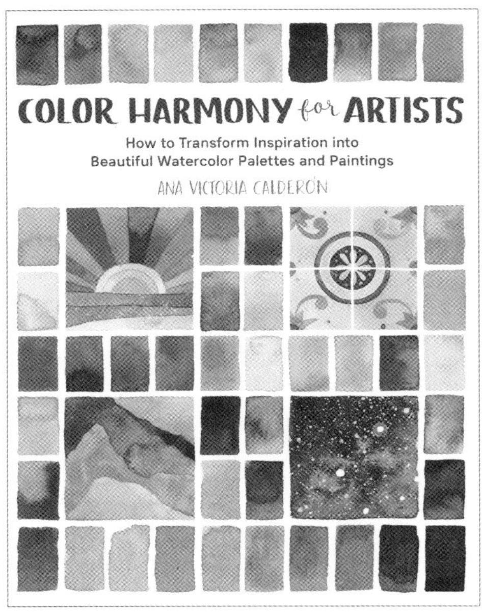

Color Harmony for Artists
978-1-63159-771-8

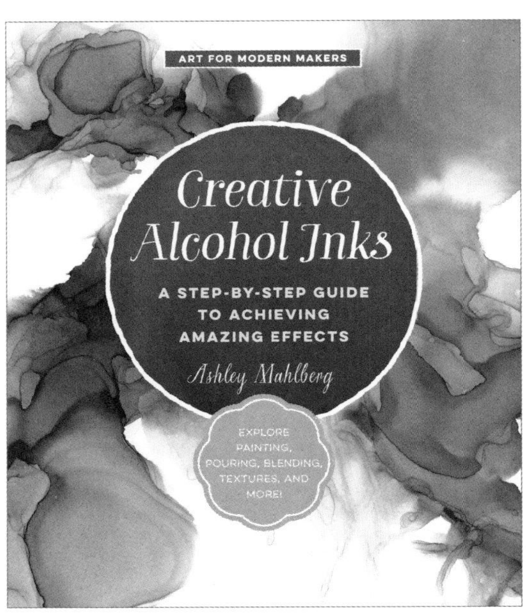

Creative Alcohol Inks
978-1-63159-791-6

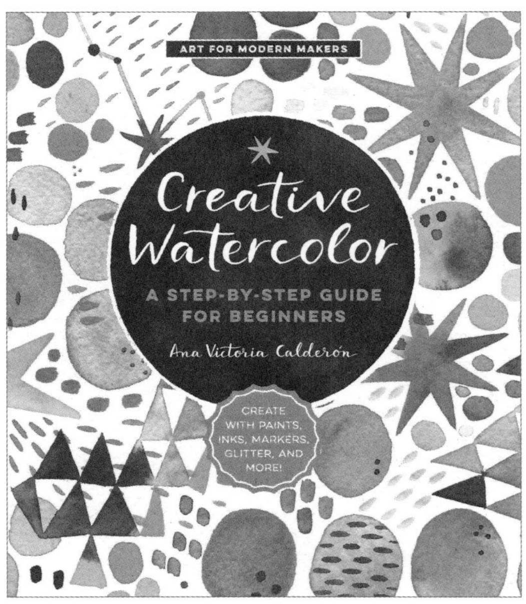

Creative Watercolor
978-1-58923-969-2

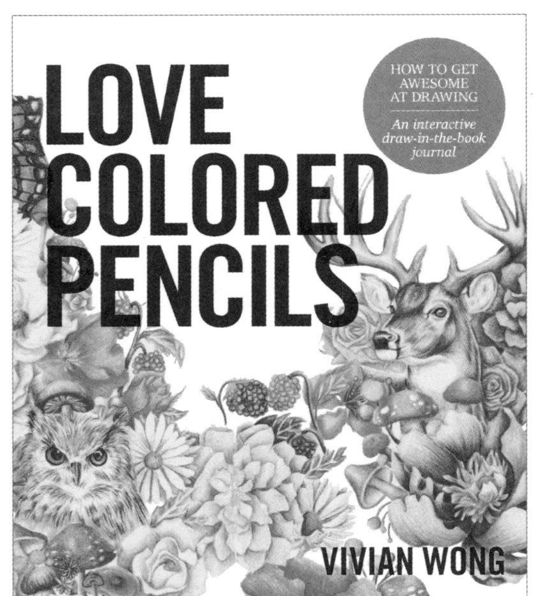

Love Colored Pencils
978-1-63159-375-8